THE NORTHERN BANTU

I   2   3   4

(1) Four Bantu Kings, with their Chief Ministers

1, Andereya Ruhanga, King of Banyoro; 2, Daudè chwa, King of Uganda
3, Kamswaga, King of Ankole; 4, Kasagama, King of Toro

(2) King of Banyoro, with his chiefs, in modern Arab dress

THE
NORTHERN BANTU

An Account of some Central African Tribes
of the Uganda Protectorate

JOHN ROSCOE

FRANK CASS & CO. LTD.
1966

Published by Frank Cass & Co. Ltd.,
10 Woburn Walk, London W.C.1
by arrangement with Cambridge University Press.

First Edition   1915
New Impression   1966

Printed in Great Britain
Thomas Nelson (Printers) Ltd., London and Edinburgh

PREFACE

IN a former work I described at some length the Baganda[1], the most advanced and most powerful Bantu tribe of Central Africa: in the present work I give a more summary account of some other important and far less known Bantu tribes in the Uganda Protectorate. Like its predecessor, this volume is based on observations made and notes taken by me during the many years when I resided in Central Africa in the service of the Church Missionary Society. Being stationed at Mengo, the capital of Uganda, I naturally had most facilities for acquainting myself with the Baganda, among whom I lived; but even at Mengo I enjoyed many opportunities for acquiring a knowledge of other tribes of the Protectorate, and I availed myself of my vacations to visit them in their own countries and investigate their customs and beliefs by personal converse with the natives. My acquaintance with the Bantu languages enabled me in every case to dispense with an interpreter: all the information concerning Bantu tribes presented to the reader in this, as in my former, volume was obtained at first hand from the people in their own language. Yet I am well aware that the account which I have given of these tribes, other than the Baganda, is fragmentary and incomplete: the short time which I could devote to the study in my vacations precluded the possibility of a thorough investigation. I feel that I have done little more than scratch the surface of a wide and fruitful field, which will yield an abundant harvest

---

[1] *The Baganda, an Account of their Native Customs and Beliefs.* Macmillan & Co., London, 1911.

to those who may have the good fortune to cultivate it hereafter. For the tribes in question are as yet comparatively
little known and they represent a great variety of stages in
social, mental, and material evolution, from the aquatic and
fishing Bakene, through the pastoral Bahima and Banyoro,
to the almost purely agricultural Bagesu and Basoga. In the
Bakene, living actually on the water of the lakes and rivers,
we see the modern equivalents of the lake dwellers of ancient
Europe: in the pastoral tribes, with their cows, we trace a
sort of reflection of the Hebrew patriarchs with their wandering
flocks and herds; while from the primitive agricultural tribes
we seem to catch a glimpse of our remote ancestors tilling
the patches of soil which they had cleared in the vast primaeval
forests. Again, a knowledge of the cannibal Bagesu, dwelling
on the slopes of the mighty Mount Elgon, with its great caves,
its rushing streams, and foaming cataracts, may perhaps throw
light on the meaning and origin of cannibalism in general.

But in order to reap the full benefit which a study of these
deeply interesting tribes offers to the student of man's early
history, it is essential that an exact and thorough investigation
of them should be undertaken without delay; for every year
sees a further encroachment of European influence on their
once secluded domain, every year witnesses a corresponding
disintegration of their ancient customs and beliefs, and unless
the investigation is undertaken soon, it will be too late to
attempt it at all: a priceless record of human history will
be lost for ever. It is lamentable to reflect, that while large
sums are annually devoted by Governments, learned societies,
and the generosity of private benefactors to the study of
merely material and comparatively permanent relics of ancient
civilisation, so little is given to the investigation of the mental
and social state of those primitive living races of men who
are melting away before our eyes, and who can still tell us
secrets which we shall never wring from all the tablets of
Babylon and the pyramids of Egypt. To the student of
man's early developement the tribes of Central Africa offer
one of the best fields still open for research, but in a few years
hence they may have ceased to do so.

Much of the information in this volume concerning the
Bahima, the Bagesu, and the Bakene has already appeared
in the form of papers contributed by me to the *Journal of
the Royal Anthropological Institute*. I wish to thank the
Council of the Institute for kindly allowing me to make use
of these papers in the present volume. For that purpose
the articles have been recast and enlarged, but their original
substance remains. The two chapters on the Banyoro and
Basoga, together with those on the Nilotic tribes, are new,
though my friend Sir J. G. Frazer has, with my full permission,
used some of the information in his comprehensive work
Totemism and Exogamy before these chapters were compiled.
The two chapters on the Nilotic tribes (the Bateso and Nilotic
Kavirondo) have been added as an appendix. They are the
result, not of researches purposely undertaken among the
people, but merely of short visits which I happened to pay
them in the course of my missionary work. Finding myself
among the tribes I availed myself of the opportunity to glean
a little information about them, and rather than keep my
notes locked up in my desk, I have added them to the volume
in the hope that they may prove useful to others. That is
my excuse for publishing them in a book otherwise devoted
to Bantu tribes.

My grateful thanks are due to my two friends, the
Rev. W. Cox, Fellow of St John's College, Cambridge, and
Sir J. G. Frazer, for valuable assistance. The former kindly
undertook the trying task of reading through the manuscript
and revising it for the press. The latter read through the
proofs, and pointed out some omissions, inconsistencies, and
obscurities, which I have endeavoured to rectify.

I am deeply indebted to the Syndics of the Cambridge
University Press for their liberality in undertaking the publication of the book. I thank them gratefully, as also a number
of friends who kindly guaranteed a sum towards the expenses
of publication.

For the photographs I am indebted to F. Knowles, Esq.,
C.M.G., District Commissioner in Uganda, the Revs. H. Brewer,
R. H. Leakey, and E. Millar, Miss Brewer and Miss Morris,

members of the Church Missionary Society in Uganda. These friends have been at considerable pains to obtain the photographs and to forward them to me in England. My own camera broke down and I could obtain no photographs with it.

To the Right Rev. Dr Willis, Bishop of Uganda, I am indebted for a table of Nilotic relationships, and also for the kind assistance he gave me as interpreter when I was taking notes among the Nilotic Kavirondo. To the Rev. A. L. Kitching, the Rev. A. B. Fisher, the Rev. H. Mathers, and Miss Attlee I am indebted for tables and other information of the most valuable nature.

JOHN ROSCOE.

THE RECTORY,
OVINGTON, NORFOLK.
20 *March*, 1915.

CONTENTS

PART I

THE BANYORO A PASTORAL PEOPLE

PART II

THE BANYANKOLE A PASTORAL TRIBE OF ANKOLE

PART III

THE BAKENE, LAKE DWELLERS

PART IV

THE BAGESU A CANNIBAL TRIBE

PART V

THE BASOGA

PART VI

NILOTIC TRIBES. THE BATESO AND THE KAVIRONDO

LIST OF ILLUSTRATIONS

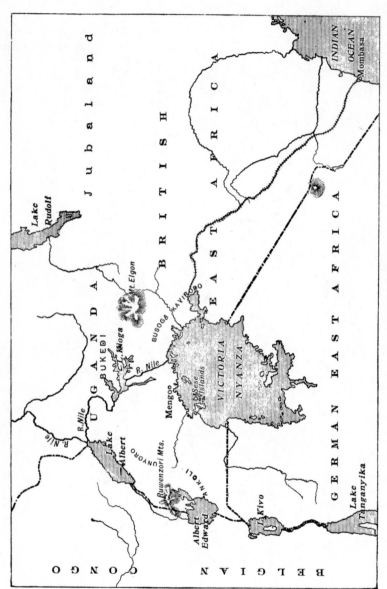

Uganda and British East Africa

PART I

THE BANYORO A PASTORAL PEOPLE

CHAPTER I

THE COUNTRY, THE PEOPLE, THE KING

Description of the country—its geographical position—its former
   area—pastoral and agricultural people—the boundaries of the
   country—native accounts of their kings and royal house—the
   mother of the second dynasty—disappearance of king Kagoro—
   the new dynasty—status of the king—sacred cows for the king's
   food supply—the king's evening meal of beef—the king's mode
   of spending the night—death of the king—war of the princes
   for the throne—crowning the new king—custom of killing or of
   banishing a prince—list of kings.

Geographical position of Bunyoro. To the north-west of
Uganda, ranging from a little south of the equator to the
Victoria Nile on the north and between 30 and 32 degrees east
of Greenwich, lies the kingdom of Bunyoro. Like Uganda,
it is one of the oldest kingdoms in Central Africa and has, for
many generations, been able at once to resist the inroads of
adjacent tribes and also to extend its own boundaries. It is
one of the few kingdoms of the Bantu tribes that possess an
established monarchy with subordinate chiefs and subchiefs
governing large districts. These chiefs command numerous
clans, many of whom are entirely pastoral, while others, though
mainly agricultural, own large flocks of goats and sheep ;
but all alike, both pastoral and agricultural, acknowledge the
king's supremacy.

Extent of Bunyoro. The kingdom originally comprised
tracts of land which now belong to Uganda proper : certainly
the Budu district and also parts of the district of Bulemezi,
Kyagwe, Singo and Gomba once belonged to Bunyoro, while a
large district of Busoga, lying to the south-east of Bunyoro

and tributary to it, was conquered by Uganda. For many years the Baganda have been slowly pushing back the Banyoro and occupying the lands thus acquired, and for some years Busoga and Budu have yielded to the superior arms of the Baganda. When British rule began in Uganda, a new kingdom was established on Mount Luinzori, and land which formed part of Bunyoro was given to the newly appointed king Kasagama, who is a nephew of Kabarega the exiled king of Bunyoro. This new king, Kasagama, was a rebel prince from Bunyoro, who was living in exile on the slopes of Mount Luinzori. Further deductions from the country were made when king Kabarega resisted the British and was finally captured and exiled to the Seychelles in 1899, soon after the British Protectorate was established in Uganda. A great part of south and east Bunyoro was given to Uganda in recognition of the services it rendered the British in suppressing king Kabarega. To-day Bunyoro is in extent about one-third of the original kingdom when at the height of its prosperity.

The pastoral clans. The Banyoro are a tribe of the great Bantu family, though they combine two distinct classes of people, the pastoral and the agricultural clans. Careful observation and enquiry lead to the opinion that the agricultural clans were the original inhabitants, and that they were conquered by the pastoral people who have reduced them to their present servile condition. The pastoral people are a tall, well-built race of men and women with finely cut features, many of them being over six feet in height. The men are athletic with little spare flesh, but the women are frequently very fat and corpulent : indeed their ideal of beauty is obesity, and their milk diet together with their careful avoidance of exercise tends to increase their size.

Agricultural clans. The agricultural clans, on the other hand, are short, ill-favoured looking men and women with broad noses of the negro type, lean, and unkempt. Both classes are dark, varying in shade from a light brown to deep black, with short woolly hair. The pastoral people refrain, as far as possible, from all manual labour and expect the agricultural clans to do their menial work for them, such as

building their houses, carrying firewood and water, and supplying them with grain and beer for their households.

Dress. The dress of the pastoral clans was, until quite recently, restricted almost entirely to cow-skins which were
dressed until quite supple. The women are more particular
about their clothing than the men and wear long robes extending
from the shoulders to the feet, often tied with a girdle in a way
that permits them to expose and use their arms, though more
frequently the arms are covered by a second robe of cow-skin
thrown over the head and hanging down to the waist. The
men are less careful about their dress : they wear smaller
skins hanging from the neck, covering the shoulders and upper
part of the body only and leaving the lower part nude. The
agricultural clans, both men and women, wear either sheep- or
goat-skins round their loins or roughly made bark-cloths.
In both sexes the dress of the agricultural clans is barely
sufficient for decency.

Boundaries of Bunyoro. The Banyoro have proved themselves to be a strong barrier on the north against the incursions of the Nilotic tribes, and to them doubtless belongs the
credit of diverting the migratory streams of those tribes from
passing south and of causing them to take an easterly route,
thus preserving the highlands of the great lakes region for
the Bantu tribes. Bunyoro is bounded on the north by
Bukedi, on the south-east by Busoga, on the west by the River
Semliki and Lake Albert, and on the south and south-west by
Uganda. The physical features of the country are much the
same as those of Uganda : it is hilly, well watered and has
some forest-land. To the south-west there are some rocky
hills which are venerated by the people, and among them is
the burial-place of the kings.

Origin of the royal house. There is no reliable account of the
origin of the kings ; this is probably due to the custom of
never mentioning the name of a king after his death and of
obliterating the word from the language. As in Uganda so
also in Bunyoro, the people have mythical stories of the first
king having come from God, originating their race and providing
them with cattle and food. Four distinct dynasties of kings

are given by the old people for the first few generations of the royal house ; yet they are unable to trace the origin of these lines, nor can they account for the disappearances of certain of them. The story of the first two kings is as follows :

A man appeared among them who because of his ability and superior knowledge was acclaimed king. He was given the name Isaza and continued to live in the country and rule it for some years. He married a wife but had no children. After some years he disappeared suddenly, and the people, who were unable to trace him or to account for his disappearance, after a prolonged search and continued waiting in the hope that he would return, made the prime minister (Bukulu) king in his stead.

The story of Nyinamweru. King Bukulu had one child, a daughter. While she was still a girl, a medicine-man came to the king and warned him against allowing his daughter to marry, saying that, should she marry and have a son, the king would die. King Bukulu accordingly guarded his daughter and, when she was old enough to marry, he built a house for her and surrounded it with a strong, high fence, with no gate or outlet, setting a man with his wife to guard the road leading to the house and thus prevent the girl from holding intercourse with the world. Inside the enclosure king Bukulu placed his daughter, whose name was Nyinamweru, with her maid Mugezi, and warned them against holding any communications with men. Food, that is to say milk, was brought daily to the guardian Lumbumbi, who climbed the fence and handed it down to the maid inside. For several years all went well, until one day a man belonging to the priestly clan called *Bacwezi* arrived. The man was a stranger in the place and wandered to the enclosure seeking some one to tell him the way. He had his dog with him and, as he could find no entrance to the enclosure, he walked round calling to the two women inside and enquiring for the entrance. They explained to him their situation and told him how they were secluded to avoid men. This, however, only increased the man's curiosity, and being struck by the beauty of the princess, he made love to her. Gathering some wild flowers he presented them to her, and finally gained the women's permission to climb into the enclosure. Simbu was the name of this man: he became the husband of the princess Nyinamweru and remained with her several months in concealment. He then left the place secretly. In due time the princess gave birth to a son and named him Ndaula. Nyinamweru nursed her child for two years without the infant being discovered. At the end of that time her nurse became afraid that the child would be seen playing in the enclosure and that its presence would endanger their lives, should king Bukulu learn of its existence. She therefore persuaded Nyinamweru to give the child to the guard Lumbumbi, who was bidden to take and cast it into a stream and drown it. The mother most reluctantly yielded to this advice, and little Ndaula was taken by the guard and cast into the river. Fortunately the child's umbilical cord was tied to his wrist and, when Lumbumbi cast him into the river, the string by which the cord was tied to the wrist caught on the branch of a tree and saved the child from drowning. Later in the day Lumbumbi passed the place and heard the child crying, and went to see how it could still be alive. When he saw what had happened, he regarded the child's preservation as an intervention of the gods, took it home to his wife and told her to nurse it. When Nyinamweru was told how her son had been preserved from death, she was delighted and gave Lumbumbi a milch cow to supply milk for the child. The boy Ndaula grew up to be a man and was commonly known as Lumbumbi's son. He herded the cattle and was a dauntless youth, full of mischief, delighting above all things to tease the king's herdsmen, who were haughty and expected everybody to give way to them and their cattle at the watering-places. It chanced one day that the king had ordered his cow-men to give his cattle salt to eat at a certain place, saying that he would be present to examine the cattle. At the appointed time Ndaula also appeared with his cows and drove them to the spot to eat salt. The king's herdsmen tried to keep the cows away, and a struggle ensued between them and Ndaula, in which the king was fatally speared. At the trial which followed Ndaula explained who he was. He then sent for his mother Nyinamweru who confirmed his story, and the people not only pardoned his offence but also crowned him king. From the time of king Ndaula it has been the custom for a mother to make her child an amulet and put it on his neck in remembrance of the string which saved Ndaula's life. King Ndaula reigned a short time and then sent for his father and brought him and his relatives into Bunyoro. Ndaula married and had a son whom he named Wamala. When Wamala grew up, his father abdicated the throne in favour of his son, in order that he might be free from the responsibilities of government and able to make war upon the surrounding tribes. Ndaula was constantly victorious in the wars he undertook, enlarged the boundaries of his country, and enriched the people. In his old age he is said to have disappeared, because it was not customary for kings to die.

King Wamala continued to reign until he became an old man when, like his predecessor, he disappeared, and his son Kyomya succeeded him on the throne. Kyomya also increased the size of the kingdom by conquering many of the surrounding tribes. Wamala appointed three men named Mugarara, Ibona and Mugenyi to be priests, and two women, Nakalanda and Nabibungo, to be priestesses to the chief gods. These men were the first of the class of people afterwards known as the Bacwezi, who are the priests of the country.

Nothing else is known of Kyomya except that, in his old age, he too disappeared as his forefathers had done, and that his son Kagoro succeeded him on the throne.

Kagoro warned by ghosts to leave his country. When Kagoro had reigned some years, he was warned by the ghosts of his ancestors that they were displeased with his people, because they robbed each other and lied to one another. The king called the people and told them that, unless they ceased from these bad habits, he must leave them. They, however, took no heed of the warning, and accordingly king Kagoro called together his near relations and departed with them secretly, carrying with him two baskets containing truth and love, and leaving behind him two baskets containing lying and hatred. One young woman who refused to go with the party was left in a house with certain sacred drums named *Kajwimbe*, *Nyalabe* and *Kyamukumbwiri*, which are still retained as royal drums. For some years the people hoped to find one of the princes whom they could induce to become king, but after a prolonged search it became evident that they must find some other person to rule over them. Accordingly the prime minister Nakolo was sent to the Bukedi country to seek a prince who would come to reign in Bunyoro. Nakolo found a prince named Nakoko and returned with him to Bunyoro, where he became king.

King Mpugu. When prince Nakoko was crowned he was named Mpugu by the people, because one side of his body was dark and the other light. He came with three brothers who with himself formed the Babito dynasty. It is said that, when the Babito family first arrived in Bunyoro, they did not understand cow-keeping. They had to learn the art from the Banyoro and also how to live on a milk diet.

Royalty and their state. The king is held in great veneration by all classes who bow low when coming before him, and no person dares take a weapon into his presence. Weapons are laid on the ground at a distance, and the owner approaches and prostrates himself to greet the king. When the king is on a journey and wishes to rest, one of his subjects immediately kneels down on one knee and offers the other as a seat for the king to sit upon.

The king lived in an enclosure very much like a cattle kraal. It was surrounded by a fence, in most instances, composed of thorny bushes intended to keep the cattle together by night and also to prevent wild animals from attacking the cows. The king's houses were divided from those of his wives and servants by roughly built fences of elephant-grass, which were merely screens to hide him from view rather than to afford protection against an armed force. By night the cows belonging to the king were taken into different court-yards and guarded by special cow-men. At each gateway to the royal enclosure there was a hut in which a guard lived, and one man was expected to be always awake and guarding the gate by day and by night. From the body of police who supplied the guards for the gates the king's personal guard was chosen, some of whom had to be on duty during the night to guard his house against any danger.

The sacred herd of cows. The king's diet was strictly regulated by ancient custom. He subsisted on milk and beef, but chiefly on milk. Vegetables and mutton he might not touch, and for his use a special herd of cows was kept. These were sacred animals which had to be guarded against coming into contact with other cows, and no one was permitted to drink the milk from them save the king and his servant appointed for the duty. The sacred herd of cows had special men to herd them and to attend to them constantly in order to prevent them from mixing with other cattle. They were kept in a part of the country where they could be kept from contact with the large ordinary herds of the king and from mingling with the cattle of chiefs. From this herd nine cows were taken to the capital to provide milk for the king's use, the animals chosen being young cows with their first calves. When a cow was ready to travel after giving birth, she was taken to the royal residence to join the select number, and one of the nine was then removed to the general body of the sacred herd in the country. This most sacred herd of nine was called *Nkorogi* and had to be jealously guarded against contact with a bull. The period for which each cow was kept in the *Nkorogi* herd was about two months, during which time both cow and calf had to be maintained in perfect condition. At the end of two months her place was taken by another cow and she was removed as already stated to the country and there kept for her milk to make butter for the king's use and for breeding purposes: she never returned to supply the king with milk.

Men belonging to the sacred herd. The *Nkorogi* cows had three special men to care for them, in addition to a boy who brought them from the pastures daily. These men had assistants who took charge of the cows during the day when they were out at pasture. The boy chosen for the office of driving the cows to and from the pasture and of drinking the surplus milk from the king's supply was known as the "Caller," so named because he had to call out to warn people to leave the path, as he passed along with the cows. He thus announced their presence and gave people time to escape out of the way of the herd. He was taken from the Abaitira clan, had to be a strong healthy boy seven or eight years old, and retained the office of " Caller " until he was old enough to marry, that is to say about seventeen years old, when the king ordered the Abaitira clan to bring another young boy. The former boy who was now deposed was given a wife by the king and settled to ordinary pastoral life. Should the boy fall sick during his term of office and the medicine-man consider the illness to be of a serious nature, he would be strangled ; or, again, should he have sexual relations with any woman, he would be put to death. He had to guard against scratching his flesh or doing anything that might draw blood. On this account he was not allowed to go into tall grass, nor might he leave the path when going to bring the cows from the pasture lest he should prick or scratch himself. To strike this boy was an offence punishable with death, because the boy's life was bound up with that of the king and anything that happened to him was liable to affect the king. Each afternoon before sunset the boy went for the *Nkorogi* cows, which were brought from the pastures to some place about a mile distant from the royal residence, when they were delivered to the boy who then began to drive them thither, raising, as he did so, his cry to warn people from the path. Men and women now hurriedly hid in the grass and covered their heads until the herd had passed. The cry was repeated from time to time until the boy reached the kraal at the royal residence, where one of the three cow-men awaited him. Another important duty of the boy "Caller" was to drink up the milk left by the king from his daily milk supply. No other person but this boy was permitted to drink any of the milk from the sacred cows, nor was the boy allowed any other food. The three milk-men in charge of the cows had special titles, *Mukologi, Munyuwanga* and *Muigimbirwa*. Each day before going to milk the cows they purified themselves by smearing their heads, arms and chests with white clay, and during their term of office, which lasted a year, they observed the

strictest rules of chastity. They were never allowed to wash
with water, but had to rub their bodies over frequently with
butter, and any infringement of these rules was punishable
with death. The cow-man *Mukologi* took charge of the sacred
cows as soon as they arrived from the pasture, and drove them
into the enclosure where *Munyuwanga* spread a mat, and the
cow to be milked was made to stand upon it. The calf of the
cow was brought and allowed to suck for a short time, and was
then held before its dam while she was milked. *Muigimbirwa*
rubbed each cow's udder with butter and cleansed it before
she was milked, and stood holding the cow's tail lest she should
flick it during the time she was being milked and cause dust
to fall into the milk. Two women, wives of the king, now
came forward, each of whom had been smeared over with
white clay in a similar manner to that of the cow-men, one of
them carrying the milk-pots and the other a bowl of water
for the milk-man to wash his hands with before milking.
Mukologi having washed his hands with the water which the
woman poured over them and squatted by the cow, the second
woman then placed a milk-pot between his knees and he milked
the amount he considered advisable from the cow into the
milk-pot. The milk-pot was encased in a wicker cover to
protect it from coming into contact with the man's flesh
during the time of milking. When the cows were milked, the
two women carried the milk into a special house which was
used as a dairy, into which the king also went to drink milk.
During the time the cows were being milked there were no
other persons permitted to be present, and none of those who
took part in the milking ceremony might cough : to do so was
considered injurious to the king and was a criminal act punishable with death.

   Royal visit to the dairy and meal. In the morning, after
the cows were milked, the king went into the dairy to drink
milk ; and no sooner did he rise to go to the dairy than all
the visitors hastily left the royal enclosure and all residents
in the enclosure withdrew from sight, while the king's wives
knelt and covered their heads until he returned. In the dairy,
the wife who was in charge uncovered the milk-pot and wiped

it with a leaf taken from a particular kind of tree, a supply of leaves from which was kept ready for use. The wife then handed the milk-pot to the king and, turning her head aside while the king drank, waited until he tapped with his hand upon the pot to indicate that he had finished, when she took it from him and gave him another pot of milk, if he wished for more. All the royal milk-pots were made of clay, though a few wooden pots were to be found among them and were the kind commonly used by other people. After the morning meal the king went to a reception-house, to which the cow-man *Muigimbirwa* came and asked him, "Are you free to see people, sire ?" If the king answered in the affirmative, *Muigimbirwa* replied, "King, live for ever," and withdrew to tell the people that they might return to the king. About noon the king again went to drink milk and afterwards retired to rest for two or three hours.

The king's evening meal of beef. In the evening a meal of beef was brought by a man-cook. The beef had to be meat from a year-old animal taken from the sacred herd. It was cut into small pieces and roasted on wooden spits or skewers before a fire. When the cook took the food to the king he smeared his head, face, arms and chest with white clay after the manner of the milk-men when going to milk the sacred cows. He had two iron prongs with sockets to fit on his first finger and thumb, these prongs being used to lift the meat and put it into the king's mouth, as the king was not permitted to touch his food with his hands. The cook had to be careful not to touch the king's teeth with the iron prongs, as such an offence was punishable with death. After the meal the king drank a little beer and retired to rest for a time. In the evening, after he had rested, certain chiefs were admitted to see the king or, if he wished, he would see some of his wives and talk with them until the time to retire for the night. Before retiring he had another meal of milk.

The king's mode of spending the night. The king was not left to sleep the whole night in one house, for, about midnight or soon after, one of his wives aroused him and conducted him to a second house and again, before dawn, he was conducted to a third house in which he completed his rest. Each morning he was attended by one of his wives, who rubbed his body over with butter instead of a bath.

Death of the king. The king never attained old age, his mental powers and bodily vigour never being allowed to decline or fail, nor did the king die from any lingering illness. Did he feel unwell or think he was about to be seriously ill, he would call his leading chiefs and hold a council to consider state affairs and would leave them under the impression that he was quite well. When the chiefs were dismissed, the king would retire to a special house, call his principal wife and ask her to bring the poison-cup. She would understand that he wished to have the poison-cup to end his life, and accordingly prepared a potion from a drug she kept ready to hand. This she gave to the king, who drank it and in a few moments was dead. The death of the king was kept secret as long as possible, and everything went on as before in the royal enclosure. To account for his absence it was said that the king was unwell and could not be seen or hold his usual courts. The principal wife took one or two chiefs into her confidence, and together they provided a cow-hide and stitched up the body of the king in it. They then made preparations for crowning a new king. This custom lasted down to within living memory.

War of princes to secure the throne. When the arrangements were ready for announcing the death, the chief cow-man was called and told the king was dead. He hereupon mounted the house in which the king's body lay, carrying a pot of milk which he raised above his head, calling in a loud voice, "The milk of the cow is lifted up. Whom is it for? Is it for you or for God?" He then dashed the pot to the ground where it broke and the milk was spilled. At the same time all the milk-pots which had been used by the king were broken. The widows took up the death-wail and the princes rushed to arms. The people now joined their favourite prince, and fighting commenced. Each prince was expected to fight for the throne. Those who feared to do so would flee into some remote part of the country, there to live a life of seclusion despised by the people. These civil wars continued for several

months. The princes met and fought. First one and then
another of them fell in battle until at length two princes only
were left. When a prince fell, his followers joined another
prince and these later battles became more serious as the
number of princes decreased and their armies increased. The
final battle was always the most severe, when the two remaining
princes fought to decide who should live and reign. No
peasant feared the blood-avenger when he killed a prince in
any of these battles, for no notice was taken afterwards of the
death of a prince who was killed in battle fighting for the
throne. The principal chiefs (Bamasaza) were not expected
to take any part in the wars, their duty being to guard the
body of the late king, await the result of the wars and prevent
any prince from taking the body before the final battle had
been fought. The retainers of chiefs might, however, join the
forces of any prince they wished to see on the throne.

Crowning the new king. When the final battle had been
fought, the victorious prince went to the capital and claimed
the body of his father. The chiefs who were guarding it first
satisfied themselves that all the princes had fallen or fled into
other countries before they delivered the body to the claimant.
They then proclaimed the prince king and set him on the royal
rug which was composed of lion-, leopard- and cow-skins, and
took the oath of allegiance to him. The new king took his
father's body for burial immediately he was crowned. All
sorrow was now ended and there was nothing but rejoicing.
The joy for the new king's victory and the knowledge that the
wars were ended, property safe and the normal life of the
community restored, entirely drowned the more solemn thought
of the late king's death. The new king next walked from his
capital to the place where the deceased king was to be buried.
It was customary for the king to walk when making any journey,
and the paths were cleared and carpeted with newly cut grass
for him to walk on. As soon as the king had buried his father,
the chiefs came to congratulate him upon his succession and
to swear allegiance to him. The name of the dead king was
not mentioned after his death, and, if the name was a word
used in the language, it was dropped and a new word coined to

take its place. The king ascended a hill called Ipeime after the funeral and mounted a rock, only a few princesses and his wives accompanying him. Should any man do so he was captured and speared to death on the rock, that his life might go to strengthen the new king.

Custom of killing or banishing a prince at the crowning ceremony. It was customary, when the princes had fallen in battle, for the new king to send a chief to one of the princes who had refused to fight, should there be any such, and for the chief thus sent to try to induce the prince to come to the capital and claim the throne. Should the chief succeed in finding a prince willing to accept the throne, the prince was taken bound before the king who had him put to death. Should the chief fail to find such a prince, he would take a boy-prince before the king, and the latter would charge the boy never to come into his presence again. This boy-prince was called *Mulagwa :* he was given an estate in some distant part of the country and never allowed to visit the king. All other princes who were found after their brother's accession were put to death.

List of kings. The first recorded king was a man of the priestly clan (Bacwezi) named Isaza who died childless.

The second king had been the prime minister of Isaza. This king's name was Bukulu : his daughter was Nyinamweru and married Simbu, and their child was Wamala Ndaula.

3. Wamala Ndaula =

4. Kyomya =

5. Kagoro =

Here the line ended and Nagwa, whose husband is unknown, became mother of the present line of kings: she belonged to the Ngabi clan.

7. Mpingu or Mpugu = Nyagiro

8. Oyokambaigulu = Ilimera of the Mulisa clan

9. Wumyabubayira = A woman of the Munyakwa clan (name unknown)

10. Nyalwabavirahaigulu = A woman of the Mugwari clan
(name unknown)

11. Cwamali = Gawa of the Mukwonga clan

12. Lugurukamacoli = Nyatworo of the Mcwa clan

13. Lukedi = Kyendeki of the Musaigwa clan

14. Kyebambi = A woman of the Wabanga clan

15. Isansayabigogo = Nkera of the Basagi clan

16. Ruhaga-ne-ngoma = A woman of the Mcwa clan

17. Kyebambi = Kajaja of the Bazira clan

18. Nabongo = Kigero of the Musita clan

19. Mirundi = Kanyange of the Muyonza clan

20. Kabarega = Katabanga of the Musita clan

21. Andereya Ruhanga

CHAPTER II

GOVERNMENT

The king the sole possessor of land—district chiefs—no land taxes—
the law of succession to chieftainships—chiefs as magistrates—
names of districts—minor or sub-chiefs—princes and princesses
land owners—the king's mother—the king's place of residence—
courts of appeal—punishment for adultery—the poison ordeal—
trial of princes and princesses—punishment for murder—punishment for homicide—treatment of the relatives of a suicide—wife
beating—treatment of theft—method of discovering theft—
imprisonment—inheritance.

The king the sole possessor of land. The land belonged
solely to the king who could dispose of it as he willed. Peasants,
however, were free to settle anywhere in the country without
asking for permission from the chief to whom the oversight
of the district belonged, for even the king did not regard his
land with any such pride or as of such value as the king of
Uganda regarded his. The king and the upper classes of the
people valued land for its pastoral rather than for its agricultural qualities. Those districts which were good as pasture-
lands were esteemed as of greater value than districts only
suited for cultivation.

District chiefs. Chiefs were appointed to govern large
tracts of country. They were given, when elected, the title
Musaza, pl. *Bamasaza*. These district-chiefs had sub-chiefs
under them, each of whom was known by the title *Ndibalaba*,
and these again had minor chiefs under them. Princes were
sent from the capital, when they were eight or nine years old,
into the country and there placed under responsible herdsmen

who trained them in the arts of cattle-breeding, milking herding and treating cows when sick. These princes were expected to learn all about cattle, and to be in no wise inferior to the most skilled herdsman.

No land taxes. The king levied no yearly taxes or rates from his subjects, and chiefs were not allowed to levy any definite annual sum from their peasants, though it was an understood rule that each peasant should take a quantity of grain to his chief after each harvest, and that the chief should take the larger portion of this to the king. It was contrary to custom for a peasant to make a gift to the king direct : it had to pass through the district-chief. When therefore a peasant made his yearly offering to his chief, it was on a scale that would suffice both king and chief. Chiefs were expected to give liberally not only grain, but more especially cattle, for the king's household. In addition to gifts of food, each district-chief was responsible for building and keeping in repair a number of houses in the royal enclosure, and he arranged with his sub-chiefs the number of men that each was to supply for any particular work.

The roads were merely tracks through the country worn by people going to and fro between the capital and their country residences, no attempt being made to construct them or to keep them clear from grass. They were only widened and hoed when the king wished to make a tour to some distant place, on which occasion men were set to cut down the grass on either side of the paths, to widen them, hoe up the weeds, fill up holes, and generally to smooth the road and carpet it with grass for the king to walk upon, for he was never carried. At other times the grass grew, leaving only a narrow track trodden hard by the feet of pedestrians.

The law of succession to chieftainships. When a chief died, his clan appointed his successor, who was as a rule a son of the deceased man ; the king, however, had the right to appoint to the office some person in no wise connected with the deceased, and he sometimes exercised it. The king might also depose a chief from office for an offence and appoint any one he wished to the chieftainship, though such cases were

rare : should the king have cause to depose a chief, he invariably put the offender to death, because it was feared the man
might avenge himself by killing the king.

Chiefs as magistrates. Each chief and sub-chief was a
magistrate in his own district, his magisterial duties being in
fact his principal work. He was also called upon to supply
warriors for punitive expeditions. Any litigant might appeal
from a lower court in a district to a higher court and finally to
the king's court, which was the final court of appeal.

Names of districts. During Kabarega's reign the country
was divided into fourteen districts named as follows :

1.	Buhimba	8.	Busongolo
2.	Ise ya Bacwezi	9.	Bugungu (Munyabara)
3.	Kyaka	10.	Bugaya (Ibanda)
4.	Bagakhya	11.	Lukongoja
5.	Bagangaizi	12.	Mbogo
6.	Mwengi (Mugalula)	13.	Bugoma
7.	Toro	14.	Buruli

Each district-chief (Musaza) had his residence at some
well-known place on the border of his district nearest the
capital, in addition to his chief residence in the capital itself ;
and it was at the latter place that he spent the greatest portion
of his time.

Minor Chiefs. Sub-chiefs were commonly called *Batongole*, though their official title was *Ndibalaba*. In their case,
as in the case of the superior chiefs, it was usual for a son to
succeed his father in office, though any son of a deceased person
might be elected by the members of the clan to which he
belonged, who then submitted the name to the king for his
approval. In arrangements for state duties, such as building
royal houses and warfare, the Batongole were responsible to
the district-chiefs, but they were free to appeal to the king for
satisfaction, should they think they were being imposed upon
by their superiors. The king seldom had occasion to interfere
with the details of government. District-chiefs resided in
the capital near the royal enclosure so as to be ready to assist
the king in state affairs, should he require their assistance ;

Plate I

(1) The King of Banyoro wearing the special hat for the Secret Court

(2) Chief, who has succeeded his father as chief, approaching the
King to be confirmed in his office
(*Banyoro Tribe*)

and they were responsible for the safety of the king against any attack upon him by a foreign power. When a chief wished to absent himself from the capital, he first sought the king's permission and explained the reason for his desire to go into the country. Such a request was seldom refused.

Princes and princesses as landowners. Princes and princesses had estates in the country upon which peasants lived whose duties were to build their masters' houses and to supply them with grain, beer and vegetables, the grain and vegetables being the food of the household-slaves and also of their free servants, for the princes and princesses themselves lived entirely on milk. There was a special house in the royal enclosure where they met and awaited the king's pleasure. One of the princes was appointed to be the representative of his brothers to hear any grievance, settle disputes among them, and be responsible to the king for their general conduct : he was given the title *Muguruzi* and had power to punish by fine any of his brothers for any offence which he might commit. In like manner a princess was appointed to rule over her sisters and was given the title *Batebi*.

The king's mother. The king's mother lived in the capital near the king. She was rich in herds of cattle and had estates which made her independent of her son's help. She held her own courts and had her bailiff to manage her estates. When the king ascended the throne, his mother at the same time assumed her office and took over the estates from her predecessor. She was expected to live in widowhood, though it was well known that she was far from being chaste. Should the king's mother die, one of her sisters or, failing a sister, some near relative of her clan was chosen for the office. This woman the king called "mother," and honoured her as such. When a king died before his mother, she retained her herds, but had smaller estates given her and lived some distance from the new king, her grandson.

The king's residence. The royal residence, though dirty and badly kept owing to the numerous cows, was far superior to any other enclosure in the country. In it there were a number of large court-houses which were used for state affairs.

In one of these the king met his district-chiefs to discuss state secrets. When the king and chiefs went to this court-house, each of them wore a peculiar hat of office which he retained during the meeting, and a tusk of ivory was laid in the doorway over which they stepped as they entered the house. In this court-house every man stood. It was here that the secret affairs of the state were discussed, especially matters of war. In the other court-houses the king sat on a raised seat, which was a mound of beaten earth covered with a rug made from the skins of a lion, a leopard and a cow, and a spear was stuck in the ground near the king's right hand with which he could transfix any man who annoyed him during the sitting of the court. When the king was about to proceed to a court-house, grass mats were spread for him to walk upon, a sacred cow walked beside him to the court, and stood by the door until he returned, when it again accompanied him to his private house. Pages lined the path from the house to the court, beating drums and playing fifes. The principal cases heard during the sitting of the court were appeals, especially in matters of theft and adultery, from district-chiefs.

Courts of appeal. When a man went to accuse another person in any court he paid a fee of one hundred cowry-shells. The judge took one-fifth of the fine imposed, while four-fifths were paid to the person who won the case. When a man appealed from one court to a higher court, he paid another fee of two hundred cowry-shells, and, as stated above, one-fifth of the fine imposed went to the court in addition to the court fee; the other four-fifths of the fine went to the successful party. Cattle lifting was one of the most common crimes among pastoral clans. The thief, when caught, had to restore the number of animals stolen and was fined twice the number he had stolen.

Punishment for adultery. In a case of adultery, if the crime had been committed with one of the king's wives, both the guilty parties were condemned to death; in a case among the common people the injured husband invariably accepted a fine from the adulterer, though he might kill the guilty wife, should he desire to do so. There were some clans a

member of which, if he committed adultery with one of the
king's wives, was not put to death, but had his eyes gouged
out.   The king's wife in such a case was taken and drowned in
the River Nile, or she might be sent to Bukedi to be given in
marriage to some chief there.   This latter punishment was
considered a worse fate than death by drowning, because the
people of Bukedi wore no clothing and lived upon grain,
whereas a woman from Bunyoro, accustomed to a milk diet,
preferred death to the degradation of cultivating and eating
vegetable food.   If an unmarried woman tempted a man and
had a child by him, the man was fined a sheep, and when the
child was weaned the father took it.   If, on the other hand,
it was proved that the man forced the woman, a heavier fine
was imposed.   In each case the man was given the opportunity
of marrying the woman by paying her relatives the marriage
fee, time being given for him to obtain the sum required.
Should the man refuse to pay the fine for his wrong-doing, the
child was retained by the members of the woman's clan and
grew up to all intents and purposes a slave.   Chiefs seldom
pardoned a man who committed adultery with one of their
wives, and the guilty couple were put to death.   Should a
commoner make love to a princess and marry her, he was put
to death and his goods were confiscated, while the princess
was severely flogged.

The poison ordeal.   When the king was in doubt as to the
rights of a case which had been brought before him for trial,
or should the parties appeal to what was deemed the final
test, the poison ordeal was resorted to.   The poison-cup contained a mixture made from the seeds of the datura plant,
which were boiled and the water from them given to each
of the litigants to drink.   After drinking the potion, the
men sat for a time until the drug had taken effect, when they
were called upon to rise and walk to the judge to hear his
decision and thank him for it.   The person who was able to
rise and walk to the judge won the case.   It was seldom that
both men could rise and walk, indeed in most cases one of
them was unable to move and usually both of them suffered
from a long illness afterwards, and often one or other died.

The property of the person who died was confiscated, a portion of it was given to the successful person, and the remainder was given to the king.

Trial of princes and princesses. The king alone could try cases arising between members of the royal family, when an appeal was made from the prince or princess set over them. When princes quarrelled and fought, the king after hearing the case might order the prince whom he considered to be in fault to be speared to death. A common punishment inflicted upon a prince was to imprison him by building a strong stockade and confining him within it for a time with a single servant, the detention lasting only a few days or two or three months. He was given a daily allowance of milk, but was prohibited from intercourse with any person during his term of imprisonment.

Punishment for murder. When a murder was committed, the members of the murdered man's clan sought the murderer, and, when they had tracked him down, they demanded his surrender from his relatives and he was put to death. Should the members of the clan to which the murderer belonged try to shield the man or refuse to give him up to justice, an appeal was made to the king and he would demand the surrender of the guilty person. When a murderer escaped into some other country and the blood avenger could not secure him, a child of the murderer or some person nearly connected with him was taken and put to death in his stead.

Punishment for homicide. Any person who accidentally killed another made the fact known as early as possible and appealed to the chief of his district to investigate the case. When it was proved that there was no animosity a heavy fine was accepted by the relatives of the dead man, and when the fine was paid one or two women were included, who were given to the near relations.

Treatment of the relations of a suicide. The relatives of a person who committed suicide were fined by the chief upon whose land the deed was committed before they were allowed to remove the body, or to destroy the house in which the deed took place or to cut down the tree, should death have been by hanging. Suicide was usually committed by hanging, though a few people strangled themselves. Men and women hanged themselves either in their house or upon some tree near the house. It was said to be necessary to destroy a tree upon which a person had hanged himself and to burn down a house in which a person had committed suicide, otherwise they would be a danger to people in general and would influence them to commit suicide. Suicide was far more common among women than among men; this was especially the case with women who had been unfaithful to their husbands and feared detection. Men who had been house-breaking or who were suspected of cattle-lifting and feared detection committed suicide, and most men preferred death to parting with cattle in payment of a fine.

Wife beating. Wife beating was not considered a serious offence and there was no punishment attached to it. The woman was said to be the property of her husband, and, should he kill her, the loss was his. Chiefs and wealthy people alone could afford to kill their wives for an offence, because they alone could afford to purchase another wife; whereas peasants, by reason of their poverty and inability to pay the marriage fee for another wife, had to be content with flogging the offender. A wife's only remedy for ill-treatment was to escape to her clan and to induce the members of it to protect her. If she had cause for complaint, her husband was asked to come and state his case before witnesses, who, if the woman was in the right, fined the husband and, before they gave up the wife, made him promise to treat her better and also to make her some compensation, such as new clothes and a goat, before she returned to her home.

Treatment of theft. Petty theft committed by young children was punished by flogging, but grown up people, especially slaves, were mutilated, their ears or their hands being cut off according to the nature of the offence. Slaves who were disobedient had their ears cut off, and, if they still continued stubborn, they were put to death.

Method of detecting thieves. In seeking to discover a thief it was necessary to employ a particular medicine-man called the "Smeller." This man visited the place from which the property had been stolen, and, after hearing the account of the theft and obtaining a description of the lost property, he went down on his hands and knees and sniffed about on the ground until he discovered the direction in which the thieves had gone, when he followed and tracked them down and captured them.

Imprisonment. There were no special places of detention, justice being for the most part done by fine, mutilation, or flogging, which were inflicted at once. Should there be reason for detention, the person was put in the stocks or else bound hand and foot. The stocks consisted of a log of wood with a hole cut through it, and one of the prisoner's feet was put through the hole, a peg being run through the log at right angles to the hole which so narrowed it as to prevent the foot from being withdrawn. One foot only of a prisoner was put through the log, so that the prisoner could move about by dragging the log, but could not escape because of its weight and also because he was usually guarded. A prisoner had to supply his own food. Detention was usually given for refusing to pay a debt or for refusing to work or for doing work badly.

Inheritance. The property of the pastoral clans consisted in cattle and in women. When a person was ill, he made known whom he wished to inherit his property at his death. A son usually became heir, though not necessarily the eldest son, and if the deceased had been a chief, the heir was introduced to the king and his approval obtained. There was seldom any difficulty raised. When a peasant settled on a piece of land and cultivated it, there was no question of the king's permission or obtaining the right of tenancy, because the king and wealthy people in general were always glad to welcome a new freeman and they did not value land except for pasture, yet they might object to a stranger settling upon it. Any peasant might cultivate land in any part of the country, the only charge upon it would be a basket of grain to be paid at harvest to the chief in whose district he resided and whose land he tilled. Peasants from generosity generally paid much more grain, without any demand being made by the chief for even the basketful to which he was entitled.

CHAPTER III

CLANS, TOTEMS AND TERMS OF RELATIONSHIP

Different classes in the tribe—family names of clans—clans with their totems—terms of relationship.

Different classes in the tribe. There are two distinct classes of people in Bunyoro, with an intermediate class, drawn from the other two, whose members are free to marry into either the one or the other. The most important class is entirely pastoral, the members of it forming the aristocracy of the country. The other class is purely agricultural, and its members consist of the peasants and labouring people. The intermediate class is composed of men who devote themselves to the cultivation of land, but who also possess cattle and whose diet is partly vegetable and partly milk. They are possibly, in many cases, men who once belonged to the pastoral people but for some reason or other have taken to agriculture. Others may be peasants who, having become rich, have imitated the mode of life of the pastoral people and adopted a partial milk diet. Whatever their origin, they possess herds of cattle and some of their totems are cattle, while others are vegetable or plant totems; whereas purely pastoral people have totems relating almost entirely to cattle, and peasants who till the soil have totems taken from plants or things relating to agriculture.

Totem clans. All three classes of the Banyoro are respectively divided into a number of totem clans. No man is allowed to marry or have sexual intercourse with a woman of his own clan, and children belong to the clan of their father; in other words, the clans are exogamous with descent in the male line. The only exception to the rule of exogamy is in the case of the royal family, who are free to marry women of their own clan, which is the Babito, with the Bushbuck for its totem. So strict is the rule of exogamy in all other clans that formerly breaches of it were capital crimes : a man who married a woman of his own totem clan was put to death.

Family names of clans. In the following list it will be noticed that some clans bear the same name, but have different totems, while others have the same totems but a different family name ; and it is impossible to say whether they are related in any way, they say they are not. The first totem mentioned is the principal totem of the clan, but the people are commonly known by their family name. When people bearing the same name meet they ask what their totems are, before they are satisfied that they are related.

Clans with their totems.   (a)   Clans restricted to pastoral people :

1.   The *Babito*, whose chief totem is the Bushbuck, *Ngabi*, and the second is Rain-water from the roofs of houses, *Maleghyo*. The royal family belong to this clan.

2.   The *Balisa*, whose chief totem is the Red or the Black Cow, *Timba* ; their second totem is Rain-water from the roofs of houses, *Maleghyo*. Members of this clan may neither eat the flesh nor drink the milk of red or of black cows.

3.   The *Bafumambogo*, whose principal totem is the Grass-hopper, *Nsenene*, their second the Cows with Red Markings, their third the Buffalo. Members of the clan may not drink the milk of cows so marked, nor eat the flesh of cows, buffaloes, or grasshoppers.

4.   The *Basonga*, whose principal totem is the Grasshopper, *Nsenene*.

5.   The *Balanze*, whose chief totem is a Mother Nursing a Female Child, *Isereka*, and their second the Grasshopper. No woman during the time she is nursing her infant may enter the cattle-kraal or any house of a member of this clan.

6.   The *Basita*, whose principal totem is the Milch Cow which has been with a bull, and their second Dew upon the Grass. The members of this clan avoid for several days drinking milk from a cow which has been with a bull, and also refrain from walking in grass while dew rests on it.

7. The *Basingo*, whose principal totem is the Cow with a Hump, *Murara*, and their second totem the Cow about to calve, *Busito*. The members of the clan avoid milk and the flesh from such cows.

8. The *Bagimu*, whose principal totem is the Red and White Cow, *Mpulu*, and their second Rain-water from the roofs of houses. Members of the clan may not drink the milk nor eat the flesh of red and white cows, nor use rain-water which has dripped from the roofs.

9. The *Banyakwa*, whose chief totem is the Cow with Straight Horns, *Ngabi*. Members of the clan may not drink the milk nor eat the flesh of straight-horned cows.

10. The *Baisanza*, whose chief totem is a Woman who enters a cattle-kraal and solicits the owner's son and is afterwards found to be pregnant by him, *Butweke*. Such a woman must never again enter a kraal, nor may a member of the clan hold any conversation with her.

11. The *Basengya*, whose principal totem is the Tongue of Animals, *Lulimi*.

12. The *Basengya*, whose principal totem is the Cow with straight Horns, *Ngabi*, and their second Rain-water from the roofs of houses, *Muleghya*.

13. The *Babyasi*, whose principal totem is the Milch Cow with Calf for the Second Time, *Ekuluzi*. Members of the clan may not eat the flesh nor drink the milk of such cows.

14. The *Bakwekwa*, whose principal totem is the Cow with Straight Horns, *Ngabi*. Members of the clan may not drink the milk nor eat the flesh of straight-horned cows.

15. The *Bacwezi*, whose principal totem is the Cow which has drunk salt-water, and their second the Cow which has been with a bull. They may not, for two days, drink the milk of cows which have drunk salt-water, nor may they drink the milk of cows that have been with a bull for five days afterwards.

16. The *Baitira*, whose principal totem is the Cow called *Bazi*, which means a particular colour ; their second totem is a Woman Nursing a Female Child.

(b) Clans whose totems combine those of pastoral and of agricultural people:

17. The *Bakwonga*, whose principal totem is the Bush-buck, *Ngabi*.

18. The *Baswa*, whose principal totem is the Bushbuck, *Ngabi*, and their second Rain-water from the roofs of houses.

19. The *Baboro*, whose chief totem is the Heart of Animals, *Mutima*, and their second the Empty Basket, *Kaibo-hasa*.

20. The *Bayangwe*, whose principal totem is a kind of Monkey, *Enkondo*, and their second another Monkey, *Nkobo*.

21. The *Bagweju*, whose principal totem is a House which has been burned down, and their second any Vessel taken from a house which has been burned down. They avoid both the place where the house stood and also any article rescued from the fire.

22. The *Batongo*, whose principal totem is the Stomach of Animals, *Amara*.

23. The *Banyawagi*, whose principal totem is the Bush-buck.

24. The *Baduku*, whose principal totem is the Worn-out Skin of a Drum.

25. The *Basengya*, whose totems are the Bushbuck and Rain-water from roofs of houses.

26. The *Banyakwa*, whose totem is the Bushbuck.

27. The *Bahenga*, whose principal totem is a Bird, *Kagondo*.

28. The *Bano*, whose principal totem is a Fungus Growing on Trees, *Katozi*.

29. The *Baisanza*, whose principal totem is an Antelope, *Epo*.

30. The *Bakimbiri*, whose principal totem is a Woman Nursing a Female Child, *Isereke*. A nursing mother may not enter the house of any member of this clan.

31. The *Bawongo*, whose principal totem is the Bushbuck, and their second a Running Stream. No member of the clan may cross running water.

32. The *Bapima*, whose principal totem is the Bushbuck.

33. The *Bagombo*, whose principal totem is the Hippo-potamus, *Kiroko*.

34. The *Baisanza*, whose principal totem is the Grasshopper.

35. The *Banyampaka*, whose principal totem is a Water Bird, *Kagondo*.

(c) Agricultural clans with totems referring to Agriculture :

36. The *Basambo*, whose principal totem is an Empty Basket, *Kaibo-hasa*, and their second a Needle, *Lukata*. Empty baskets may not be brought into the presence of members of this clan. Needles must be covered before they are taken into the house of a member of the clan.

37. The *Bayonza*, whose principal totem is a kind of Bird, *Nyoza*, and their second an Empty Basket.

38. The *Bayaga-Abaruka-Omabiba*, whose principal totem is any kind of Bird, and their second Millet, *Bulo*. Birds may not be killed or eaten by any member of this clan, nor may millet which during harvest has been reaped and left in the field all night be taken away by any member of the clan the next day.

39. The *Batwa*, whose principal totem is the Milch Cow, and their second Grass which has been put into the mouth, *Nsugu*. Members of the clan must avoid milch cows and any grass which a person has put into his mouth.

40. The *Bakimbire*, whose principal totem is a Mother Nursing a Female Child, *Isereke*.

41. The *Baraha*, whose principal totem is the Wagtail, *Akanyamasole*.

42. The *Bakimbire*, whose principal totem is Potter's Clay, *Bumba*, and their second Millet, *Bulo*, which has been left in the field all night at harvest after being cut.

43. The *Bagimu*, whose principal totem is the Yam, *Ngobe*.

44. The *Baregeya*, whose principal totem is a Bird, *Ndegeya*.

45. The *Bahembo*, whose principal totem is the Empty Basket, *Kaibo-hasa*.

46. The *Basengya*, whose principal totem is the Wooden Spoon, *Lugala*, which is used in stirring porridge. No member of this clan may touch a wooden porridge spoon.

Terms of Relationship (M.S. = man speaks, W.S. = woman speaks) :

1. Forefather, (M.S.) Baisenkuru.
2. Forefather, (W.S.) Isenkuru.
3. Father's mother, Nyina-nkulu.
4. Father's father, Isenkulu.
5. Mother's father, Isenkulu.
6. Mother's mother, Nyina-nkulu.
7. Father, Ise or Tata.
8. Father's brother, Isento.
9. Father's sister, Isenkati.
10. Father's brother's wife, Muka Isento or Mukasi.
11. Father's sister's husband, Iba Isenkati or Mukoi.
12. Mother, Nyina or Mau.
13. Mother's brother, Nyinarumi.
14. Mother's sister, Nyina ento.
15. Mother's brother's wife, Muka nyinarumi.
16. Mother's sister's husband, Mukoi.
17. Brother, (M.S.) Mugenzi.
18. Brother, (W.S.) Munyanya.
19. Elder brother, (M.S.) Mukuru.
20. Elder brother, (W.S.) Munyanya or Mukuru.
21. Younger brother, (M.S.) Muto wange.
22. Younger brother, (W.S.) Muto wange or Munyanya.
23. Sister, (M.S.) Munyanya.
24. Sister, (W.S.) Mugenzi.
25. Elder sister, (M.S.) Munyanya or Mukuru.
26. Elder sister, (W.S.) Mukuru or Nyakaitu.
27. Younger sister, (M.S.) Muto wange or Munyanya.
28. Younger sister, (W.S.) Muto wange or Nyakaitu or Lugaihya.
29. Brother (same father but different mother), (M.S.) Munyanya.
30. Brother (same father but different mother), (W.S.) Munyanya.
31. Brother (same mother but different father), (M.S.) Owanyina.
32. Brother (same mother but different father), (W.S.) Owanyina.

33. Sister (same father but different mother), (M.S.) Munyanya.

34. Sister (same father but different mother), (W.S.) Owaise or Mugenzi.

35. Sister (same mother but different father), (M.S.) Owanyina.

36. Sister (same mother but different father), (W.S.) Owanyina.

37. Brother's wife, (M.S.) Muramu.

38. Brother's wife, (W.S.) Muramu.

39. Sister's husband, (M.S.) Muramu.

40. Sister's husband, (W.S.) Muramu.

41. Husband, Iba.

42. Wife, Mukazi.

43. Father's brother's son, (M.S.) Omwana wa Isento.

44. Father's brother's son, (W.S.) Omwana wa Isento or Munyanya.

45. Father's brother's daughter, (M.S.) Omwana wa Isento or Munyanya.

46. Father's brother's daughter, (W.S.) Mugenzi.

47. Father's sister's son (M.S.) Mwhiwha or Omwana wa Isenkati.

48. Father's sister's son, (W.S.) Mwhiwha or Omwana wa Isenkati.

49. Father's sister's daughter, (M.S.) Mwhiwha or Omwana wa Isenkati.

50. Father's sister's daughter, (W.S.) Nyina ento.

51. Mother's brother's son, (M.S.) Nyina rumi.

52. Mother's brother's son, (W.S.) Nyina rumi.

53. Mother's brother's daughter, (M.S.) Nyina ento.

54. Mother's brother's daughter, (W.S.) Nyina ento.

55. Mother's sister's son, (M.S.) Omwana wa nyina ento.

56. Mother's sister's son, (W.S.) Omwana wa nyina ento.

57. Mother's sister's daughter, (M.S.) Omwana wa nyina ento.

58. Mother's sister's daughter, (W.S.) Omwana wa nyina ento.

59. Son, Omutabani.

60. Son's wife, (M.S.) Muka mwana.
61. Son's wife, (W.S.) Muka mwana.
62. Daughter, Omuhara.
63. Daughter's husband, (M.S.) Mukoi.
64. Daughter's husband, (W.S.) Mukoi.
65. Brother's son, (M.S.) Omwana wa mugenzi.
66. Brother's son, (W.S.) Omwana wa munyanya.
67. Brother's daughter, (M.S.) Omwana wa mugenzi.
68. Brother's daughter, (W.S.) Omwana wa munyanya.
69. Sister's son, (M.S.) Mwhiwha.
70. Sister's son, (W.S.) Mwhiwha.
71. Sister's son's daughter, (M.S.) Mwhiwha.
72. Sister's son's daughter, (W.S.) Mwhiwha.
73. Brother's son's wife, (M.S.) Muka mwana.
74. Brother's son's wife, (W.S.) Muka mwana.
75. Brother's sister's husband, (M.S.) Muramu.
76. Brother's sister's husband, (W.S.) Muramu.
77. Sister's son's wife, (M.S.) Muka mwana.
78. Sister's son's wife, (W.S.) Muka mwana.
79. Sister's daughter's husband, (M.S.) Muko wange.
80. Sister's daughter's husband, (W.S.) Muko wange.
81. Son's son, (M.S.) Mujukuru.
82. Son's son, (W.S.) Mujukuru.
83. Son's daughter, (M.S.) Mujukuru.
84. Son's daughter, (W.S.) Mujukuru.
85. Daughter's son, (M.S.) Mujukuru.
86. Daughter's son, (W.S.) Mujukuru.
87. Daughter's daughter, (M.S.) Mujukuru.
88. Daughter's daughter, (W.S.) Mujukuru.
89. Wife's father, Isezara.
90. Wife's mother, Nyinazara.
91. Wife's brother, Muramu.
92. Wife's brother's wife, Muramu.
93. Wife's brother's son, Omwana wa muramu or muramu.
94. Wife's brother's daughter, Omwana wa muramu or muramu.
95. Wife's sister, Muramu.
96. Wife's sister's husband, Muramu.

97. Wife's sister's son, Mwana wa muramu or muramu.

98. Wife's sister's daughter, Mwana wa muramu or muramu.

99. Husband's father, Isezara.

100. Husband's mother, Nyinazara.

101. Husband's brother, Muramu.

102. Husband's brother's wife, Mukaibu or Muka muramu.

103. Husband's brother's son, Omwana wa muramu.

104. Husband's brother's daughter, Omwana wa muramu.

105. Husband's sister, Muramu.

106. Husband's sister's husband, Muko wange.

107. Husband's sister's son, Mwhiwha or Iba.

108. Husband's sister's daughter, Mwhiwha or Iba.

109. Son's wife's father, Muitwe.

110. Son's wife's mother, Muitwe.

111. Parent, Omuzaire, pl. Abazaire.

112. Child, Mwana, pl. Abana.

CHAPTER IV

MARRIAGE AND BIRTH

The king's wives—marriage of sisters—the king's mother—marriage
of princes—marriage customs in pastoral clans—the bride's dress
and marriage ceremony—seclusion of bride—marriage customs in
agricultural clans—womens' duties among pastoral people—
fetish to ensure conception—methods used to ensure motherhood
—restrictions placed on women during pregnancy—birth—food of
a mother when nursing her child—treatment of a child—naming a
child—birth customs among agricultural people—birth of twins—
death of twins—table of birth rate.

King's wives, marriage of sisters. Though the Banyoro
clans are exogamous, this rule does not apply to royalty ;
for in the royal family brothers frequently marry their
sisters, and as there is no rule to prohibit them from having
offspring, they sometimes have children by them, though
princesses usually kill their children at birth. This seems
to have been done rather to save trouble in nursing them
than from any fear or sense of guilt. The custom of marriage
with a sister is probably due to the fact that the royal
family belong to some other race than the pastoral people
a race who followed the rule of succession through the
female line, and the king married his sister to ensure his son
succeeding him. The king had usually several princesses among
his wives and often had children by them, and such children
took their places with other princes as legitimate heirs to
the throne, no difference being made between them and the
king's sons born of women from pastoral clans. The practice
of marrying a near relative was usually confined to couples
of the same generation, though there was no rule which
forbad a prince from marrying a princess who was either his
aunt or his neice ; a father, however, refrained from marrying

his daughter. When a princess became a wife of the king, she did not leave him to go to some other prince, but regarded herself as his sole property. The case was different with princes who married their sisters : with them there was no binding marriage contract, and a princess was free to leave her brother to go to some other prince, if she elected to do so. Such marriages being more of the nature of love-matches, the couple came together for a time and their union was rather of a secret than of a public nature. It was illegal for any commoner to marry a princess ; and should such a couple be found living together, they would have been put to death. When a prince married his sister and she had a child by him, she had to leave the capital for her confinement, as in the case of other women. Polygamy was general, the only restriction as to the number of wives a man might marry being the milk-supply for their food. In the case of the king and wealthy chiefs there was a plentiful supply, and therefore no limit was fixed to the number of their wives. It was considered an honour to give women to the king to become his wives, and their number was ever increasing. The king seldom had to ask for a woman, because pastoral chiefs and peasants hoped that, by giving their daughters to him, they would not only gain immediate benefit but would become related to the future king, who would advance their social position. Though the king was freely supplied with women for his harem, still, should he hear of some attractive girl, he would send her some ornament to wear, usually a few beads, which indicated that she was engaged to him. When old enough to marry, such a girl would be taken to the court and become one of the king's wives. It was not customary for the king to marry women from agricultural clans : he confined himself to members of pastoral clans.

The king's mother. The king's mother was held in great respect. She lived in her own enclosure near the king's residence. She was not allowed to remarry after her husband's death, but she had her paramours of whom no man might speak to the king. Should the king suspect any man of being

unduly familiar with his mother, he would order him to be
executed.   The king's mother, his wives, and in fact all women
regarded obesity as a mark of beauty and vied with one
another who should be the stoutest.   Their stoutness prevented
them from walking even short distances without many rests.
They took no exercise, but were carried in litters wherever
they wished to go.   The king often gave presents of domestic
slaves to his mother and to his wives, in addition to cows.
The slaves were wanted for menial work and to cultivate the
land in order to supply vegetable food for household slaves and
servants, who were seldom allowed a milk-diet.

Marriage of princes.   Princes were encouraged to marry
and were given wives by their fathers, chiefs were also allowed
to give women to princes whom they admired or to whom they
wished to be related ; and further, princes married women
from pastoral clans according to the customs of the country,
that is to say by paying a marriage-fee of cattle.   Each prince
had his herds of cattle from which he obtained his supply of
milk for himself and his wives.   Princes were given estates
by their father, the king, where they could place their peasants
and slaves and whence they could obtain vegetable food for
their households.   Their herds of cattle were free to roam
over large tracts of country in company with those of the
king, so long as the ordinary rules not to mix the colours, etc.,
were observed.

Cousin marriage.   Among the Banyoro first cousins, the
children of a brother and sister respectively, are forbidden to
marry each other ; but second cousins, the grandchildren of a
brother and sister respectively, are allowed to marry each
other, if the father of the one is a son of that brother, and if
the mother of the other is a daughter of that sister.   In other
words, a man's children may not marry his sister's children ;
but a man's son's children may marry his sister's daughter's
children.

Marriage in pastoral clans.   Among pastoral clans a father
arranged for his son's marriage.   He sought some girl, who
belonged to a clan different from his own, who was possibly still

a child, and arranged with her parents for her to become the wife of his son when old enough to marry. He would give two or more cows to the girl's parents, who would then consider their daughter as engaged to be married. It was the mother's duty to keep her daughter pure until marriage. A girl thus betrothed remained with her parents until she was marriageable. During the time the couple were too young to marry, they held no communication one with the other, and the engagement rested entirely with the parents whose duty it was to keep the bride from forming any attachment to another man. At the time of marriage some of the bridegroom's female relatives visited the bride to see her anointed with butter and to examine her and see whether she was free from diseases of the skin. In like manner some of the bride's male relatives visited and examined the bridegroom on behalf of the bride and reported to her whether he was a desirable husband. The bride's relatives decided the amount the bridegroom should pay for the marriage fee, and this amount was paid before a man took his bride. The sum demanded by the wealthier people was from ten to twenty cows, which were paid to the bride's parents. It was always pleasant to a bride to make her prospective husband pay a large sum for her, as it gratified her vanity and was a measure of her husband's desire to have her. The marriage took place in the evening. The bride was veiled with either bark-cloths or well-dressed cow-skins, and was carried on the shoulders of some strong male relative to her future home. It was customary for women of pastoral clans to wear a veil when going out, so that the dress worn at marriage was that of daily use. The bride was accompanied by some of her relatives and girl-friends who carried her belongings and sang and danced as they went. They remained for the night and often during the following day, dancing and singing. The bride was expected to be in tears when going to her husband, because she was leaving her parents. These tears were in many cases forced and feigned expressions of grief. A bride was in reality glad to marry. Parents usually gave their daughter a present of cows, some of them in milk,

to ensure her food ; relatives and friends made her presents
of clothing and ornaments. A bride was taken to live with
her husband's parents who received her as a daughter. She
sat first in the lap of her mother-in-law and afterwards in the
lap of her father-in-law, and was in all respects treated as a
daughter. Until her first child was born, she lived with her
mother-in-law. When her first baby was born, her husband
and father-in-law built her a house near her mother-in-law,
in the same kraal, and she began her duties as a wife and mother.
Marriage was consummated in the evening of the second day
after the marriage ceremony when the guests had departed.
An elderly woman, an aunt of the bride, was present to instruct
the young couple in their matrimonial duties, and remained
with them for several days.

Seclusion of the bride. The bride was secluded for a period
varying from ten days to a year, according to her husband's
wealth and position. Both husband and wife promised to be
faithful to each other, and the wife was charged to be hospitable
to her husband's guests. When the term of seclusion ended,
the bridegroom took his wife to visit her parents, and he was
admitted into their family as a son by first sitting in the lap
of his mother-in-law and afterwards in that of his father-in-law.
When a man married one of his slaves and she became a
mother, she was no longer considered a slave. Should her
husband die before her, the heir recognised her as a free woman.
Women thus freed seldom sought their relatives, if they belonged
to another tribe. They remained with their children.

Marriage in agricultural clans. In agricultural clans, when
a man attained the age of puberty, he was left to manage as
best he could to obtain a wife, though his father assisted him
as much as he was able and gave him the advice necessary to
obtain a woman who was in no way related to him. Agricultural people seldom possessed more than two or three goats
or sheep, and, as the marriage fee varied from ten to forty goats,
a father could give but little assistance, and a man required
months to obtain the sum demanded. Members of the man's
clan were requested to help, but, even with their assistance,

it often took a man ten months or longer to obtain the number of goats asked. A bridegroom paid a number of goats when he first asked the parents for their daughter. If these were accepted, the girl was considered betrothed and waited until the full number was paid, when she was claimed by the man. The nuptials were conducted by night as in the case of the pastoral people. The bride was carried veiled in the evening to her husband. She was accompanied by friends who danced and sang during the night and the next day, and by an aunt, the bride's father's sister, who lived with the young couple some time after marriage to instruct them in their matrimonial duties. At the time of marriage the guests were regaled with mutton and porridge made from millet-flour, and were given beer to drink. When the bride's father's sister returned home, the bridegroom gave her a present of a sheep. A bride among agricultural people did not remain secluded many days: it was necessary that she should go to dig in her husband's garden, so that, after a few days or at most at the end of a month, she went to her work of digging. When first going to her garden after seclusion, a bride left the house secretly in the early morning and proceeded to the garden and worked for a time before other people were up ; when they began to move, she returned as secretly to her home as she had left it, the first streaks of sunlight indicating that it was time for her to return. After the work in the morning had been done, the husband gave a second feast and both he and his wife publicly promised to be faithful to each other : the wife was then free to go about her household duties. The newly married couple lived near the bridegroom's parents, and father and son both worked for the same master. A father invariably helped his son to build his house. An agricultural peasant avoided his mother-in-law, and only spoke to her when she was hidden from sight.

Women's duties among pastoral people. In pastoral clans women do no work beyond churning and washing milk-pots. Manual work has always been regarded as degrading and cultivation of the ground as positively injurious to their cattle. There was no cooking done by women of pastoral clans. Milk was drunk fresh from the cows and, when beef was obtained, a man would cut it into small pieces and cook it on wooden spits or skewers over the log-fire. During menstruation the wives of wealthy cattle owners were given milk to drink from old cows which were not expected to have calves again ; wives of men with only a limited number of cows were prohibited from drinking milk at all and had to live on vegetable food during the time of their indisposition, because their condition was considered harmful to the cows, should they drink milk. After living on a vegetable diet a woman fasted at least twelve hours before she ventured to drink milk again. During the time of her indisposition a woman lived apart from her husband ; she was careful not to touch anything belonging to him and took care not to touch any milk-vessels. Her husband also was excluded from visiting the king and from going to war until his wife was well again.

Fetish to ensure conception and methods followed to secure motherhood. A wife expected to become a mother soon after marriage. To ensure this her husband would obtain a fetish from a medicine-man for her to wear round her waist. The fetish was generally two pieces of stick an inch long, a little thicker than a lead pencil, which were threaded on a string side by side and encased in goat-skin. They were frequently decorated with two or four cowry-shells stitched on to the goat-skin. Should a wife show no signs of pregnancy, a medicine-man was consulted and he would discover the cause of her failure to bear by resorting to one of his means of divination, either by killing a cow, sheep, or a fowl, or by a water-test. The animal was killed and its intestines examined for markings which would indicate the cause of the failure ; or, if the water-test was resorted to, the man cast a number of short pieces of stick into the vessel and watched how they floated, and according to the positions they took he gave his oracle. Women were frequently said to be prevented from having children by ghosts which had some grievance against the husband and restrained his wife from child-bearing. To remedy this defect an offering, either an ox or a sheep, according to the advice of the medicine-man, was made to the ghost, who would remove the restriction. Sometimes a medicine-man was asked to visit a sterile wife of the king or a sterile wife of a wealthy chief. He was then supplied with a fowl which had to be a male bird, killed the fowl and smeared the blood on the inside of the woman's thighs. Sometimes he also poured the blood into a shallow vessel. The woman stripped and sat in it and had some of the blood smeared on the lower part of her body. These remedies were supposed to be sufficient to bring about pregnancy.

Restrictions placed upon a woman during pregnancy. During her period of gestation a woman was given powdered herbs to drink mixed with water : she was careful not to touch the clothing of any man other than her husband, lest she should injure her child ; she slept on her own bed apart from her husband and avoided coming into contact with other men. A wife of the king at such a time was removed from the royal residence to some relative who took care of her and provided her with a woman to act as midwife when her child was born, and to continue to guard her and her child until her infant was weaned at the end of three years. At the time of birth the mother stood in a stooping position for her delivery by one of the pillars of the house.

Birth customs. When the child was born, the midwife washed its mouth out with her finger and started respiration, and she waited for the after-birth before she cut the umbilical cord. The after-birth was buried near the door of the house. If the child was a boy, it was buried on the right side of the doorway ; if a girl, on the left side of it. The mother was secluded after her confinement for four days, if the child was a boy ; for three days, if it was a girl. She lay on the floor near the fire and no person except the midwife and her husband might enter the house. The fire was watched and kept burning brightly during the time of seclusion, until the mother was taken to the back of the house for her purificatory rite. At the expiration of the mother's seclusion she was washed from head to foot by the midwife, while other relatives swept out the house and recarpeted it with newly cut grass, the old grass from the house and the dust being thrown away on the dung-heap in the kraal. During her pregnancy and until she ceased to nurse her child, a woman of the pastoral clans drank from a wooden cup : she was not given an earthenware vessel, lest her child should grow up weak or be frail and die an early death.

Food of a mother when nursing her child. A nursing mother was restricted to the milk of cows which had lost their calves, if her child was a boy ; but she was free to drink milk from any cow, if it was a girl. A small piece of the umbilical cord was encased in leather, decorated and made into an ornament for the child to wear round its neck. The child was not allowed to sit for three months after its birth : it either lay on its back on a rug on the floor, or it was carried in its nurse's arms. At the end of the third month the father's mother came and placed the child to sit on the floor alone. She did this in the presence of a few relatives, because the ceremony was considered to make the child grow strong.

Treatment of a child and naming it. A mother nursed her child for three years, unless she became pregnant again, in which case the child was weaned. In any case she began to give it cow's milk to drink when it was six months old. A child wore no clothes, but it had various amulets made into ornaments which were fastened round its neck, or its wrists and ankles, and also tied into its hair. The child was named by its paternal grandmother, when it cut its first lower teeth. It was given a name of some deceased ancestor of its father's clan and the ghost of that relative was supposed to guard the child and to make it thrive. After it was named the mother took her child a round of visits to the members of her husband's clan, who welcomed it as a member and gave it presents of ornaments. Should a female child suffer from abdominal pains, the mother was accused of adultery ; but if a male child suffered, the father was accused. In such cases a medicine-man came and, after he had made his medicine, the guilty parent had to spit into it, and the child was made to drink the medicine.   There was no punishment if a man was unfaithful to his wife, though it was believed his child would die, if he continued to live an immoral life after he had been warned. A husband would flog his wife severely and might kill her, if he discovered she had been unfaithful to him.

Birth customs among agricultural clans.   Among agricultural people a wife during her period of menstruation continued to cook for her husband and was in no way restricted from attending to his wants, but she was not permitted to approach other men, and her husband never went to the royal enclosure until his wife was quite recovered.   Similar customs to those adopted by the pastoral people were followed in order to procure children.   A wife consulted the medicine-man, wore fetishes and drank powdered herbs daily.   When pregnant, a wife avoided food which she considered harmful to her condition, though she had no special rule of food taboo to follow such as those of the Baganda.   No man might touch a woman when she was with child.   She might not even shake hands with any man, and she drank from her own special cup which she kept in some place where it would not be used by any other person.   At the time of her confinement her mother-in-law or some elderly person from her husband's clan undertook the duties of midwife.   The after-birth was buried outside the house near the door, according to the sex of the child : on the right side of the doorway for a boy, and on the left side if it was a girl.   The mother was secluded four days if the child was a boy, and three days if it was a girl ; and she slept on the floor near a brightly burning fire.   The child was nursed for three years, but after the fourth month it was given artificial food, chiefly ripe plantain made into gruel.   A man liked his wife to have sons : he even despised and neglected her if all her children were girls.   It was said to be an evil omen when a child cut its upper teeth before the lower ones, and a mother watched anxiously for the first teeth and was greatly relieved when a tooth in the lower jaw appeared first. A child had its head shaved when the hair became too thick.

Sex made no difference to this rule. During infancy the mother was responsible for dressing the hair, but when a child was weaned and taken away from its mother a paternal aunt performed the office of hair dresser until the child grew up and married. After marriage a man looked to his wife to shave his head for him. Among pastoral people a child seldom had its hair cut until it was six years old, and the ceremony of shaving the head was then performed at a special gathering of relations. A child wore bells on its ankles until it could walk freely. They were said to encourage walking and to strengthen the legs.

Birth of twins. The birth of twins was a solemn event. The children were supposed to be the gift of the gods and were received accordingly with peculiar rites to celebrate their birth. The midwife sent for a medicine-man who isolated both parents, shut them in a house and built up the doorway to prevent them from coming out and to keep others from entering the house. When possible a new house was rapidly built for this purpose and the man and his wife were kept prisoners for at least a week, and were fed through a small opening which was only large enough to permit food to be handed in. The wife had to live in the hut some six months ; the husband, however, was allowed to find a substitute, a boy from his clan who had not reached the age of puberty. When possible the boy was a uterine brother, or at least a brother by the same father. This boy entered the hut, remained with the mother of the twins and set the father free to go about his regular duties. The umbilical cord of each child was cut upon a thong used to tie the legs of a young cow when it was milked, and the cow had to be one with a female calf. Should a woman who belonged to an agricultural clan have twins, the umbilical cord was cut upon the handle of a hoe. No knife was ever used for this purpose ; it was cut with a strip split from a reed, in the case of a first-born child from a dry reed and, for other children, from a growing reed. It was a common rule for a father of twins to remain in the hut with his wife until the new moon appeared, and afterwards, when he went out of

the hut, he refrained from shaving his head until the children
were brought out and named, when the relatives were allowed
to see them. This ceremony took place at the end of six
months. At the time of the birth of twins the father sent a
messenger to let his parents know that there were twins born
and thus prevent his mother from paying a visit to see his
wife. The messenger chosen was a man swift of foot. He
proceeded to the parents' house and called to them from a distance, "Your daughter has many children," and then turned
and fled, chased by the inmates of the house. Should they
catch him before he reached the hut of the mother of the
twins, he had to pay a fine, and the disgrace of being caught
was very great. As each new moon appeared, a dance was given
at the hut in which the mother and twins lived. This lasted
for two or three days and was continued both by day and by
night by the relatives and friends assembled. At the end of
six months the husband killed an ox near the hut and the twins
were brought out and shown to the relatives. Among the
agricultural clans the parents were taken in the early morning
to some river or pool of water where they were publicly washed
and shaved clean of all hair on head and body, and their nails
were pared on hands and feet. The hair and nail-parings were
taken and deposited by the husband in some secret place
together with the sweepings from the hut. The twins also
had their heads shaved, but the mother preserved the hair.
The after-birth of a twin was kept in the house in a new cooking-pot, and, when dry, it was sealed up. The pot was covered
with a sheep-skin or a cow-skin. After the purificatory rite
the pot was deposited in some unfrequented place and left,
or it was buried in an ant-hillock. Dancing again took place
after the purificatory ceremonies were ended, and this continued for several months, as each new moon appeared. When
the moon was first seen, the twins had drum-sticks placed in
their hands and were helped to beat a few taps on a drum to
start the dancing. The only difference between pastoral and
agricultural people in the observance of twin ceremonies was
in the kind of food eaten : the agricultural people at the time

of the purificatory ceremonies gave a meal of vegetables with meat and beer, whereas pastoral people were restricted to milk.

Death of twins. Should a twin die at birth, it was buried by a medicine-man, but the after-birth was kept in the house until the other child was weaned. When both twins died in infancy, each body was put into a new cooking-pot and dried by the medicine-man, who then took the pots with the bodies to an unfrequented place and sought an ant-hillock, where he dug a hole large enough in the side of the hillock to admit the pots. He then covered the hole over with the earth he had dug from the hillock.

It has been stated that twins are regarded by the Banyoro as unlucky, and that they are exposed to the midday sun at birth until one dies. It was impossible to find any native to confirm this statement, and it appears to be contrary to the common beliefs of the people[1].

Parents were diligent in making offerings to the gods when a twin died, because they attributed the death to the god's displeasure. Parents preferred twins to be a boy and a girl, because they said the gods were pleased with both parents, whereas, if both were boys, it was a sign that the mother's clan was in disfavour and, if both were girls, the father's clan was in disfavour. The clan which was in disfavour made offerings to the gods to remove any cause of their ill-will and displeasure.

In agricultural clans the parents of twins sowed a plot of land with millet and called it "the children's plot." When the grain was ripe they cooked a meal with the first-fruits and ate it in the presence of the god, before they ventured to eat any grain that year.

Birth rate. The birth rate of girls appears to be in excess of that of boys. Twenty-seven mothers who were questioned by

---

[1] Miss Attlee of the C.M.S. Bunyoro Mission, however, writes to me : "Many women state that twins were greatly feared and that it is a custom to expose the twins until they die and then put the bodies in cooking-pots and fill the pots with cow-dung. The pot was placed on a slow fire until the whole was quite dry and the pots were retained in the house fully a year. They were afterwards thrown into a river or swamp."

Miss Attlee gave the total of children born to them as 101.   Of these, 60 were girls and 41 were boys.   Of the 101 children born, 32 died in infancy, 32 died before they reached maturity, leaving only 37 who came to manhood.   The table is as follows :

Women questioned No.	Children born	Boys	Girls	Died in infancy	Died before maturity	Grew up to maturity
1	6	2	4	3	3	—
2	1	—	1	1	—	—
3	1	—	1	—	—	1
4	6	4	2	5	—	1
5	4	—	4	3	—	1
6	3	3	—	1	—	2
7	7	4	3	3	2	2
8	4	2	2	2	1	1
9	2	2	—	2	—	—
10	1	—	1	—	—	1
11	1	—	1	—	—	1
12	1	1	—	1	—	—
13	7	3	4	4	1	2
14	3	1	2	—	1	2
15	4	2	2	—	1	3
16	1	—	1	—	—	1
17	3	1	2	—	—	3
18	5	2	3	—	1	4
19	3	1	2	1	—	2
20	7	1	6	—	7	—
21	13	4	9	3	9	1
22	5	2	3	1	—	4
23	4	1	3	—	4	—
24	3	1	2	—	1	2
25	1	1	—	—	—	1
26	3	2	1	1	1	1
27	2	1	1	1	1	1
Totals	101	41	60	32	32	37

CHAPTER V

SICKNESS AND DEATH

Death of the king—preparing the royal corpse for burial—princes fight for the throne—chiefs and widows killed at the grave of the king—cattle offered to the dead king—sickness among common people—magical influence the cause of death—sickness among pastoral people—beliefs in ghostly possession—disposal of property by sick men—ascertaining the cause of death—management of a sick chamber—death—burial customs of pastoral people—mourning customs—introducing the heir to end mourning—burial of princes and princesses—burial customs of agricultural clans—burial of women.

Death of the king. The Banyoro, in common with other known tribes of Africa, would not allow their king to lie ill of any serious sickness. They sought to end his life while he was in full strength : indeed, the king himself would, when he felt his strength declining through age, or when he feared he was about to fall ill, end his life by taking poison. The king's chief wife kept herbs ready to hand and prepared a cup at his bidding ; he swallowed the drug and in a few moments he was dead. Under other circumstances, for example, when suffering from any slight indisposition, the king kept his bed and was attended by his chief wife who obtained assistance from a chief and a medicine-man, and they nursed him until he was able to resume his duties, such slight ailments seldom confining the king to his room for more than one or two days. If after two days the king did not recover his general health, he adopted the usual custom of his predecessors by ending his life. The wife who administered the poison-cup called one or two of the leading chiefs when the king was dead and made known to them the real state of affairs, and they kept the king's death secret until they could make preparations for the

wars which would inevitably follow when the princes learned
that their father was dead and the contest for the vacant
throne began. Sometimes a king told some of his chiefs he
was about to die and named the prince he would like to succeed
to the throne, but this express wish in no wise prevented the
princes from entering upon their struggle, and the most
capable warrior invariably obtained the throne.

Preparing the corpse for burial. After the body of the
king was washed, the limbs were bent up into a squatting
position and the hands raised to one side of the head; the head
was shaved and the nails pared, and the sinews of the back were
cut out and buried apart from the body. The body was
wrapped first in a well-dressed cow-skin and afterwards stitched
in a raw cow-skin that had recently been flayed. Each day
milk was brought from the sacred cows to the dairy for the
king and each night meat was cooked for him as though he
were still alive; and the chiefs and the principal wife kept
guard over the house to prevent the true state of affairs from
becoming known while they made preparations for the coming
struggle for the crown.

Princes fight for the throne. When the death was announced,
the principal chiefs assembled in the royal enclosure and took
their posts as guards over the king's body, while princes set
themselves at the head of their followers to fight for the throne.
During the time the civil wars lasted, the royal widows mourned
daily and paid no attention to the disturbed state of the
country. No fires were allowed to burn during the period of
mourning, they were all extinguished when the king's death
was announced; a fire might be lighted by friction with fire sticks
for cooking necessary food, but it was extinguished immediately the cooking was done and fresh fire obtained when it was
wanted. When at length the victorious prince was escorted
in triumph to the royal enclosure and demanded the body of
his father from the leading chiefs who had been neutral during
the wars and guarded the body, the chiefs satisfied themselves
that no prince was left alive to contest the throne before they
admitted the prince into the royal enclosure; and when satisfied,
they proclaimed him king and gave him the body of his father.

Burial of the king. The first duty of the new king was to take the body of his father into a particular district of his country for burial. This district lay to the north-west of the capital over the important river *Kafu.* The funeral procession was conducted more like a festival than a funeral ceremony: there was no mourning, but drums, flutes and songs resounded as the procession made its way. There was double cause for joy: the wars were ended, the country settled, and there was rejoicing for the new king. When the district in which the kings were buried was reached, the new king and chiefs selected a place for the grave and a man was told to prepare a site where the grave was to be dug; this he did by measuring the space required and by digging a trench enclosing it. When this was done, he announced the fact to the king, whereupon the order was given to seize the man and he was put to death, the sinews from his back being cut out and used for cord to tie the blades on the hoes to be used in digging the grave. The grave was a large pit with a path leading into it, down which the bearers carried the body. The pit was lined with cow-skins and over these bark-cloths were spread, and a bed was made in the middle of the pit upon which the body was laid and covered with many more bark-cloths.

Chiefs and widows killed at the king's grave. Two or more of the principal widows of the dead king were led into the grave and speared to death beside the body; the boy who announced the approach of the sacred cows when coming from pasture to be milked, the chief herdsman, the chief cook and the chief who had charge of the king's well were also clubbed to death in the grave. It is a disputed question where the bodies of these various victims killed in the grave were buried: some say they were removed and buried in graves near the king's grave, but the weight of evidence is in favour of the bodies having been left to lie where they fell under the executioner's club. Many widows came to the funeral and when they saw the body covered and their companions executed, they drank poison they had brought with them and fell dead into the grave. These people who died at the grave were said to be companions of the late king's ghost: they were sent to accompany the king into the other world and to continue their services for him there.

Cattle offered to the dead king. In addition to the people who were executed, there were numbers of sacred cows killed by the grave to be the king's cattle in the ghost-world. The meat of the sacrificed animals was given to the peasants who dug the grave and built a temple over it. Before the grave was filled with earth, there were numbers of bark-cloths thrown into it. When filled a mound of beaten earth was made over it and a large hut was built over the place. A guard was appointed to live in the hut to present the offerings sent to the ghost of the departed. The earth-mound over the grave was made with a flat surface, covered with a grass carpet and overlaid with cow-skins and leopard-skins. This was the throne where the ghost was said to take its seat at any ceremony. Before this throne offerings were made to the departed king, and there also requests were made when the reigning king wished to consult his father upon state matters or when sickness appeared in the royal household. The departed king was commonly spoken of as being asleep, but never as dead. Upon the king's return from the funeral of his father, sacred fire was brought to him by the keeper of the sacred fire, who had the title of *Nsansa Namugoye*; the king took the fire from the keeper and held it for a few moments; he then returned it to the keeper and told him to light the fires in the royal enclosure. All the fires in the country were supposed to be lighted from this fire. The original fire was said to have been brought to the country by one of the first kings.

Sickness among the common people. Among common people sickness was believed to have its origin in magic worked by some evil-disposed person, or it might be due to a ghost which had been neglected in some way; but it was seldom attributed to natural causes. Before any serious illness could be treated, it was essential to discover the cause whether it was due to magic or to a ghost. A wife dared not allow her husband to lie ill many hours without calling in some of his relatives, lest they should accuse her of being the cause of the illness. In cases of indisposition such as headache, cold or mild attacks of fever, the wife and relatives resorted to bleeding or blistering with hot irons, or they tied a band tightly round the head, but did not seek the aid of a medicine-man. Should these remedies prove ineffectual, the medicine-man was called in to diagnose the case.

Magical influence the cause of death. One common mode of magical influence was to bury bones of animals or birds, over which incantations had been made, near the house or to hide them in the thatch of the house of the person to be influenced. It was firmly believed that sickness would follow. A medicine-man was able by his tests to tell whether there were such magical bones causing the sickness or whether the illness was due to magic of some other kind, or whether it was caused by a ghost: this he did by the test obtained from a pot of water into which he cast pieces of stick, or by the markings on the entrails of an animal or a fowl which he was given to kill for the purpose. Should he declare that bones had been hidden near the house, he sent for a special medicine-man known as the "Smeller" and told him what had happened. This man, after hearing the details of the oracle, began to sniff about like a dog, first in one place and then in another, until he discovered the spot where the bones were concealed and unearthed them. This work often took hours, because the man might dig in various places where he detected some peculiar scent and afterwards find that it was not the right place. When the bones had been discovered, they were taken away by the medicine-man and destroyed: the sickness would then yield to ordinary treatment and the patient would recover. Sometimes a sick man accused by name some person of having worked magic, when the test pointed to magic; the medicine-man would then call the accused person and take two fowls, one to represent the sick man and the other to represent the person accused of magic, and the fowls would be shut up without food for two days after which time the medicine-man would administer an amount of poison, such as was used in the poison-ordeal, to each fowl and watch to see the effect. The fowl that died was said to prove the person it represented to be guilty: should it be that of the sick man, he was said to have made a false charge and was fined heavily; but if it was the fowl of the accused man, he would be burned to death.

Sickness among the pastoral people. When a man of a pastoral clan fell ill, a medicine-man was called in to transfer the sickness to some cow provided by the sick man's relatives. The sick man was then taken by his wives and relatives to some place at a distance from the kraal, where the medicine-man rubbed him all over with herbs and then tied the herbs to the neck of the animal chosen, thus transferring the sickness to the animal. The animal was killed, and its blood was caught in a vessel and smeared over the company, who then returned home leaving the medicine-man to dispose of the meat as he wished, either by eating it or by throwing it on to waste-land. Sometimes a medicine-man selected a sheep to which the sickness was to be transferred. He forced it to drink some fluid he had made from herbs into which the sick man had expectorated, and the sheep was then turned loose and driven into some uninhabited part of the country, carrying with it the man's sickness.

Beliefs in ghostly possession. In a case where a medicine-man of the agricultural clans was said to be possessed by a ghost which could not be exorcised, the medicine-man told him to order a feast to be cooked and to invite a number of guests to the meal. The food was prepared and the guests were made to sit in the open near the door of the sick man's house. When the food was served and the guests were about to eat the meal, the medicine-man would rush out from some place of hiding, snatch up the food and run away with it, leaving the guests disappointed and hungry. This action was intended to appeal to the ghost and make it understand that it would cause similar distress by taking away the head of the house and leaving those dependant upon him without food. In some cases when a ghost possessed a man, a medicine-man was called in and given a sheep which he tied to the head of the sick man for a time, until the ghost was said to have left the sick man and entered the animal. The sheep was then taken and kept in a shrine at the grave of the person whose ghost was said to have been causing the trouble. Another important method of exorcising ghosts was to call in a special medicine-man noted for his success in capturing ghosts. This man was allotted a house near that of the sick man and he was given a black goat, which he tied in the house until the following day. He then collected a quantity of herbs, and laid them in a heap on the floor of his house. In the early morning, having killed the goat on the heap of herbs by cutting its throat, he made a fire in the house and placed meat round it to roast on sticks which were stuck into the floor. When the hut was filled with a savoury smell of the cooking meat, the sick man was carried in, laid on a bed near the fire and two of his relatives were told to sit and watch a water-pot in which a piece of cooked meat was put, and over the mouth of the pot a few blades of grass were tied in such a position that they waved with the slightest movement in the air. The men were told that the ghost would be tempted to leave the sick man in order to have a meal of meat and would enter the pot to eat the meat in it, and that when it entered the pot it would cause the blades of grass to wave. They were warned to let the medicine-man know when the grass moved, so that he might capture the ghost. The medicine-man took his seat on the opposite side of the fire and chanted a song in soft tones, and kept time to his song with a gourd-rattle, bidding the ghost to leave the man and eat the food. The smell, combined with the chant, caused the ghost to leave its victim and enter the pot which was an inviting place with its morsel of meat. When it entered the pot, it caused the grass to move and the men notified the fact to the medicine-man who quickly covered it with a skin, smeared it over with clay, carried it away to the nearest river and thus drowned the ghost. Should there be no river near, he cast the captive ghost on waste-land and burnt it to death. The sick man would afterwards be treated for his illness and recover.

Disposal of property by sick men. Sick men usually appointed a son to be heir to any property they had, and their express wishes were followed, if possible: even the king would recognise the wishes of the departed, confer his title upon the heir and give him the land of his predecessor, unless he had some definite reason for rejecting the man. Among wealthy pastoral people whose property consisted in cattle, the question of a successor was one for the clan, and it was theirs to decide whether they would accept the dead man's wishes or not. It was, however, more usual for men to divide their cattle among their children during their illness. Should a man neglect this precaution, the elders of his clan appointed his heir, but in most instances they gave the property to the eldest son of the deceased. Women did not inherit property among either pastoral or agricultural clans; but girls of pastoral clans were given a number of cows from their father's estate when they married. The heir to property, whether from a pastoral or from an agricultural clan, was in each case presented to the king, and the king confirmed him in the office or rejected him, should he have good reason for so doing. When a man succeeded to property, he visited the king to take the oath of allegiance and gave him five or six cows and two slaves from the estate of the deceased.

Ascertaining the cause of death. Whenever a death took place, it was necessary for the relatives to consult a medicine-man to discover by some test the cause of death, and should a person be accused of working magic, he was clubbed to death, unless the relatives of the deceased man accepted a fine or the accused was able to disprove the accusation by a counter-oracle. Should a ghost be supposed to have caused the death, it had to be propitiated lest it should continue its destructive work upon other members of the clan.

Management of a sick chamber. A sick chamber was usually full of relatives and friends who talked freely about the illness and the patient's chances of recovery, and from time to time they made sympathetic remarks to the patient, so that the sick man had little quiet. Should a friend be unable to go in person to the sick chamber, he would send a representative, lest he should be denounced as unsympathetic and run the risk of being charged with having worked magic to cause the illness[1].

[1] Syphilis has for many years been a scourge in Bunyoro. The people attribute the source of the disease to Bukedi and say it was brought into that country from Egypt. Women whom the Banyoro captured in war in Bukedi introduced the disease among the Banyoro. It was the custom of mothers

Death. When death was announced, the wail for the dead
was raised, the widows being conspicuous by their loud calls
upon the dead to return and by smearing their chests with
wood ashes. The body of the dead man was washed, the head
shaved and the nails pared on hands and feet and the parings
preserved; the legs were bent up into a squatting position
and the hands raised under the right side of the head.

Burial customs of pastoral people. Among pastoral clans
and agricultural clans burial took place within twenty-four
hours after death. The dung heap in the cow-kraal was the
burial-place for a member of a pastoral clan. The men dug
the grave and the women remained in the house preparing the
body for the grave and bewailing their loss; the body was
never left from the time of death until burial. During the
actual burial there was no sound of mourning anywhere;
silence reigned until the body was committed to the grave,
when it began again. The weapons of the dead man, his food
vessels and milk-pots were brought and placed in front of the
house in which the body lay. When the body was ready for
burial, the relatives and friends filed into the house, gazed a
few moments on the face of the dead and rubbed a little butter
upon the forehead from a pot placed for the purpose by the
bedside: this was called taking leave of the dead. The body
was wrapped in a cow-skin and carried to the grave by male
relatives. The grave was lined with cow-skins; and the
widows, children and relatives stood round until the body was
laid on a prepared bed in the grave and covered with cow-
skins and bark-cloths. They each scraped a little earth with
the elbow into the grave before the men finally filled it, and
the mourners afterwards returned to the house to fast and
mourn. In the evening when the cattle was brought from the
pasture, the milch cows were not milked but were left lowing
for their calves which were shut up in huts near; a bull was

to practise a kind of inoculation upon their infants to ensure their growing
up, which was effected in the following way: some mothers wrapped their
infant in clothing from a person known to be suffering from the disease while
others placed the child to sleep in the same bed with a patient until the child
showed signs of the disease when they nursed it. The custom greatly increased
the infant death-rate, but the survivors generally grew up to maturity.

selected from the herd of the deceased and a cord was tied tightly round its scrotum, which caused it to low with pain. The rule not to milk any cows of a deceased man on the day he was buried was carefully observed, and the animals were left lowing in discomfort during the night. The widows and children put aside all ornaments and wore girdles made from dry plantain-leaves. During the night after the funeral no one in the kraal was allowed to go to bed or to sleep, fires were made outside the kraal in the open and the relatives and friends gathered round these and wailed unceasingly the whole night. In the early morning when the first glow of the rising sun appeared, the eldest brother of the deceased man entered the kraal and speared the bull that was chosen the night before and killed it; and the meat was cut up and divided among the mourners who cooked it at the watch-fires and ate it on the spot. The cows were milked and driven to pasture and the eldest brother of the deceased man entered the house, cut down the wall which divided the sleeping-room from the living-room, and broke up the bedstead of the deceased. The milk-pots and weapons were left outside the house, and the widows and mourners slept outside until the heir appeared to end the mourning.

Mourning customs. Mourning continued from two to six months and during this time the mourners were not allowed to drink milk, relatives and friends of the deceased providing oxen for meat and beer to be drunk. The oxen were in fact offered to the ghost, the blood of the animals being poured on the ground, which was contrary to the usual custom of catching and cooking it and the meat was divided among the mourners. Rules of chastity were carefully observed by the mourners, who avoided contact with other people who were not mourning.

Introducing the heir to end mourning. When the mourning was to end, the head of the clan introduced the heir to the mourners, who offered an ox to the deceased and told the mourners they were to purify themselves and end the mourning. On the third day after the heir was introduced, several oxen were brought and killed and the meat was given to the mourners; a quantity of beer was also given to them. The next day the heir took his seat in an open place near the kraal and heard the claims of any creditors upon the estate of the deceased. Should any creditor fail to make his claim on that occasion, he was unable to do so at any future time. After this ceremony the grave was enclosed with a reed-fence and a few huts were built at a short distance from the house of mourning. The mourners had their heads shaved and nails pared, the hair and nail parings being taken and deposited with those of the deceased by the grave in the enclosure. The pots and weapons of the deceased were also placed by the grave. The mourners went to live in the huts which were built for their use, remained in them four days, and washed daily. On the fourth day they had their heads shaved again and their nails cut, and the hair and parings were again taken to the grave. After this purificatory rite the relatives of the deceased came with the parents or, should they be dead, with some elderly couple who represented the parents of the dead man, with a large supply of milk and new clothing for each mourner. The mourners dressed in new clothing, drank the milk brought and were escorted to a house where they might meet their friends and talk freely with them, for during the season of mourning they had been separated from all members of the clan. The mourners remained in the house provided for them the following three days, seeing their friends, and on the fourth day they were escorted to the king, to whom they took a cow and calf and a few pots of milk, after which they were free to return to their ordinary life. No grave except that of a king was ever repaired or remembered when mourning ceased: even the place of burial was deserted by the clan and gradually became overgrown with shrubs and forgotten. When a man died suddenly, an ox was strangled on the spot where the death occurred; the animal's throat, nose and mouth being held so that it could not breathe until it suffocated. A medicine-man performed this ceremony and took the meat of the animal.

Burial of princes and of princesses. When a prince or a princess died, he or she received greater honour in burial and the time of mourning was longer than for any ordinary member of a pastoral clan. The king sent a representative to the

funeral, but he never visited any sick person or went to a
funeral: in fact any person who fell ill in the capital was
removed at once to some place at a distance from the royal
residence, lest the king should be affected by the disease.

Burial customs of agricultural clans. In an agricultural
clan any man who died was washed and his head shaved, as
was the custom with the pastoral clans, but the dead man was
buried on waste-land near a garden. The dead was wrapped
in bark-cloths, without any butter being used when taking
leave of the dead. The relatives entered the house and gazed
on the face of the dead man and passed out into the open.
After the funeral the mourners washed near the grave and
continued to mourn for two or three months. Even with the
poorest person the relatives appointed some member of the
clan to be heir and he came to end the mourning: he broke
down the doorposts of the house, and if it had a wall inside, he
cut it down and destroyed the bedstead of the dead man.
A sacred meal was prepared consisting of millet-flour, goat-
flesh and beer. The mourners afterwards shaved their heads
and cut their nails, and the hair was taken and placed by
the grave. All the pots used by the deceased either for
cooking his food or for carrying his water were taken and broken
by the grave, and his sleeping-mat, spear and stick were taken
and placed by the mound over the grave.

Burial of women. When a woman died, her body was
washed and her head shaved, her legs were bent up into a
squatting posture and her hands raised and placed under
the left side of her head. The wife of an agricultural peasant
was seldom washed after death, but her legs were bent up and
her hands were placed under her head on the left side. After
the burial of a wife the husband broke down the house in which
she had lived and built a new house a little distance from the
old site; he might, however, use the materials from the old
house in building the new house, if he wished to do so: few
materials were rejected, only those unfit for use being thrown
aside.

CHAPTER VI

INDUSTRIES

Cow-keeping—the kraal—milking and herding cows—making butter—
distribution of milk—fasting after eating beef and drinking beer—
milk restrictions—agriculture and food of agricultural people—
harvest and threshing—granaries—flour and the use of it—food
of pastoral people—the love of blood for food—use of grain in
pastoral clans—beer and brewing—iron working—smithing—salt
making—fisher-men and fishing—dress and ornaments—pottery
and potters—canoes—basketry.

Cow-keeping. The chief industry of the Banyoro has
always been cow-keeping: in this occupation all classes of
people may take part without any feeling of loss of prestige
in the eyes of the nation. In the ranks of herdsmen princes
and men of mean birth may alike be found; whereas no prince
nor indeed any poor person from the pastoral clans would
willingly take any part in building, and they carefully avoid
all agricultural pursuits. The king owns the largest number
of cattle in the country, though some of the wealthy chiefs
also own large herds. In addition to the sacred herd which is
reserved solely for his own use, the king has many large herds
which are kept in different parts of the country and from these
cows are brought to the royal residence to supply milk for the
king's wives and household. The cows are divided into herds
according to their colour, each herd being kept apart from
other herds which differ in this respect, because, in breeding,
colour is the chief feature looked to. Little regard is paid to
the breed of cows which give the most milk: if a cow is good
in rearing her calves, and especially if she gives birth to cow-
calves, she is considered to be a good one; whereas a cow that
has bull-calves is not liked so well, even though she gives

a better supply of milk. To remedy the latter evil, that is that of bearing male calves, herdsmen usually change the bull because they charge him with the responsibility for the sex of the calves which are born. One bull was said to suffice fifty cows, though in large herds numbering from one to two hundred cows several bulls are kept. The bulls are left to fight their own battles for the supremacy in a herd, but the herdsmen try to prevent one bull from killing another. No care is taken to prevent inter-breeding, and a bull may pair with his own offspring without hindrance. When bull-calves are in excess, or when bulls are born which the herdsmen do not like, they perform an operation which has similar effects to castration, the scrotum being crushed between two stones and the testicles so injured as to render the animals imperfect. The operation is performed while the animals are still young: they do not appear to suffer considerable pain from it and are soon lively and strong again. Many such animals are reared for killing purposes only.

The kraal. The pastoral people are essentially nomads. They move about within given areas on account of the pasture and health of the cattle, though the king and chiefs have fixed centres of residence. The herdsmen are limited in their range of districts because they are obliged to avoid mixing their cows with those of another colour; still the large extent of the country offers them ample change of pasturage. The kraals are only used for keeping the cows together by night: they are very easily constructed and are of a temporary character, there being little idea of protecting animals from wild beasts by these structures. The huts of the herdsmen are first built, forming a circle a little distance from each other with their doorways opening into the kraal. These huts are small, seldom more than ten feet in diameter and eight feet high. They are quickly built by using any kind of tree-branches near to hand that are suited to make the frame-work, which consists of branches stuck in the ground to form a circle, bent inwards and tied together at the upper end. This frame is thatched with any kind of grass; between the huts thorn-bushes are dragged and stakes planted at the intervals to keep the bushes in place: a gateway is left between two of the huts and thorn-bushes are again dragged into the opening to close it during the night. The number of huts and the size of the kraal depends upon the herd it is intended to receive: four and often five men inhabit a hut with sometimes one or two women. There is little thought given to comfort in the huts: they are merely a protection against rain or cold by night. The bed is a heap of grass upon which a cow-skin is thrown by night and which is rolled up by day: in each hut two or three calves are tied during the night, and a fire in the middle of the floor completes the furniture of the place. Cooking is seldom required, because vegetable food is forbidden to herdsmen, and it is said to be dangerous to the health of the herd for them to partake of such food: hence cooking-pots are not often wanted and the milk-pots are not numerous, two or three earthen pots, several gourds, and some wooden pots being all they need. It is not customary to keep milk many hours, except the pots set aside for churning: herdsmen drink milk while milking or as soon after as possible and fast until the cows are again milked, unless they can obtain meat and beer, when they abstain from drinking milk for a period of about twelve hours after the meal of meat and beer. Each day the kraal is swept and the sweepings are heaped on one side of the kraal with the exception of some droppings which are spread in the sun to dry to be used for fuel. A large fire is kept burning constantly in the kraal near the entrance. By this fire the cows are milked in the early morning and again in the evening; it is also a watch fire, because some of the men are awake during the night, watching over the cows, though they seldom set any special guard. It is not often a kraal is visited by wild animals and it is contrary to the methods of warfare among the adjacent tribes to make an attack during the night. When the ground in a kraal becomes full of holes and soft from the feet of the cows, the men move on to some new place; or again, if some member of the kraal dies and is buried in the heap of droppings, the herdsmen remove to new ground, the peasants who live in the neighbourhood being hired to build the new kraal, which they are glad to do for butter or for pay in weapons, hoes or salt which the herdsmen give them; some herdsmen, however, have slaves whose duty is to build for them, and usually the owner of the cows will send his peasants of the agricultural clans to build a new kraal.

Milking and herding cows. Herdsmen rise with the dawn (about half-past five) to milk the cows. They first bring out the calf of the particular cow to be milked and allow it to suck for a few moments. It is then held by one man before the cow while another man milks her, the milkman squatting on his haunches by the cow's side and milking into a gourd, using both hands to milk and gripping the pot between his knees. Should the cow be inclined to kick or be restless, he binds her hind legs together and milks as much as he considers sufficient. After the cow is milked, she is turned out near the kraal with her calf where the latter may finish its meal at leisure. In this manner all the cows are milked in quick succession and turned out of the kraal, near which they are left one or perhaps two hours with their calves before they are driven to the pastures. The milk-vessels are almost entirely either of wood or gourds, though a few earthen pots may be found in a kraal for reserving a little milk for use at mid-day. Gourd milk-pots are freely used and a particular sized gourd is the measure by which to gauge the amount of milk to be taken from each cow. Few cows yield more than a quart of milk in the morning and a similar amount in the evening, the remainder being left for the calf, which is considered of much greater value than the milk. The chief object is to raise a number of cows and by their number to increase the amount of milk rather than to improve the cows individually. Milk is carried daily to the owner of the cows for his consumption, though chiefs keep a number of milch cows near their residence to supply their immediate needs. Milk-vessels are washed daily, when possible by women, though in some kraals there are no women and the men have to perform this duty. After being washed out the pots are drained and, when dry, are held over a smoke-fire in which grass is burned to give a special flavour to the pot and milk. One part of the cleansing of pots is to wash them with cows' urine. The mere fact of this custom was all that could be obtained, the people being unwilling to give details. No metal vessels are used: pastoral people do not allow such vessels to have milk poured into them lest the cows should suffer. Women are not permitted to herd cows nor to milk them: their duties are restricted to washing the milk-pots and to churning.

Butter making. Each day a quantity of milk is set aside in large bottle-gourds and, when the amount required has accumulated, it is churned by one of the women or, failing a woman, by a man. The gourd for churning rests on an old garment, or the person in charge of it sits on the ground and nurses it, rocking it gently to and fro until the butter separates from the milk. When churned, the butter-milk is poured off into some vessel and drunk by the herdsmen, and the butter is shaken from the bottle into a wooden dish and slightly worked to get the milk from it. Butter is not washed, as it is only wanted for anointing the body; and a little milk, if left in it, is not considered detrimental. The butter is either made up into packets bound with plantain-fibre or put into large wooden pots to be carried to the chief. Herdsmen take turns in going out by day to herd the cattle, four or five men controlling a herd of two hundred and guarding them during the day against the attacks of wild animals Herdsmen go out in all weathers and do not return until sunset even when the day is wet: they are usually armed with a long stick with which to drive the cattle and also carry a spear for use in case any wild beast attacks the herd. The men who remain behind in the kraal sweep it out, take out the grass used for bedding for the calves to dry, and prepare the fire-wood for the evening; others carry the day's milk and butter to the chief; the rest guard the calves as they roam about near the kraal and pick up what herbage they can find. The grass the cows prefer is a short kind growing on the plains. The animals move along as they graze, and have often covered several miles when they are turned back and led to some watering-place to drink before they are taken into the kraal for the night. No food is given to the animals by night in the kraal, and there is no attempt made to provide artificial food for them.

Distribution of milk. Pastoral people are particular about the distribution of milk: those who drink it are careful to avoid vegetable diet, and no stranger is offered milk when visiting a kraal, because he may have previously eaten some kind of food which they consider would be harmful to the herd, should he drink milk without a fast to clear his system of vegetable food; their hospitality is shown by giving the visitor some other food such as beef and beer, which will prepare him for a meal of milk on the following morning. Should there be insufficient milk to supply the needs of the men in the kraal, some of them will be given vegetables in the evening and fast until the following morning.

Custom of fasting after eating beef or vegetables. Should there be no plantains and the people be reduced to eating sweet potatoes, it will be necessary to abstain from milk for two days after eating them, until the system is quite clear, before they may again drink milk. Chiefs and wealthy men usually eat meat in the evening and abstain from drinking milk until the following morning. They drink beer after eating meat and then retire to sleep. They say it is necessary to allow an interval of several hours after eating meat before they venture to drink milk. For the first four days after a cow calves the milk from it is set aside for women to drink; on the fifth day men may drink it without injury to the cow or herd. Women are forbidden milk during their menses and live upon vegetable diet, unless the husband is a wealthy man, when they are given the milk from an old cow which is supposed to be past bearing: and the milk from such a cow is kept separate from the common lot of milk and reserved for the use of the sick wife alone. No milk may be cooked nor may it be warmed by fire, because of the harm likely to happen to the herd. A woman at childbirth may drink milk, but, if the child is a boy, she is given the milk from a cow that has lost her calf; whereas, if the child is a girl, she is free to drink the milk from any cow. There is no prohibition placed upon peasants of agricultural clans keeping cattle: in fact some peasants do keep them, but they will not herd them themselves. This task they leave to their sons, and also that of milking them, if they are old enough and know how to milk. Peasants of the agricultural clans prefer to keep goats and sheep and only use cows to purchase wives with. It is quite contrary to custom to kill cows: even the king and the wealthy people refrain from doing so, unless a cow is past bearing or barren. Bulls are frequently killed for food, but the loss of a cow is as painful to a man as the death of a member of his family and his sorrow and despondency will be as great: the death of a favourite cow is at times so trying to a man as to cause him to commit suicide. In cases of sickness among cows the men treat them with as much care and anxiety as they would a child, seeking the aid of the medicine-man, trying remedies and sitting up to watch the sick animal by night.

Agriculture, food of agricultural people. The Banyoro are unlike the Baganda in the matter of agriculture in that they grow grain freely and live upon porridge made from flour of millet, whereas the Baganda live entirely upon plantains and despise all other kinds of food. In Bunyoro, it is true, there are groves of plantains but they are poorly cultivated, indeed few women understand the cultivation of the tree. Again, in Bunyoro cultivation is avoided by the pastoral peeple: it is said to be harmful for a wife of a man belonging to a pastoral clan to till the land as, by doing so, she may injure the cattle. In Uganda princesses not only possess gardens but are frequently to be found at work in them. In Bunyoro the agricultural peasant may be found side by side with his wife tilling the ground and preparing it for seed, whereas in Uganda no man works in the field and the cultivation of all vegetable-food is left to the wife. The fields are dug and prepared for the first rains which begin to fall about September. The chief grain grown is the small millet (bulo) which has to be kept free from weeds until it is a foot high, when it is strong enough to resist the growth of weeds and only needs protection against wild animals. No other method is employed in working the fields than that of hoeing the ground with short-handled hoes two feet long. Peasants spend most of their time in their fields when the crops are growing and they build huts in which to live and protect their fields from wild animals, especially

from pigs which do much harm if left to invade them.   As the
crops begin to ripen, it is necessary to guard them against
flocks of birds, pigeons being the worst enemies of the grain.
As these birds would do great harm if left undisturbed, children,
chiefly girls, are employed to scare them away and are provided
with iron bells or some instrument, such as rude wooden
clappers, for the purpose.

Harvest and threshing corn. The harvest begins about
March and is a busy time for the peasants: both men and
women again work together to reap the corn.   They cut off
the heads of the corn with small knives and carry them to
some prepared place for threshing.   There is seldom any fear
of rain during harvest time, so that the grain can be left
outside in heaps on the threshing-floors during the night until
the field has been reaped.   The threshing is a slow process,
the heads of grain being held up singly and the grain beaten
out with a stick.   When the threshing is complete, there is
the winnowing, which is effected by pouring the grain from one
basket to another, one basket being held up and the grain
slowly emptied from it into the other basket on the floor, thus
allowing the wind to carry off the dust and chaff.   The clean
grain is then carried home and stored.

Granaries. The granaries are large wicker-baskets raised
from the ground upon stones or upon a wooden frame resting
upon posts which are let into the ground, the baskets being
placed upon the frame.   The granaries are some four feet
deep and from two to three feet in diameter, and have a heavily
thatched lid to carry off the rain.   They are smeared inside
with clay and cow-dung to make them water-proof and to
prevent the grain from running out through the crevices.
As a rule each wife has her own granary near to her hut, not
only for convenience but also that she may be able to guard
it.   In addition to these granaries the peasants dig pits similar
to wells: these are round holes from eight to ten feet deep and
three feet in diameter and are dug in secret places with some
tree or other natural feature to mark the spot.   Grain is
kept in these pits for use during disturbed times and especially
during civil wars, when it is impossible to cultivate the land.

The grain stored in these pits is put into small baskets which can easily be raised to the surface and the grain dried and kept from being spoiled by damp. Millet and sweet potatoes are the principal vegetables grown, though maize and yams with sesame, beans and marrows are to be found in the gardens of the more careful and particular house-wives.

Flour-grinding. Millet is ground into flour in the common mill, which consists of a large stone upon which the grain is placed by the handful from a basket by the side of the worker and rubbed with a smaller stone until it is fine enough, when it is pushed into a basket placed at the end of the large stone. This method of grinding has the disadvantage of making the flour full of grits and is unwholesome, especially to those who are unaccustomed to the food. The meal is made into thick porridge and eaten from the pot, round which the family gather and take the food with their hands from it. A pot of sauce made from vegetable-leaves boiled and flavoured with salt accompanies the porridge, or, when possible, meat or fish is added to flavour the meal, the family taking a little porridge from the pot and dipping it into the sauce as they eat. Beans are freely grown but are seldom eaten green, being allowed to ripen and dry when they are soaked in water and the husks removed before they are cooked. Sweet potatoes are boiled with the beans and they are mashed together. Maize is grown by most peasants, but it is grown in small quantities and is seldom ground into flour to be made into porridge, the corn being eaten in the cob when young, or, at times, fried in earthen pots and eaten in small quantities more as a sweet than as a real meal. Plantains are grown by some women in small quantities, but few women know how to cook them as the Baganda women do: they usually boil them as they do potatoes, without peeling them, in a pot with water. The meals are not served up so nicely as the Baganda women dish up theirs, nor are the women so cleanly in their persons or so particular in their methods of cooking: this is probably due to the fact that the upper classes seldom have any cooking done for them. The middle classes who keep cows and also cultivate are most careful in their diet not to eat vegetables and to drink milk near together.   Persons who drink milk in the morning do not eat other food until the evening, and those who drink milk in the evening eat no vegetables until the next day. Sweet potatoes and beans are the vegetables they avoid most of all, and each person, after eating such food, is careful to abstain from drinking milk for a period of two days.   This precaution is taken to prevent milk from coming into contact with either meat or vegetables in the stomach; it is believed that food eaten indiscriminately will cause sickness among the cattle.

Food of pastoral people.   In the upper classes milk is the chief diet though men who can afford to kill an animal eat meat in the evening and drink beer after the meal.   They may drink milk several hours after eating beef before going to rest, if they wish to do so, but this is seldom done.   More often men continue to drink beer until late at night before they retire to rest.   Meat is always roasted on wooden spits, the meat being cut into small pieces, the spit run through them and then stuck into the earthen-floor at an angle over the fire. The meat is cut into small pieces about two inches square so that, when roasted, it can be handed to the chief and he can bite it off the spit and eat it without any further trouble in cutting it.   Children live entirely upon milk and are taught to drink large bowls full at a time: mothers are strict with their children as to the amount of milk they force them to drink and often scold and sometimes smack them to make them drink more, when they wish to leave it.   Women live almost entirely upon milk and become enormously stout, partly from the amount of milk they drink and partly because they take so little exercise.

Love of blood for food.   Herdsmen frequently bleed young bulls and cook the blood, though they rarely ever bleed cows. For the purpose of bleeding they tie a cord tightly round the animal's neck until the arteries stand out, when one is opened and the amount of blood which it is thought the animal can spare without suffering harm is drawn: the cord is now removed and the bleeding stopped.   When an animal is killed, its blood is caught and cooked, none of it being lost.   When animals are offered to either a god or a ghost, the blood is poured on the ground at the temple or shrine and not eaten by the worshippers.

Use of grain in pastoral clans. The king and wealthy pastoral people need large supplies of grain for brewing and for the maintenance of their household servants and slaves whom they cannot supply with milk: the grain is supplied by the agricultural peasants who tenant their estates. When the king wants grain, he kills several oxen, cuts up the meat into portions for the different districts and sends these as presents by special messengers to the peasants whom they tell that the king is in need of grain. The peasants readily respond by sending gifts through their district-chiefs. Fowls and eggs are rarely eaten by agricultural peasants and never by members of the pastoral clans, as these last consider fish and fowls to be harmful to their cows, though they frequently keep fowls and sell them to other tribes in return for spears and salt.

Beer and brewing. Beer is drunk by all classes, it is the principal drink of the agricultural peasants, who have no milk and fall back upon water when beer fails them. Every peasant understands the method of brewing. Beer is brewed either from millet or from plantains. The latter kind is brewed in much smaller quantities than the former. When millet is to be used for brewing, it is put into water to soak until it begins to sprout when it is spread on grass or mats to dry in the sun; when quite dry, it is ground into coarse meal and soaked for three days when the water is poured off and the meal dried and gently baked. The meal is again put into large pots filled with water and stands for two days; when it ferments, the liquid is strained off and is now ready to drink. When millet is plentiful, large quantities of beer are brewed and the agricultural peasants give themselves up to pleasure-making, dancing and drinking for several weeks, visiting first one and then another part of the country where it is known that beer is to be obtained. Though there is a great amount of beer drunk each year, there is not much open drunkenness: when a person gets under the influence of drink, he retires to sleep off the effects. There are not often quarrels of any serious nature because it is a recognised rule to lay aside arms when beer-drinking takes place, in order to avoid bloodshed in heated quarrels over the cups. Plantain-beer is made, as in Uganda, from the pulp of the fruit, the juice being fermented with millet.

Building. In Bunyoro the dwellings are most primitive, easily constructed and of perishable materials: they are bee-hive huts, designed to protect the people from the cold night air and the rainy weather rather than for affording comfort to their inmates. In fine weather people spend most of their time in the open air. The king and the wealthier classes have larger and better-built huts, though the architecture of their houses is the same as that of the peasants' houses, and there is a similar lack of furniture, light and ventilation. The materials used in building are timber and reeds for the frame-work, which is thatched with grass. The larger houses are about fourteen feet in diameter and fourteen feet high, but peasants' huts are only twelve feet in diameter and twelve feet high, while the huts of the poorer pastoral people are not more than eight feet in diameter and eight feet high. A chief's house and a peasant's house alike are poorly built when compared with either the Buganda or the Busoga house, and they are dirty and badly kept. In place of a bedstead there is in some huts a mound of beaten earth covered with grass, but others have only a heap of grass for a bed. The floors are of beaten earth carpeted with grass, and in the middle of the floor is the fire-place where a fire is kept burning constantly.

The king's residence. The king had a number of huts built for his wives and retainers around his own private house. The huts were divided into lots, each lot with a court-yard fenced in with elephant-grass, leaving cow-kraals in different places for the many cows required for his household. By means of these fences the retainers were kept apart from the women and the king enjoyed a certain amount of privacy, because his houses were fenced off from others. The entire group of the king's houses was encircled with a grass-fence intended more for privacy than security. The principal chiefs had their houses around the king's enclosure, and they also had their

wives and retainers around them. The chiefs were expected
to protect the king from danger, should it be necessary to do
so, that is to guard him against sudden attacks from other
nations rather than from any internal foe. Both the king and
the chiefs kept large herds of cows in milk in the capital, the
animals being constantly changed by relays from the country-
herds where the pasture was better than that about the
capital. This custom was followed in order to keep the cows
in health and to save the calves from dying from lack of
proper nourishment, because more milk was wanted from the
cows kept in the capital than from those in the country districts where the calves were chiefly considered. There were no
well-kept roads to be found anywhere, only tracks made by
people travelling to or from districts in the country or by the
cattle going to their pastures. In the country the agricultural
peasants had their fields dotted about and lived in or near them,
but they seldom lived in communities: the pastoral clans
were more inclined to live in communities than the agricultural clans, because they could thus better defend their cattle
against attacks from enemies or wild beasts.

Modern methods of building. Since the advent of the English and the subjugation of the country the capital has become
more of a town with shops and a market, and there are roads
from one part of the country to another; the chiefs have also
been induced to build houses of sun-dried bricks roofed with
corrugated iron in place of their old grass-huts.

Iron working. From very early times in the history of the
country the Banyoro have had a knowledge of iron-work,
having for many generations supplied many of the surrounding
Bantu tribes with iron. It is impossible to discover how
the people first learned the art of iron-smelting: they had
their furnaces and men who made iron-smelting their life-
work as far back as their legends carry them. The iron
ore is dug from the hills where it is abundant; though at
times the smelters follow a vein of good ore some distance
under the ground, in many instances it is found lying on the
surface or only two feet deep. It is smelted and passed on in
the rough to the smiths who work it into spears, hoes, knives,

Plate II

Iron smelting
(*Banyoro Tribe*)

bells and bracelets, which are the chief things required in iron. The men who quarry the ore smelt it. They are a distinct class from the smiths and rarely work iron after smelting it; and conversely smiths rarely smelt it. Iron smelters generally work in companies. They first prepare their charcoal by felling and burning the special kind of trees until the amount of charcoal required is obtained. The fires which have been made to char the wood are extinguished by covering them with green boughs and grass and heaping earth on the top when the workers consider the wood sufficiently charred. When cool, the charcoal is broken up to the size of walnuts and carried to the place selected for smelting the ore. The chief upon whose land the iron ore is dug is paid in iron at the rate of a piece big enough to make a hoe for each furnace of metal smelted. The iron-smelters offer a fowl to the spirit of the hill when they are digging ore from a pit, lest they should be buried in the mine by the angry spirit causing the earth to fall in and entomb them. When the amount of ore required has been dug, the workers dig a pit two or three feet deep and two feet in diameter which they fill with dry reeds. Round the mouth of the pit the ground is beaten hard and a dome of clay built over it, leaving a small hole in the centre to serve as a chimney. Holes are made round the dome for the nozzles of the bellows and the iron is put into the pit in layers with charcoal between them, and the fires are now lighted. More charcoal and iron-stone are added as required and the blast is kept going until the amount of iron-stone to be dealt with has been smelted, when the pit is broken open, covered with green boughs and grass and left to cool. During the time that the smelters are engaged in making charcoal, digging the iron-stone and smelting, they live apart from other men and their wives and observe strict rules of chastity. The smelted metal is cut into pieces large enough to make a spear or a hoe and the smiths purchase the pieces with goats, vegetable food or cowry-shells.

Smithing. Smiths are to be found in all parts of the country. They work up the rough metal received from the smelters into spears, hoes, knives or ornaments, as required.

Smithies are mere sheds to protect the smith from the heat
of the sun or from rain. The workman squats when at work
or sits on the floor. His fire-place is a hole in the middle of
the floor of his hut, and his bellows are a pair of covered pots,
as in Uganda, with a stick attached to the middle of the skin
covering the pot. The pots have a nozzle on one side which
is connected with a tube made of clay which goes into the fire.
The blast is made by raising the sticks and drawing the air into
the pot, the downward stroke forcing it through the nozzle
into the fire. The anvil is a stone, and the hammer for heavy
work is another stone; but for finer work a piece of iron ten
inches long and an inch thick, tapering to a point, is used. A
smith often has a boy-assistant to blow his fire and use the
large heavy stone to hammer bigger pieces of iron: the boy
is an apprentice who is being taught the work.

Salt-making. Salt-making was an important industry and
the salt had as great a sale as the iron and was possibly more
widely known because the demand was greater. Many men
and women found employment in this trade and made a fairly
good living by it. The two best-known centres for salt-making
were in the north, on a branch of the Nile locally known by the
name of the River Kabiga, and at Katwe on the shores of Lake
Albert Edward, to the south-west of the capital of Bunyoro.
The method of making salt was much the same in each place,
and the account that now follows was given by one of the
workers from the River Kabiga. The surface sand on the
river bank is scraped up and put into large pots specially made
with small holes in the bottom of them. These pots are raised
on wooden stands high enough to receive another pot under-
neath them; water is poured over the sand in the pot on the
stand and finds its way through into the pot below. The sand
is thus thoroughly washed two or three times, is spread out to
dry and afterwards taken and scattered again in its former
place on the river where it is left for a few days before it is
again scraped up for renewed washing. The water in the lower
pots is evaporated over slow fires and the salt which is left
encrusted in the pots is scraped out and tied in plantain-fibre
packets weighing from thirty to fifty pounds each. Women are

Plate III

(1) Brackish stream. Scraping up sand to extract salt
(Banyoro Tribe)

(2) Washing sand to extract salt
(Banyoro Tribe)

the chief workers in collecting the sand and washing it, though men assist them to gather fire-wood, boil the salt, tie it into bundles and dispose of it in the markets. No attempt has ever been made to purify the salt, which has a brown colour and contains other chemical substances which make it unpleasant to the taste of any person unaccustomed to it. During the rains the salt-workers are compelled to cease work because the river is in flood and no salt-laden sand can be obtained from the river-bank. The king and the pastoral people require large quantities of salt for their cows: they give the animals salt in water to drink almost monthly. When the king wants salt he sends a present of meat to the workers who, in return, send loads of salt. Each year the king sends an offering of a white cow to the river god Wansemba to induce him to give a plentiful supply of salt. Salt is sent to the principal markets on the borders of Bunyoro, and in this way it is carried far and wide to supply the needs of peoples who live upon a vegetable diet.

Fishermen and fishing. The peasants living on the shores of Lake Albert and along the banks of the River Nile combine fishing with agricultural pursuits: their chief method of fishing is with traps similar to those used in Uganda, lines being also used by some men. The sale of fish is limited in Bunyoro because pastoral people may not eat fish, nor indeed may they have it in their kraals: all people who drink milk abstain from eating fish and from touching it. The agricultural peasants, therefore, are the only people able to eat fish and they cannot afford to purchase it except in the smallest amounts. This limits the industry to the few people living near the Lakes or the Nile, and to various markets on the frontier which are attended by people of other nations.

Dress and ornaments. The pastoral people wear almost entirely cow-skins carefully dressed. Women are most particular to cover their entire persons; they wear one skin tied round the waist and another thrown over the shoulders and, when they go out, another thrown over the head hanging down to the waist and leaving only a small opening through which to see. Men are less careful about their clothing than women:

they seldom wear more than a small piece of skin or a calf-skin thrown over the shoulders. Women of agricultural clans wear a small goat-skin or sheep-skin roughly dressed tied round the waist, and the men wear a small skin hanging in front. Some agricultural peasants make bark-cloth of a thick coarse kind and wear it as a long garment like a toga. These garments are square sheets of bark-cloth tied together by two corners, passed over the head and tied round the waist with a strip of plantain-fibre. Most clans use a thick roughly made bark-cloth for their beds. The pastoral people place a cow-skin upon the floor or make a mound of earth and cover it with grass and spread their cow-skin upon it. Agricultural peasants often lie upon grass and cover themselves with bark-cloths. All the people are fond of ornaments and wear brace-lets of iron, brass and copper. The women of the pastoral clans wear numbers of anklets of fine iron wire twisted round elephant-hair from the tail of the animals. Beads are worn by all who can obtain them. These are strung round the neck with necklets of elephant-hair. Many people have markings on their heads, foreheads and temples which they say are chiefly made by burning-irons when they are ill, and not with any idea of ornamentation. These scars are almost universally upon the foreheads of the pastoral people and are made in a special way by the different clans, so that the people know to which clan each person belongs. The scars are made in childhood either by cutting the skin for cupping purposes to bleed them or by using the burning-iron for blistering, but always in cases of sickness. Both in pastoral and in agricultural clans the people extract four teeth in the lower jaw, medicine-men being experts at extracting them. The teeth are extracted at puberty when boys and girls are taught various tribal customs by elderly men. People of other nations who do not extract their teeth are said to be like dogs.

Pottery and potters. Bunyoro[1] pottery is well known in the neighbouring countries and many people prefer it to that of their own country. Potters are of the agricultural peasant class who obtain their clay from swampy ground where they

---

[1] Bunyoro is the country, Banyoro the people.

get clay of a whitish grey, experience having taught them that this is the best kind for their purpose. Potters are a distinct class from the ordinary peasants, and, though they may be called upon to perform certain duties for their chiefs, yet regard pot-making as their chief employment. The clay is dug and carried to the potter's house and kept in some damp place, portions of it being taken as required. A potter's tools are few and simple: a pointed stick, a curved piece of gourd, a small portion of a broken pot are all a man requires. He uses no wheel but, with his hands or with the curved piece of gourd, he works the clay into shape. All his clay he kneads with his hands, mixing as much powdered stone into it as he thinks necessary to prevent the pot from cracking when drying. The method of making pots is the same as in Uganda: the bottom is first made and the sides are built up from it by adding snake-like coils of clay on to the portion already made and smoothing them out with the piece of gourd and the pointed stick as he turns it round. One kind of pot used in the houses of the wealthier pastoral people is of a pretty greyish tint. The colour is obtained by grinding a stone like mica into powder and mixing it with the clay. The best pots are made much thinner than those in common use and are reserved for holding milk. The pots are polished by holding them in the smoke of fires made so that they give a thick juicy smoke. The pots when thoroughly blacked and shining are rubbed over with a rag and take an excellent polish. A potter is careful to place his pots when drying where they shall not be stepped over and where no pregnant woman shall come near them. Should either of the above precautions be disregarded, it is thought the pots will break when being baked.

Canoes and canoe-men. Canoes are used on Lake Albert, Lake Edward and on the Nile, but in all cases the canoes are solid "dug-out" canoes. Some canoes are large and must have been made from gigantic trees. Before a tree is felled for the purpose of making a royal canoe, the king sends a man or an ox to be offered to the tree-spirit; the victim is killed beside the tree in a place where the blood runs on the tree roots; if it is an animal that is offered, the flesh of the victim is cooked and eaten beside the tree by the medicine-man and the workmen who are to fell the tree and build the canoe; the body of the human victim is left by the tree roots. The prow and stern of a "dug-out" canoe are slightly rounded and bevelled from the top to the keel, making the upper part of the canoe much longer than the keel. As a matter of fact there is no real keel: the outside bottom of the canoe is rounded and made thicker and heavier than the sides, and the sides are thicker near the bottom than at the top, though even at the top the sides are left quite an inch thick. The bottom of the canoe is flat inside to enable cattle to stand with comfort, because canoes are frequently required to ferry cattle over the lakes and the Nile. When a canoe is complete and ready to be launched, a sheep or a fowl is killed in it and the blood left inside for the spirit of the canoe; the flesh is cooked and eaten by the canoe-men, as they sit either in or near the canoe. On the river Nile the method of crossing is as follows: canoes are usually punted into the current of the stream with the bows kept pointed up the stream and are carried by the water to the opposite side; the man who holds the punting-pole uses it as a rudder to steer the canoe and, when he reaches the shallow water, he again punts the canoe to the landing place. On the lakes long-handled paddles are often used and the men stand to paddle, though when they are crossing the lakes the paddlers sit on the sides of the canoes and use the common short-handled paddle with a leaf-blade. The canoe-men are peasants who live on the shores of the lakes or on the Nile; those on the river are ferry-men and spend most of their time in ferrying people over the river for a small fee.

Basketry. Baskets are made by women belonging to the agricultural clans, who supply pastoral peoples with any baskets they require. Baskets are extensively used by agricultural peoples who require them for carrying grain and food, whereas pastoral clans have little use for them. Baskets are made from papyrus-grass and from twigs of a cane-like nature. They are plaited or worked into cane-baskets by women during their leisure time.

CHAPTER VII

WARFARE

Civil wars the most serious in the national history—the king leading the army in person—weapons of war—duties of women at home—omens which guided a warrior when starting on an expedition—treatment of fallen comrades and of foes—return of the army—treatment of a general when an expedition failed.

Civil wars the most serious in the national history. The Banyoro have not for years been an aggressive people, though there were occasional punitive expeditions sent against adjacent nations. The civil wars which took place at the death of each king to decide the question of succession were the most serious events in the national history. There have, however, been war expeditions which were directed against either the Bakedi, one of the Nilotic tribes lying to the north-east of Bunyoro and bordering on Lake Albert, or against the Banyankole whose country lies to the south-west of Bunyoro; they had also to resist the inroads of the Baganda on their southern borders. The Banyoro state that they have not made attacks upon the Baganda for years, but have only resisted the attacks made by that nation, whereas upon the other two nations they made organised attacks in order to capture cattle.

The king leading the army in person. For many years it has been customary for the king to remain at home and not to accompany the army. The people discourage their king from leading the army in person because they fear that he might be killed or wounded, and he therefore appoints a deputy to whom he delegates special powers during the expedition. The general thus appointed is selected by the king in consultation with the mediums of gods. Chiefs are ordered to go to war in person, unless the king excuses them and tells them to send a deputy with a number of men. Chiefs belonging to pastoral clans call upon their assistant herdsmen to join them in any war expedition, and agricultural peasants are also collected from all parts of the country.

Weapons of war. Warriors armed themselves with two spears, one for throwing and one for hand-to-hand fighting, should it be necessary, and with a shield made of wood and decorated with cane-stitching upon the face and a pointed boss in the centre. When the army started on an expedition, offerings to the war-god were sent in advance to the border of the country to be attacked. The offering might be an ox, or a human being, or a fowl. The medicine-man chosen to take the sacrifice, killed it on the border of the enemy's country and invoked the aid of the war-god to destroy the foe and to bless the army. Chiefs led their retainers in battle but there was no order and little discipline in these expeditions, the chief aim of the army being to capture cattle and to steal women or children, when possible. The king sent a royal drum and war-fetishes, and each warrior carried his own particular fetish. Only chiefs took women with them: they had one or perhaps two wives accompanying them to nurse them in case of sickness or should they be wounded; these women carried their husband's clothing and assisted to prepare their food. During punitive expeditions chiefs had to live on a vegetable diet and the wives selected to accompany them were those who had some idea of cooking. Peasant warriors marched with as little baggage as possible and they generally managed to wear a bark-cloth which they could use as covering by night.

Duties of wives at home. It was incumbent upon all wives who were left behind to live chaste lives, to make offerings to the gods and to abstain from cutting their hair and to put away all vessels used by their husbands until they returned. Should a wife shave her head during her husband's absence on an expedition and he be wounded or killed, she would be blamed as the cause, and the heir to the property would send her back to her relatives and claim the original marriage fee; and she would find it difficult to obtain a husband in the

future. Should a warrior strike his foot against a tree root
or against a stone, he would attribute the cause of the accident
to his wife who, he would say, was going about visiting and
enjoying herself, instead of making offerings to the gods to
protect him.

**Omens supposed to guide a warrior when starting on an
expedition.** No warrior would start on an expedition if,
during the night, his fire went out, or if the brown biting-ant
nsanafu invaded his house during the night; and should he
meet a woman when he was starting or should he see two
guinea-fowls, he would return and wait until the next day.
Again, if a man owned a dog and it gave birth to puppies
during the night, he would wait a day before starting on the
expedition. When a man fell in battle, no attempt was made
to take the body home by his companions, who buried him
where he fell. Should a wife be proved to have been unfaithful
to her husband during his absence on a punitive expedition,
he either put her to death or sold her into slavery.

Treatment of fallen companions and of foes. Those of the
enemy slain in battle were decapitated, but the remains were
left on the spot where they found the body. The warriors
who buried any comrade who fell in battle were given an ox
to eat, when the task was ended, by the general. They killed
and ate the ox at some place apart from the army and did
not mingle with their comrades during the day of the funeral.

Return of the army. When an expedition was successful,
the captives and the cattle were led in triumph to the king
and the army returned home with rejoicing. When the army
was some distance from the royal residence, the general sent
a report to the king telling him how the army had fared and
giving an account of the spoil taken. The king at once consulted
the priest whether it was safe for the army to return to the capital or whether any offering was necessary to cleanse it and to
propitiate the gods before the warriors entered the capital.
The king gave the chiefs and warriors presents of slaves and
some of the cattle taken during the expedition.

Treatment of a general when an expedition failed. Should
the expedition be a failure, the general had to retire into the

country for ten or twelve months until the king's anger abated. Any chief who was accused of cowardice and failed to justify his actions before the king was deposed from office and deprived of all his goods and wives.   The accused person had to sit before a crowd of warriors, wearing a thin skin, taken from the region of the heart of an ox, across his chest and was scorned and jeered at by the other warriors who were feasted with meat and beer.   A warrior who killed one of the enemy was highly praised at the time by the general and, upon his return home, his father made a feast in his honour and his chief made him some present, a slave or a cow.

CHAPTER VIII

HUNTING, DRUMS AND THEIR USE .

Agricultural people only hunt animals for food—elephant hunting—
precautions taken by the wife of a huntsman—pits and traps for
game—methods of hunting small game—the use of drums—royal
drums—the war-drum.

Agricultural people only hunt animals for food. We should
scarcely expect a pastoral people to be hunters, their life is so
contrary to that of a hunter. The meat of most wild animals
is forbidden them, which at once limits the object of hunting
to pure sport and leaves the wider aim of obtaining food
from the chase to people of agricultural clans. On the other
hand it is customary to hunt beasts of prey not only from the
love of sport, but also from necessity, that is, when lions and
leopards become dangerous to the herds. The herdsmen never
hesitate to hunt them and show no lack of courage during the
hunts: they will face the fiercest lion and spear it as they would
the most timid animal. Hunting is therefore in the main
limited to members of agricultural clans and is engaged in by
them for the sake of meat, there being few men who make the
chase their principal calling in preference to other work.

Elephant hunting. When hunting elephants, the huntsman
first discovers the locality of a herd and chooses one or two
trees in the track the animals will be likely to take to go to
water. He climbs one tree and his companions climb other
trees near, hide in the branches and wait until the animals
pass under them, when they spear the animal chosen, if possible between the shoulders, and withdraw the spear if they can.
Sometimes they are unable to spear and bring down an animal

at one blow and if it also escapes the other men, they then have to follow it until through weakness it is separated from the herd and they can surround it and spear it to death. When ivory is obtained, one tusk is given to the king, the other the chief-hunter takes for himself, the other hunters with him sharing the meat, which is dried in the sun to be sold in the market or retained for home use. Hunters visit the god of the chase before they undertake an expedition, to secure a blessing upon their weapons and protection against dangerous attacks of the animals; they also offer a goat and a pot of beer to the god. Irunga is the chief god of the chase and has power over all wild animals: he is the same as Dungu of the Baganda.

Precautions taken by a hunter's wife. During his absence, a hunter's wife has to remain at home: she may not visit her friends nor allow any man to come to see her, and she has to make an offering daily to the fetishes for her husband's safety. Should a hunter meet a woman when he is going to hunt, he strikes her: otherwise his expedition will fail and he himself will run the risk of being killed by an animal.

Pits and traps. Sometimes hunters make deep pits and put spikes into them to impale animals; they also use foot-traps which are holes dug in the tracks of animals with a spike at the bottom. The holes are covered and the animal steps on the covering, slips into the hole and is lamed by the spike breaking off in the foot. The hunter then follows up any such animal and kills it. When hunting buffalo, two or three men go out together and stalk the animals until one of the men gets near enough to spear one of them. When it turns to attack him, one of the other men rises and also spears it and saves his companions from its charge by diverting the animal's attention. After spearing an animal the hunter lies flat upon the ground and awaits his companions to save him from the attack of the infuriated animal. The man who first spears an animal takes both legs, the man who spears it afterwards takes the shoulders, the breast goes to the chief of the district, and the rest of the meat is divided up among the other hunters who may be present. Dogs are often used in hunting buffalo to keep the attention of the animals while the hunter gets near enough to spear them. The dogs are given the entrails of the animal killed, and at times some of the meat, if they have done good work.

Method of hunting small game. In hunting small game such as antelope, pigs and the large rat, nets are used and the animals are driven into them by beaters who have dogs, while other men stand in hiding at intervals along the net ready to spear any animal that rushes into it. In dividing up small game the man who first strikes an animal is given a leg, the second man takes a shoulder, and the rest is divided up and the dogs are given the entrails. Some meat is reserved from any good bag for the god.

Drums and their use.

The use of drums, royal drums. Drums are used both for pleasure and for work. The king has the monopoly of drummers. The chief use to which a drum is put is some religious purpose or other. A number of them is attached to each temple. They are sounded merely to invigorate the king, and each of these drums has a fetish in it which is made when the king comes to the throne. The fetish in the drum gives it its importance. In outward appearance a sacred drum differs in no respect from others. They all alike have a hollow shell of wood, usually two feet in diameter and two feet six or three feet deep, the bottom being smaller than the top. They are covered with cow-skin at top and bottom, the skin being laced together on the sides of the drum by twisted thongs of hide. Inside the drum, however, is a fetish. This may be only a small object, like a ball of medicated clay, or a stick to which a number of objects are fastened, but over the fetish the blood of some victim is poured; in the case of royal drums it is the blood of human beings who are decapitated over the drum for the purpose. The chief of these sacred drums is named *Nyakangubi*, and in olden days the blood of three human beings was allowed to run over the fetish when a new king was proclaimed. During the life of the king, should the leather of the drum wear out by beating it, an ox was killed to provide a new skin and the blood of the animal was poured into the drum over the fetish. Several other drums had one human sacrifice killed over them when the king began to reign, and a number of others had blood of oxen poured over them.

The war-drum. There was a special war-drum which was lent to each general who went to war. This had a peculiar rhythm. Other drums are used to indicate the office of different chiefs; and again, special rhythms are used by people when dancing or beating a drum for pleasure.

CHAPTER IX

RELIGIOUS BELIEFS

The undeveloped state of religious beliefs. Religious beliefs are not nearly so developed in Bunyoro as are those of the Baganda: still, so far as they have advanced, the cult is very similar. The principal gods, whom the people assert to be superhuman, were most probably human beings who for some cause were held in veneration and were deified after death. So far as the present generation of people know, there never have been any material objects to represent the gods: they have ever been merely names, and only a few of the gods had temples in which priests and mediums resided. The influence of a god was confined to some locality, as in Uganda, and it was necessary to have some object to which the mysterious presence and power of the god could communicate itself so as to be taken into other parts of the country. For this purpose fetishes were made and kept in the homes of the people or carried about for particular purposes. Amulets were worn to ward off disease or as a protection against wild animals or reptiles, while others were intended to be used medicinally by scraping or by rubbing them on stones and mixing the powder thus obtained with water for internal use, or by mixing it with butter for external application.

The principal gods. There were innumerable gods in the country, each clan having its favourite god; and in many cases there were gods belonging to private members of a clan, to whom the members resorted for special aid. In addition there are a number of gods to whom the people gave particular honour, and whom they call their national gods. Such are:

Wamala, the god of plenty. Wamala, the god of plenty, gave the increase of man and cattle, and of crops He had a temple near the king's residence, with priests and a medium. When the medium was about to give an oracle, he wore two bark-cloths, one tied over each shoulder; he also tied two white calf-skins round his waist, the skins having a row of small iron bells along the lower edge. On his ankles he also wore small bells, and upon his head a special hat. It was customary for the king, and also for the chiefs, to consult this god, and cows with bull-calves were offered when they wished to consult him about their herds and to ask his blessing. Never less than two cows with their calves were sent to the temple at a time. These were taken in the evening about sunset and were milked by the door of the temple, and a pot of milk was taken into the temple from each cow. The priest placed the milk in a special place before the throne of the god and also scattered a little millet on the floor. After this the medium became possessed by the god and gave the oracle, telling what should be done if there was sickness among the people, or what remedies they should apply should there be some plague in a herd. Should sickness break out among the people or a plague among the cattle, it was said that the god Wamala needed an offering. The priest was then consulted and told the king what colour the ox should be which was to be offered. The ox was taken to the temple and killed by the door, the right shoulder of the animal was presented to the priest, and the heart and male organs were hung over the door. The priest now entered the temple with the meat, and cutting off some small pieces threw them about before the god's throne, saying "Peace, Peace." The remainder of the shoulder the priests and medium ate by the door of the temple. The rest of the meat was eaten by the people who gathered for the ceremony. They lighted a fire and cooked the meat near the temple and sang and danced during the night. From time to time the medium mixed with the crowd bellowing like an ox and uttering the words, "Peace, Peace," in deep tones. In the early morning the crowd dispersed to their homes. Sometimes a white ram was offered in addition to the ox. This animal, however, was kept alive at the temple and was allowed to roam about at pleasure during the day and was taken into the temple for the night.

Ruhanga the Creator. The god Ruhanga was said to be the creator of all things. He was held in esteem by all the people, but he had neither temple nor priest. People did not call upon him for assistance, because he had done his work and there was no need to ask further favours of him. Other gods could assist in multiplying men, cattle, and crops; they could also heal sickness and stay plagues. Hence the creator was not troubled about these matters, nor indeed was he thought of except when they desired to give him the honour that was due to him as the Maker of all things.

Muhingo, the god of war. Muhingo was the god of war. His priest was never allowed to appear before the king. Each general sent an offering to him before starting on an expedition and received his blessing; and again, when he returned, he sent an offering of cows and sheep. A priest accompanied the general on any punitive expedition, carrying a special drum which was beaten during the expedition to encourage the warriors and to make them realise that he was with them.

Ndhaula, the god of small-pox. Ndhaula, the god of small-pox, was one of the most powerful of the gods. He had a female medium who seldom left the temple precincts. The temple of Ndhaula was built in the vicinity of the king's tombs to the south-west of Bunyoro. The Baganda were accustomed to send offerings to the god to propitiate him and to stay a scourge of small-pox in Uganda.

Mugizi, the god of Lake Albert. Mugizi was the god of Lake Albert. His medium was a woman who wore a fringe of cowry-shells and small iron bells on her leather garment. The fringe was so made that it moved about like the waves of the lake, when the medium walked. It was to this god the people went to make offerings when they wished to cross the lake by canoe.

Kauka, the cattle-god of foot-disease. Kauka was a cattle-god, whose special duty it was to keep the herds free from foot-disease. The herdsmen resorted to him and sought his assistance, when any animal fell lame.

Nyalwa, a cattle-god to preserve the health of the herd. Nyalwa was a cattle-god whose duty it was to keep cows in good health: occasional offerings were made to him.

Kagoro, the god to cause cows to increase. Kagoro was the cattle-god who was able to make cattle prolific and he was frequently resorted to by herdsmen to assist with particular animals, to make them breed quickly. He was also the god of thunder. The people sent offerings to him when any one was struck by lightning and begged him to spare the people and not to be angry with them.

Kigare, the god interested in the welfare of cows. Kigare also was a cattle-god. He was in fact one of the most powerful of the cattle-gods. His priest did not fear even the king and would order him to investigate any supposed carelessness on the part of the herdsmen. The priest of this god waked the herdsmen in the morning to go to milk the cows and to take them to their pastures.

Mulindwa and Nyinawhira, goddesses who cared for royalty. Mulindwa and Nyinawhira were goddesses. They had a temple within the royal enclosure. Their special duties were to watch over and care for the health of the royal family.

Kaikara, a goddess of harvest. Kaikara was the goddess of harvest. Her medium was a woman. Before the harvest could be reaped, the people brought some cooked millet into the temple, when the medium, dressed with a special head-dress and a mantle of two cow-skins, took the food into the temple. She scattered a little of the food about in the temple and the people ate the remainder by the door, after which the harvest might be reaped.

Lubanga, the god of health. Lubanga was a god of healing to whom the pastoral and agricultural people resorted for help in any sickness. His temple had a strong stockade of growing trees. When a suppliant went he took a pot of beer in which was a drinking tube. The medium sucked a little of the beer from the tube and squirted it from his mouth on each side of the temple. He carried a stick decorated with pieces of bark-cloth, beads, brass ornaments and other things worn by the people.

Munume, the god of weather. Munume was the god who had control over the weather. To him the king sent an offering of an ox and the people sent sheep and fowls which were sacrificed to the god, the blood being poured out by the temple and the people eating a sacred meal of meat with the priests at the temple-door. These offerings were sent when rain was wanted or when there was a continuous fall of rain and the people desired fair weather.

Gods of clans. There were many gods known to the various clans to whom members of the clan went to seek assistance. These gods, however, did not help the nation at large and could only be approached by members of the clan to which the god belonged.

Sacred pythons. Pythons were regarded as sacred in certain places. Other pythons outside the area were not sacred. They were spoken of as cows and their young as calves. No one would kill one of these sacred reptiles nor drive it from his house, should it enter. The king had a special temple for pythons named *Kisengwa*, where the reptiles were daily fed with milk. It is said that the pythons never killed any one, or at least very seldom. Should it happen that a person was caught by a python, the people besought the priests to remove the reptile because they said, "It has proved itself to be no god but a dangerous reptile."

Cause of earthquakes. Earthquakes were said to be caused by the ghosts of departed kings. When the monarchs moved they caused the earth to tremble.

The fear of ghosts. Ghosts were feared in a lesser degree than in Uganda and consequently graves were not kept in repair nor were they remembered. The graves of departed kings, princes and a few important chiefs only were cared for and kept free from weeds. When the king had any slight ailment, he attributed it to the influence of the ghost of an ancestor, sent an offering to the grave and had the grave repaired, if necessary. Sometimes ghosts caused people to fall ill. This was, however, at the instigation of the living.

Medicine-men and their duties. Medicine-men were required to make offerings and perform ceremonies to stay sickness and to prevent the gods from being angry with the people at large. It was especially necessary for priests to guard the agricultural people at harvest-time, because they were then constantly feasting and drinking to excess. When sickness made its appearance in the royal family, the medicine-men told the king which priest to send for and the priest told the king what offering to make to stay the sickness. The offering was usually an ox of some special colour. The ox was brought before the king, who spat upon a piece of plantain-leaf and the ox was forced to swallow it. It was then kept by the king's house all the night and, on the following morning, the priests brought branches from special trees and herbs into the main entrance of the royal enclosure and spread them on the ground. The king with the royal family assembled at the entrance and the ox was marched round them four times. It was afterwards thrown on its back on the branches and herbs, and one of the priests quickly cut its throat and watched to see how the blood flowed from the arteries. Should it spurt out and afterwards flow gently, it was a bad sign; if, however, it flowed quickly, it was a good omen. Again, should the artery on the left side bleed more freely than that on the right side, it was a bad sign; to flow evenly from both, or for the right artery to bleed quicker than that on the left, was a good sign. The blood was caught and set aside until the animal was opened and the entrails were examined. If all was well, the priest took some of the herbs from under the ox, dipped them in the blood and touched the king's forehead, throat and the

back of his shoulder with blood; he also sprinkled each
member of the royal family between the shoulders with blood
and poured the remainder of it over the gate-posts of the
entrance-gate. The priests and the medicine-men took the
meat as their portion. Should the omen be bad, the king
sent for a second animal and went through the ceremony a
second time, to see whether it confirmed the first or whether
the result of the first was accidental; if the second was a good
omen, the results obtained from it were accepted and the first
were ignored.

Ceremony to avert famine. When famine appeared to be
imminent and the cattle were also suffering from lack of food,
the medicine-men looked for the house of a poor man who had
neither wife nor child. The door was taken from the house,
and they also provided themselves with an empty milk-pot,
an empty butter-dish, a potato, a few beans and some millet.
These were then placed in front of the chief medicine-man
with a bunch of herbs. A procession was next formed, headed
by the medicine-man who carried the door, with the various
articles and herbs laid upon it, to some adjacent country in
order to banish from the country hunger, famine, and any
cause that was bringing famine and want, and to cast them
upon another nation.

Rite to prevent evil from happening during feasts. A ceremony was observed by the people when feasting and dancing
took place, to prevent the gods from being angry or from
sending evil, should any one incautiously offend them during
the feast. The chief medicine-man would also visit the king
and tell him that the year had been one of plenty and that
the cattle and crops had been blessed, so that food would be
abundant. After the visit the king would appoint a day for
the people to come together and would present the medicine-
man with two white sheep and two white fowls. The medicine-
man would thereupon kill one fowl and one sheep and examine
their entrails for a confirmation of his previous oracle. If the
desired confirmation was obtained, he sprinkled the people
with blood and offered the living sheep and fowl to the god
Wamala to be kept alive at his temple. The people were then

free to enter into the pleasures and joys of harvest. Sometimes, before the harvest festivities were celebrated, a barren cow, the fattest that could be found, was brought and killed. Its entrails were then examined by a priest and the blood of the animal was sprinkled upon the people. The priest also made a tour round the capital, saying, "We must speak for the god. Let sickness, evil, war and famine grow fat at a distance and never come to us or ours!" The priest took the meat of the animal and ate it in the temple.

Ceremony to prevent war. Should a report arise that an enemy was about to invade the country, or when some portion of the country had been raided and some people killed and others carried away into slavery, the medicine-man procured a blind cow, a puppy with its eyes still closed and a basket of food which was carefully wrapped up so that no one could tell the kind of food it contained. The animals were killed and cut up into small portions and the food was also divided into a corresponding number of portions. These were taken and buried in every road by which it was possible for the foe to enter the country. This was supposed to be sufficient to ruin the powers of perception of any expeditionary force, when the members of it stepped over the hidden portions of food, minced cow, and minced puppy, in the road.

Fetishes. Members of each clan held fetishes in great veneration and believed them to be possessed of supernatural powers. The fetishes were identical with those in Uganda in appearance and use, though the owners would not acknowledge that they were possessed by the same gods as those whom the Baganda worshipped. When some catastrophe happened such as failure of a punitive expedition, it was said that the victorious party possessed some stronger fetish; the conquered party never confessed their fetishes to be useless. The common fetishes were made of horns of animals filled with ingredients by medicine-men. Some were intended to be carried about, while others were meant to be kept in the house. Offerings of sheep and fowls were made to them, and at such time the blood of the victims was smeared over them.

Amulets. Amulets were freely used and, as in Uganda,

Plate IV

(1) **Royal drum containing human blood**
(*Banyoro Tribe*)

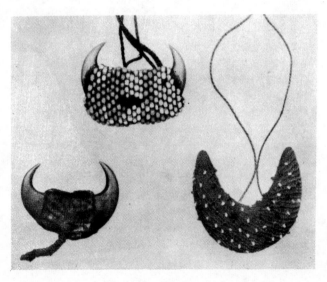

(2) **Amulets**
(*Banyoro Tribe*)

they were obtained from medicine-men in cases of sickness, to be powdered and taken internally or externally, as the case might be. After the illness, the remaining amulets were worn to stave off similar sickness in the future.

New moon. Each new moon was observed by the king and all his subjects, more especially by agricultural peasants. The king made an offering of two or more sheep. In the evening, when the moon appeared, the meat of the animals was given to the peasants who were present, and all work was suspended during the day after the moon was seen.

Dreams. Great faith was placed in dreams. Good dreams betokened good fortune and bad dreams warned a man to be on his guard. After a bad dream he would take a handful of ashes from his fire and holding them in his hand would blow them away before he attempted to touch his face in the morning. He would afterwards seek the aid of his fetishes.

A man's shadow was supposed to be a part of himself. He therefore took care it should not be speared, trodden upon or in any wise injured, lest he too should suffer in like manner.

PART II

THE BANYANKOLE

A PASTORAL TRIBE OF ANKOLE

Plate V

(1) The King and Prime Minister of Ankole

(2) Banyankole warriors

CHAPTER X

THE COUNTRY AND PEOPLE

Geographical position of Ankole—physical features—the climate,
forest-land and agricultural people—the Bahima—dress and habits
of the Bahima—weapons used by herdsmen—cattle-kraals—salt
given to cows as a tonic—milk-vessels—kraal watch-fires—sheep
a protection to cows against lightning—treatment of calves—the
duties of women—food and milk taboos—relationship of the
Bahima to the Banyoro.

Geographical position of Ankole. Ankole is a country
lying between the 30th and 32nd degrees of longitude and
between the first degree south and the first degree north of the
equator. It is a very small kingdom when measured by our
western ideas and is indeed scarcely worthy of the name. It
is bounded on the north by Toro, on the south by Ruanda, on
the east by Uganda, and on the west by the Albert Lake and
the Congo State. On every side the adjacent tribe is stronger
than that of the Banyankole and might with ease crush them
and reduce them to a state of slavery; their preservation is
possibly due to the friendship made with these surrounding
tribes who are kept in an amicable frame by frequent gifts
of cattle.

Physical features. The country is undulating, a feature
which is pleasant to the traveller and gives something fresh
to gaze upon as he travels along; and though the hills are none
of them very high, he occasionally climbs some loftier emi-
nence which affords him a more extensive view of the land
lying before him with its waving grass and its few clumps of
forest-land. There are no great swamps like those in Uganda,
the drainage is better, the water is not held up by the vegetable
growth, and consequently papyrus-grass has not had opportunity to grow and form permanent dams to the floods
caused by rain. The water escapes by the main outlets into
the lakes, and hence the country is much drier, and the atmosphere less humid than in Uganda, where swamps are frequent

and papyrus forms wide marshes extending for miles between the hills. Then, too, there is an absence of elephant-grass and a greater abundance of short grass more suited to the large herds of cattle which roam through the country and keep down the quickly growing herbage. The seasons are also more marked than in Uganda: fewer showers fall in the months known as the dry season. During these rainless periods the grass becomes dry and withered and towards the end of the dry season is burned off by the herdsmen, who have to use discretion when burning tracts of land in order to retain a sufficient extent where they can pasture their herds, until the young and tender blades have sprung up again on the burnt area before a second tract may be burned off. This method of burning the grass serves several good purposes: it not only clears off the dry useless grass, but it also provides a manure to the grass roots and stimulates them to fresh growth, while many kinds of insects and reptiles which are injurious to cattle are cleared off, the excessive growth of shrubs is checked and the lairs of wild animals are destroyed.

The climate, forest-land and agricultural people. During the day the heat is frequently greater than is comfortable, though it does not often run to one hundred degrees in the shade; by night dew falls heavily and the valleys are very cold. It is always advisable to camp on more elevated ground to escape the cold, which is not nearly so great on the hills by night. There are a few clumps of forest on the borders of the country, but timber is scarce in the interior and the trees are of little value for building purposes. It is well for the people that their huts require little timber and that the short branches of shrubs supply their needs, while the dung from the herd forms an important part of their fuel. The land is not so good for cultivation as in Bunyoro or in Uganda, though there are a few agricultural people who eke out a miserable existence upon scanty crops of millet and a few plantain they grow. These agricultural people are commonly called 'Slaves,' *Baheru,* and were in all probability the aborigines who were not strong enough to resist the incursions of the pastoral people and thus sank into a state of subjugation which is little removed

Plate VI

Litter for carrying a princess, with the men bearers
(*Banyankole Tribe*)

from domestic slavery. They are the workers who do all the menial tasks for the pastoral clans, all the drudgery whether of transport, or of house and cattle-kraal construction, in addition to supplying them with beer and any vegetable food they may require. These peasants cultivate the smallest amount of land possible for their existence and adopt the most primitive methods of cultivation, so that the results they obtain from the land can scarcely be said to be a satisfactory test of what the produce would be if it were properly tilled and given a fair trial.

The Bahima. The pastoral people are commonly called Bahima though they prefer to be called Banyankole; they are a tall, fine race though physically not very strong. Many of them are over six feet in height, their young king being six feet six inches and broad in proportion to his height. Yet this young giant does not appear to be remarkably tall until some other person stands near him and is dwarfed by the contrast. It is not only the men who are so tall, the women also being above the usual stature of their sex among other tribes, though they do injustice to their height by a fashionable stoop which makes them appear much shorter than they really are. The features of these pastoral people are good: they have straight noses with a bridge, thin lips, finely chiselled faces, heads well set on fairly developed frames, and a good carriage; there is in fact nothing but their colour and their short woolly hair to make you think of them as negroids.

Dress and habits of Bahima. Men go scantily dressed: they are often destitute of clothing except for a small skin-cape thrown over their shoulders. Women, on the other hand, are completely clothed with well-dressed cow-hide mantles covering their heads and reaching to the feet, with only a small aperture left through which to see. Women are also as corpulent as the men are thin and spare in flesh; indeed they consider stoutness to be a mark of great beauty and strive to attain the largest possible proportions. Women do no work beyond washing milk-vessels and churning the small amount of milk that has been set aside for butter. Neither men nor women wash, as it is considered to be detrimental to the cattle. They therefore use a dry bath for cleansing the skin, smearing butter and a kind of red earth over the body instead of water, and, after drying the skin, they rub butter well into the flesh. For the purpose of smearing the body butter is required in large quantities in each family. The more wealthy people are able to perform their anointing more frequently than the poorer who can only afford to anoint their persons profusely at long intervals, though they put a little butter on their faces and hands daily. The chief occupation of the men is cattle rearing and guarding the herds against attacks of man and beast at pasture, and providing fuel for the kraal and litter for the calves to lie upon. Men become warmly attached to their cows: some of them they love like children, pet and talk to them, coax them, and weep over their ailments. Should a favourite cow die, their grief is extreme and cases are not wanting in which men have committed suicide through excessive grief at the loss of an animal. As herdsmen they can manage two hundred cows when grazing with comparative ease, though it is usual for two or three men to accompany a herd, their duty being to lead the cows to the best pasture, and to guard the herd from wild beasts and from the ravages of hostile tribes. The cows so thoroughly understand the men that they will come or go as they are told, and thus give little trouble to the herdsmen.

Weapons used by herdsmen. Herdsmen are armed with one or two spears and with a long stick with which to drive the animals. The stick is useful to reach an animal in front when the cows are crowded together at watering-places, or when entering the kraal, if an animal is stubborn and resists when spoken to and has to be tapped gently to remind it of its duty to walk on and let the others in. When herding, the men have a peculiar habit of standing on one foot, with the other leg raised and the sole of the foot placed against the calf of the leg upon which they stand, while they lean upon the spear or stick. One man stands while the others, who may be accompanying him in herding, squat about on their haunches and smoke or talk. Herdsmen do not build permanent houses, they move about with the herds from place to place according

Plate VII

(1) Banyankole women resting

(2) Banyankole herdsmen

to the state of the pasturage, and build grass-huts which are all they require for the time. At each camping-place huts are built a short distance from each other so as to form a circle. The doors all open into the circle, and between the huts thorny shrubs are placed to keep the cattle from roaming and also to prevent wild animals from invading the herd by night. The kraal has only one entrance which is closed at night by drawing large thorny bushes into the opening which prevents any one from entering or from leaving the kraal. A kraal may be occupied for two or three months if there is good pasturage in the district; or it may be left after two or three weeks, should a better centre for grazing be found. The herds go out early each morning after milking is done, and return in the evening at sunset, and all the day the cows roam about grazing, often making a circuit of twelve to fifteen miles. They are taken to water twice in the day, about noon and again towards evening before going into the kraal for the night. The site chosen for a kraal is as near to water as possible, though in some places the water is inaccessible to the animals and has to be drawn by the men; under such circumstances long clay troughs are dug and two or three men are appointed to draw water and fill the troughs, whilst others keep the animals in order that they may not crowd together, and further to see that each animal has sufficient to drink. At watering-places grass fires are lighted to create a smoke which keeps flies from biting and tormenting the animals; men also stand about among them with leafy branches to whisk off the flies and prevent them from settling while the cows are drinking. As each batch of cows is watered they move from the water to the fires a little distance away and wait until all the others have had sufficient. It is amusing to see how soon the animals learn to know the benefit they derive from the smoke and struggle with each other to obtain places nearest the fire.

Salt given to cows as a tonic. Cows have no artificial food given them in the kraal, nor are they fed after entering it at night until they go out again to the pasture in the morning. Sometimes, if sickness appears in a herd, a little salt is added to the water which they drink in the evening. This mixture is supposed to be an excellent tonic, and from observation it certainly appears to do good. The amount of milk each cow yields is very small, about five pints in the morning and perhaps a little more in the evening. The calves are always reared by the dam and allowed most of the milk; they are never reared artificially. Should a cow with a calf die, the herdsmen try to save the calf by teaching it to drink milk; more frequently they try to make some other cow act as foster-mother instead of having to feed it by hand. Herdsmen assert that a cow will not yield her milk unless her calf is with her, and for this reason the calf is allowed to suck before the cow is milked. When a calf dies, the skin is preserved and produced each time the cow is milked and is held before her during the time she is being milked. The men know numerous herbs which they administer to cows for various diseases, and one herb which they insert into the uterus to make a cow yield milk when its calf dies. This medicine has to be administered with care and not too often, because too frequent applications are said to cause barrenness.

Milk-vessels. No vessel of iron is allowed to be used for milk, only wooden bowls, gourds, or earthen pots. The use of other kinds of vessels would be injurious, they believe, to the cattle and might possibly cause the cows to fall ill. Not only are milk-vessels restricted to the special kinds mentioned, but even these have to undergo a daily purification of washing and fumigating with a special kind of grass smoke, which imparts a particular flavour to the milk and makes it palatable to the people.

The kraal watch-fire. Each morning and evening a fire, which is constantly smouldering in the kraal, is stirred up into flame, and around it the cows arrange themselves to be milked. The fire gives off quantities of smoke which soothes the cows and keeps flies from them. It is fed with grass which has been used for bedding for calves and with dried dung from the herd, the men seldom using wood or ordinary grass on this fire. The ash-heap is left undisturbed in the kraal, a little dung fuel being added during the day to keep it alight while by night the glow is kept bright by the watchmen. I have

Plate VIII

(1) Banyankole milk pots

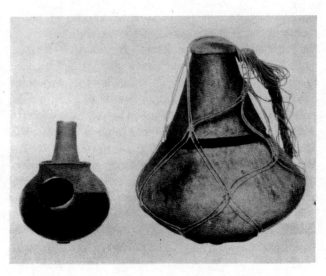

(2) Wooden milk pot, with fumigating furnace
(Banyankole Tribe)

never learned whether this fire has any ceremonial significance, but the nature of the fuel employed seems to point to a certain sanctity. Each morning, when the herd has left the kraal, some of the men who remain at home sweep up the enclosure, and the refuse is swept to a heap on one side, after the droppings, which are to be dried and used for fuel, have been removed and spread out to dry.

Sheep as a protection against lightning. A large sheep is often kept with a herd of cows and goes to graze with the animals daily. This sheep is said to be a protection to the herd during any thunder-storm, and it is thought to ward off lightning. The sheep is made a pet of by the herdsmen, and always sleeps in one of the huts.

Treatment of calves. Calves are not taken to the pastures with the herd until they have been weaned. This happens when a cow is nearing the time to have another calf and discards her former one. For the first few days after birth a calf remains shut up in a hut and is only brought out in the morning and again in the evening to be suckled. At the end of ten days it is allowed to wander about the kraal and pick up what herbage it can, and is brought under shelter during the heat of the day. Some of the men who rest at home watch the calves grazing near the kraal and see that they are not attacked by wild beasts. Calves are suckled twice daily, in the morning and again in the evening. In the early morning, as the sun rises, each cow is taken in turn to be milked, the calf is loosed from the hut in which it sleeps and is allowed to begin its meal, and after it has sucked a little it is taken away. For this purpose a man drags it forward and holds it before the dam, while another milks into a gourd milk-pot as much as he considers wise, when the calf is again turned loose with the cow and both are driven outside the kraal where they are left for an hour or more, while the others are milked and the men enjoy their own repast and pipe before going out for the day with the herd. Again in the evening there is the same task to perform as in the morning, and after its meal the calf is shut up for the night.

The duties of women. Women are never allowed to touch

cows: the men alone milk and herd them; the duties of women are to wash the pots, or to see that they are washed, the work itself generally falling upon their maids. The pots are washed with boiling water and left to dry in the sun; they are afterwards fumigated. The method of fumigating is to use a small furnace made like a small milk-pot with a narrow neck three inches long and a flange at the base upon which the inverted milk-pot rests with the neck of the furnace inside it. The furnace is six inches in diameter, having in the side a hole two inches wide, and into this is pushed dry grass which has a sweet smell; a hot ember is then put into the grass and gently fanned until the smoke rises into the milk-pot. Sometimes milk-vessels are purified with cows' urine besides the water. When men are away herding cattle and have no women with them to cleanse their vessels, they invariably use urine for washing their pots and smoke them afterwards. Women also churn. Their churns are large bottle-gourds into which a little milk is poured daily as it can be spared. The neck of the gourd is corked and the gourd rocked to and fro either upon a grass-pad or upon the knee until the butter separates. The buttermilk is poured off and the butter shaken out into a wooden dish or upon a plantain-leaf; it is then worked a little until the water and milk are got out of it. The chief use of butter is for anointing their bodies, though at times it is eaten.

Food and milk taboos. Milk is the food of the Bahima, and only when there is a shortage will they resort to vegetable food. Chiefs and wealthy men add beef to their milk diet, and there are a few kinds of wild animals they will eat, though these are limited to such as they consider related to cows, for example buffalo and one or two kinds of antelope, water-buck and hartebeest. Beef or other flesh is eaten in the evening only, and beer is drunk afterwards. They do not eat any kind of vegetable food with the beef, and milk is avoided for some hours: usually the night intervenes after a meal of beef and beer before milk is again drunk. There is a firm belief that the cows would sicken should milk and meat or vegetable mix in the stomach. Milk is drunk while it is fresh: they prefer

Plate IX

(1) Milk vessel being fumigated
(*Banyankole Tribe*)

(2) Gourd milk measures and milk pots
(*Banyankole Tribe*)

it warm from the cow, but drink the morning's milk at noon if it is still sweet; should it have turned sour, it is put into the churn for butter. Any milk that is over from the meal at noon is put into the churn, though usually a child is made to drink it. A mother will scold a child when it refuses to drink the milk given it and will force it to drink the amount she thinks it ought to consume. When cattle are scarce and there is little milk for the family, the men drink the morning's supply and the women that of the evening. Men then seek meat of some kind; and only when pressed by hunger will they resort to plantains and beer, and then fast until early morning when they obtain their portion of milk. Women are permitted to eat beef, but no other kind of meat, and should they eat vegetables they refrain from drinking milk. During her menses a woman may not drink milk, except from an old cow past bearing; should her husband fail to procure such a cow she eats vegetables until she is well again. Should a woman continue to drink milk during her indisposition it is thought she would injure the cows, especially their generative powers. Meat is never boiled nor cooked in any other way than by roasting it upon spits over the wood fires. It is eaten from the spit without any flavouring. The most intoxicating drink used by the people is made from honey; they also make a kind of drink from milk which is said to be intoxicating.

The Bahima related to the Banyoro. These Bahima are closely related to the Banyoro. The royal family claim a common ancestor. Their language is a dialect of the same family group, and members of the one tribe can converse freely with those of the other. Again, many of their milk customs are similar. There seems to be no doubt that the two tribes are derived from a common stock, and that the fact of living in another part of the country with different surroundings has modified some customs and beliefs. In certain cases one tribe has preserved customs while the other has abandoned them.

They have legends which state that their forefathers came from another country, some say from the east, while others point to the north-east.

CHAPTER XI

GOVERNMENT, CLANS AND TOTEMS, MARRIAGE

Estimation of wealth—difficulty in obtaining the names of kings—the
king the real owner of all cattle—the king's court—the royal
enclosure—the king's duties—electing a new king—educating
princes — inheritance — rape — divorce — murder — manslaughter —
clans and totems—slavery among pastoral people—long-horned
cattle—marriage—descent through the male line—a mother's care
for her daughter's morality—betrothal of poor pastoral maidens—
marriage customs—polyandry—high code of morality among young
unmarried women—morality among married women—adultery—
treatment of women during their menses.

The king's estimation of wealth.   The Bahima will recognise
no man as king who is not of the blood royal, and it is absolutely impossible for a woman to rule.   Contrary to the usual
custom of kings and of the tribes surrounding Ankole, the king
does not reckon his greatness by the area of his kingdom nor
by the number of his subjects nor yet by the amount of land
cultivated, but by the cattle he possesses.   His chiefs are
appointed to rule a certain number of cattle with lesser chiefs
under them.   True each chief has a district over which his
cattle roam.   Such boundaries, however, are only guides
which serve to separate each chief's cattle from those of other
chiefs and to prevent disputes between the herdsmen as to the
best places for pasturing their herds.   The land is not regarded
as of any value apart from the qualities of pasturage.   Neither
the king nor people ever talk of the land as belonging to
any particular chief; his chieftainship is always described in
terms of the number of cows he has under his control.   What
the land is to other kings and chiefs, so their herds are to
the Bahima.

Difficulty in obtaining names of kings. Owing to the custom of avoiding any mention of the dead and of removing the name of a departed king from the language, should it be the name of something in ordinary use, which thereafter receives a new name, it has been found impossible to obtain a very reliable list of their kings. Should the name of a dead king be the same as that of some animal, the name of that animal must be changed; for example, one king was called a lion, so after his death the name of the lion was changed; and in like manner if the name should be used in any other way in ordinary language, a new word has to be coined and the old word falls into disuse. The following list of kings was obtained from an elderly person who was induced to impart the information; it is not guaranteed to be correct, all that can be said is that such men were known to have been kings at some former time:

1. Luhinda   2. Kasaira   3. Mirimai
4. Lumongi   5. Machwa   6. Kahiya
7. Wabisenge   8. Gasiyonga   9. Mutambuka
10. Ntale   11. Kahaya

The king is the real owner of all cattle. The king had power over all cattle in his kingdom; no man considered any cattle his own, though to all intents and purposes he had sole right to the herd under him during his lifetime. The king could depose a chief; but it was always deemed wise to inflict capital punishment when a man was deposed, because such a person would certainly seek to kill the king. When a man was deposed, his means of livelihood were gone as well as all else that he cared for in life; he would therefore rather die than be parted from his cattle. There was in the past little in the manner of life and in the surroundings of a king to mark him as sovereign. He had his kraal like any of his subjects, which only differed in that it was a trifle larger than that of his chiefs who lived near him, and he had a few more huts for his wives; in other respects the king lived much in the same way, surrounded by his cattle.

The king's court.   The king's courts were held in the open, under some tree where he sat on a rug made of lion-skin, while his chiefs arranged themselves around him, squatting on their haunches, and the poorer pastoral people remained at a distance.   When any man came to a gathering, he first greeted the king by going down on his knees, prostrating himself before him and asking him how he was; afterward he would step aside to some vacant place either near the king or more remote according to his rank.   Arms and all kinds of weapons were left at a distance, no person being permitted to come into the king's presence with any weapon or instrument which could be used against him.   The poorest subject might approach the king, there was no attempt made to restrict any man from coming and speaking to him if he so wished.   After such a meeting or court the king retired into his kraal, where he was accompanied by his wives, one or two of whom always attended him at court, sitting immediately behind him.   These wives alone had free permission to pass into the enclosure. The king would invite any chief he wished to see, or any person with whom he wished to confer, to follow him.   Others might remain under the tree and continue their meeting or retire to their own homes as they wished.

The royal enclosure.   Inside the king's enclosure there were a few miserably poor huts into which he welcomed any visitor or chief and where in bad weather he held his councils.   The king's huts were beehive shaped, bigger than those of a chief and slightly better built, the floor being carpeted with grass. On the right side upon entering the hut was a mound about a foot high, some six feet long and four feet wide; grass was laid on this mound and upon the grass a rug was spread on which his majesty sat while any visitor took his seat in front of him.   On the other part of the dais milk-pots were arranged after they had been washed and fumigated and were ready for use at the next milking-time.   In the king's private house part of the dais was taken up with the king's fetishes, which were spread out ready for special use.   The hut had a wall of elephant-grass dividing it.   On the back side of the division was a bed, generally a mound of earth covered with grass upon

Plate X

(1) Herdsman carrying milk
(*Banyankole Tribe*)

(2) Banyankole huts

which bark-cloths could be laid when it was wanted for use to sleep upon. Each house had a courtyard through which cows wandered, because even the king liked to have his cattle near him and see them, though he did nothing more than coax them and talk to them. The odour from cows, which to most people would be offensive, is pleasant and welcome to a man of the pastoral clans, and the loss of it is a great deprivation.

The king's duties. During the day the king would hear any cases of appeal from a chief and decide any matters which were brought before him. He talked about the welfare of his herds, and also learned if there were any complaints among his people. Most matters of litigation between chief and chief were in reference to cattle, with an occasional case relative to a wife or daughter; possibly a case of theft was brought before him and sometimes rumours of war or of raiding parties had to be dealt with. The rest of the day was spent in drinking milk, sleeping or talking any gossip that might be going about.

Electing a new king. The choice of a king lay with the chiefs, though a sick king made known which of his sons he wished to reign after him, and his wishes were followed unless there was some good reason for not doing so. The choice was not determined by seniority but by other qualifications, age having no part in the consideration.

Educating princes. Princes were placed during their minority in different parts of the country under the guardianship of some responsible chief, who was expected to train them in the art of cattle-rearing, and also in the customs of the tribe. When a prince came to the throne, he invariably raised the chief who had brought him up to the rank of first-grade chief and gave him one of the best offices, and he was called "King's father" by the people.

Inheritance and levirate customs. When a man dies, the representatives of his clan appoint his eldest son to inherit any cattle he may have had. When there is no son, a brother of the deceased marries the widow or widows, and the first male child born becomes heir to the property. A brother by the same parents is sought to inherit the widows; but should such a man have the full number of wives he can support or should he not wish to increase their number, he may refuse to have them. Under such circumstances, the widows continue to live on the milk from their late husband's cattle or go to live with relatives, and the man is expected to visit them as their husband, and any children they may have are called the children of the deceased. Again, should there be a son, the deceased's brother is expected to visit the wives as their husband even though they live with their husband's son. When a man inherits children of a deceased brother, he takes the children and places them one by one in the lap of his chief wife, who receives them and embraces them and thus accepts them as her own children. Her husband afterwards brings a thong which he uses for tying the legs of restive cows during milking and binds it round her waist in the manner a midwife binds a woman after childbirth. After this ceremony the children grow up with the family and are counted as part of it.

Rape. Should a man force an unmarried woman, the injured woman will complain and the man will be tried and if guilty must bring a number of cattle to her parents and marry the woman. Should a man refuse to marry the woman, he forfeits all his cattle and is reduced to the status of a herdsman; this is a serious punishment which any man fears more than death; in many instances a man will commit suicide rather than part with his cattle.

Divorce. Divorce is almost unknown; there are, however, a few known cases where a man had divorced his wife because she had become a prostitute. There are also a few instances on record where men have sought to put away their wives owing to their having become quarrelsome and abusive: in each case the wife was sent back to her clan and the marriage money demanded. Instances are not wanting in which women have been irritable and abusive; the husband has then accused his wife in court where she has been tried, and when found guilty she has been sent to the sacred lake of Karagwe for purification. The priest who undertakes the cleansing first administers a strong emetic, and, after the woman has been made violently sick, he gives her a purgative and allows that to work; she is afterwards washed in the lake and restored to her husband. The mere fact of being sent to the sacred lake is a punishment a woman dreads so much that she returns a changed character.

Murder. When a murder has been committed, it is the duty of the members of the clan of the murdered man to seek their brother's murderer and to bring him to justice. Should positive proof be lacking who the murderer is, the relatives seek a diviner who by his arts discovers the guilty person. The diviner names the man, and the relatives accuse him to the chief in whose employ he may be at the time. The accused man has to prove his innocence or else be condemned. It is almost impossible for a man to clear himself when accused, unless he can do so by taking the poison ordeal and by running the risk of dying from the poison. Any man who premeditates murder seeks to carry out his decision when he feels sure he can escape and flee the country; he then commits the deed and leaves his native land never to return. The avenger of blood, when he has traced the deed to a man who is absent, accuses the murderer's clan and they have to pay compensation. Should a murderer be caught by his accusers, the relatives of the accused must act promptly and have the case tried, if they wish to save his life, or he will be condemned and executed. The king's court alone can save such a man from death and decide what the fine shall be for the murder. When a suspected murderer is captured, he is put on his trial and opportunity is given him either to deny the charge, or, if he confesses, to tell why he committed the deed. A man who denies a murder is given the test-ordeal and, should he survive, he is acquitted. When a fine is imposed upon a clan for murder, part of the sum is paid at once, the remainder is left to be paid by instalments, as opportunity arises. Sometimes a clan refuses to pay the fine imposed by the king, and this is a *casus belli* between the two clans. The injured clan awaits its chance until it is either strong enough to settle the question by force of arms, or else some person is captured belonging to the other clan, who is then killed without trial: this ends the grievance and the clans may become apparently friendly again. Still there will be an under current of bitter feeling which may break out at any moment. When a case of murder is settled by a fine, the murderer is free to visit and hold friendly relations with the clan he has injured; there is often a ceremony when a fine is paid to which he is invited and when he is publicly proclaimed free from any blame or further incrimination.

Manslaughter. It sometimes happens that a man may injure another by accident and the injured man die. The safest plan is for the person who caused the injury to go at once to his chief and state the facts, leaving him to call the relatives of the deceased and try the case. If they are satisfied that the injury which caused death was accidental and that there was no malice, they accept compensation and the matter ends.

Clans and Totems.

Clans and their totems. The nation is divided into clans each of which owns a common parent and has common totems, and the line of descent is reckoned through the male line, that is, men and women belong to the clan of their father, not of their mother. No man may marry a woman of his own clan; in other words, the clans are exogamous. There are fourteen clans, each of which bears a special name by which it is known and called. The totems of a clan are not often mentioned publicly though they are well known to each member of the nation; with few exceptions the totems refer to cows or to some part of a cow which has to be avoided by the clan. The only explanation given for the origin of clans and totems was that an ancestor was made ill by eating or by drinking the thing they now avoid and regard as taboo. Clanship carries many benefits and privileges with it, especially during times of distress and sickness, or when a person is wronged by a member of another clan, or should a man be murdered.

The clans are:

1. *Abahinda*, whose totem is a Monkey, *Nkima*; this clan is the royal clan.

2. *Abasambo*, whose totem is a Cow, *Ngabi*. Cows with straight horns.

3. *Abagahiya*, whose totem is a Cow, *Ngobe*. Striped cows.

4. *Abasingo*, whose totem is a Cow with black stripes from neck to tail, *Kitale*.

5. *Abasito*, whose totem is a Cow, *Kigabo*.

6. *Abasaigi*, whose totem is a Cow's tongue, *Lulimi*.

7. *Abami*, whose totem is a Cow with black or white spots, *Ente luzimu*.

8. *Abagai*, whose totem is a Striped Cow, *Ngobe*. Members of this clan may not drink the milk from such a cow nor even touch it.

9. *Abasingo*, whose totem is a Cow with markings running from head to tail.

10. *Abasikatwa*, whose totem is a Cow of dark brown colour, *Ente ya lukungu*.

11. *Abakimbiri*, whose totem is a Cow born feet first.

12. *Abatalogo*, whose totem is Entrails of a Cow, *Ebyenda*.

13. *Abatwa*, whose totem is Twins, *Abalongo*.

14. *Abaitira*, whose totem is the human breasts, *Mabere*.

Number one is the royal clan which, as with the Banyoro, has a totem unconnected with cattle.

Number thirteen, that of twins. When a woman of this clan gives birth to twins, the members of the kraal in which she is living send her to her mother, with whom she remains until the twins have cut their first teeth. After the twins have cut their first teeth, the husband restores his wife to her home and has intercourse with her. The members of the kraal move away from their old kraal in which the twins were born, and build a new kraal at once.

Number fourteen. The human breasts. When a woman of this clan gives birth to a female child, the husband brings a piece of cow-dung, draws a little milk from his wife's breast upon the dung, and throws it into the kraal for the cows to walk upon during the night.

Slavery among pastoral people. No member of the nation may enslave another member; they are free born and therefore cannot enslave one another. They possess as slaves men and women from other nations whom they have purchased or captured.

Long-horned cattle. The Bahima have a kind of long-horned cattle of which they are justly proud; some of them have extremely fine horns measuring five feet from tip to tip. It is interesting to watch a herd of these animals enter the kraal through a narrow doorway; they turn their heads on one side to get their horns through. Their colour is dark red, almost black, though some are light and sometimes a striped or a white cow appears. The totems refer chiefly to the colour, though some refer to the shape of their horns.

Men alone come into immediate contact with cows, women only wash the pots and churn. The men are responsible for all work which brings them into contact with the animals.

Marriage.

Betrothal takes place in many instances in infancy. When parents have a son born they arrange with parents of some other clan who have a daughter also an infant, that these children shall marry when they grow up. The compact is ratified by the boy's parents giving the other parents one and sometimes two milch cows. It is the duty of a girl's mother to watch over her daughter's morals in any case, whether she be betrothed or not. Marriage restrictions observed by most Bantu people are observed also by these pastoral people, to wit: a man may not marry a woman from his father's clan, nor yet from his mother's clan.

Descent through the male line. All children belong to the father's clan and take his totems: their father's brothers are called their fathers and his sisters are called aunts on the father's side, *sengawe*. Members of his clan who are of his own generation a man calls his brothers and sisters, and all children a generation below him he calls his children. His father's parents and older people a man calls his grandparents. On his mother's side a man calls his mother's sisters mother and her brothers by the term *Mujwa*. On the mother's side children

Plate XI

(1) Long-horned cattle of the Banyankole

(2) Royal milk pans and water ladle
(*Banyoro Tribe*)

soon cease to think of relationship after the generation below them, whereas on the father's side the relationship remains. These exogamous rules do not apply to royalty, for in the royal family endogamy obtains, in so far as princesses may only marry their brothers, or members of the royal family. Princes marry their sisters and have children by them, but they are not restricted to marry sisters only, they may marry as many wives as they choose from other clans.

A mother's care for her daughter's morality. Every mother is responsible for her daughter's conduct until she marries. Wherever the mother goes the daughter must accompany her if she is to spend the night away from home, so that she may guard her. Before marriage a girl does not cut her hair, nor is she permitted to wear any ornament on her waist or legs. As her hair grows beads and cowry-shells are worked into it and are a token that she is unmarried.

Betrothal of poor pastoral maidens. Among the lower classes of pastoral people there are many parents who are unable to betroth their sons in infancy; these grow up to manhood and obtain the necessary means for marriage as best they can. When a young betrothed couple grow up to maturity and the youth wishes to marry, he brings his future father-in-law a milch cow and a heifer. This gift confirms the first promise made by the parents on his behalf and gives the girl's parents to understand that he means to hold to the early promise made for him. The young couple do not meet or see one another. From the time this second gift is taken to the girl's parents until the time of marriage the girl is kept constantly veiled; no man, not even her brothers, may see her face. The number of cows to be given for the marriage gift is named and a provisional date fixed for the marriage. The prospective bridegroom is given several months in which to obtain the full number of cows, and when these are paid the actual day for the marriage is fixed.

Marriage customs. Relatives and friends of both parties meet at the house of the bride's parents: they represent many clans. The bride's father supplies a fat ox for a feast before the marriage takes place. The ox is killed near the kraal, fires are made and the meat is roasted and eaten by the guests who afterwards betake themselves to the kraal for the next ceremony.   The bridegroom enters the kraal and is conducted to the hut in which the bride stands waiting, wearing the usual dress of women which covers her from head to foot.   He takes her right hand and leads her from the house and out of the kraal to the assembled guests.   A strong rope is produced by one of the bride's relatives and tied to one of the bride's legs. Sides are then chosen by members of the bride's and bridegroom's clans and a tug of war takes place.   The bride's clan struggle to retain their sister, and the bridegroom's clan strive to carry her off.   During this contest the bride stands weeping because she is being taken from her old home and relatives; it is the correct thing to do.   The bridegroom stands by her, still holding her hand, and when the final pull is given in his favour he slips the rope from her ankle and hurries her away a few yards to a group waiting near with a cow-hide spread on the ground.   The bride sits upon this and the young men raise her up and rush off with her in triumph to the bridegroom's parents' house, chased by friends and relatives.   During the struggle for possession of the bride the bridegroom's parents have hurried away from the scene of the feast to prepare for the reception of their daughter-in-law and sit awaiting her When the party arrives with the bride the bridegroom takes her and places her in his mother's lap, and after she has embraced her and welcomed her as a daughter he puts her in his father's lap and she is received into the family with every token of affection as a daughter.   She is taken by her mother-in-law and put to rest for a time as a child.   The party of friends dance and celebrate the wedding with rejoicing during the day and night.   An aunt, the father's sister, accompanies a bride to her new home and remains with her three nights.   On the third night the marriage is consummated and the aunt returns to her home.   When she leaves there is an affectionate parting and the bridegroom's father gives her a cow as a present. On the day of her marriage a bride's father gives his daughter a present of a number of cows, never less than six, to ensure her having food.

Polyandry. It happens at times that a poor man cannot afford to pay the necessary number of cows to obtain a wife and still have sufficient left to supply him and his wife with milk for their daily need. He therefore seeks the aid of one or more brothers to join him and together they pay the marriage fee and the woman becomes the wife of the party. The eldest brother goes through the marriage customs, but it is understood that she is the wife of all the men in the contract. The woman lives with each in turn until she is with child, when she remains with the eldest until the child is born. Any children born of such a marriage are called the children of the eldest brother. An agreement of this kind does not prevent any member of the party from relinquishing his share in this arrangement and marrying another wife himself, if he wishes to do so when he has obtained the means.

High code of morality among young women. It is remarkable how careful women are to avoid all connections with men until after marriage. Should any woman commit fornication and have a child before marriage, she is disgraced for life. The clan condemns and disowns her as soon as the fact is known. She is sent away to the sacred lake Karagwe, where she remains until her child is born, after which she may return to her tribe to the man who disgraced her; and should he refuse to take her, she becomes a menial, whom no man will marry except some person who has been disgraced and is unable to obtain a wife, or perhaps some slave may marry her.

Morality among married women. Though the rule for a woman to be careful in her relations with men before marriage is so strict and though after marriage she will cover herself from head to foot when going out, yet once married every woman consents to be the wife of any visitor who may come to see her husband. It is a widely recognised rule for a man to allow his visitor to sleep on the same bed with him and his wife, and in the early morning for the husband to go to attend to his cattle, leaving his wife for the guest's use. Should a husband be absent from home and a guest arrive, it is the duty of the wife to entertain him and live with him. The rules of hospitality are such that a man must provide his visitor with a wife during his visit: should even a younger brother come, he also has the use of his brother's wife during his stay. Again when a man visits a friend taking his wife with him, the men exchange wives during the visit. This is one of the few tribes in Central Africa where polyandry exists side by side with polygamy. The number of wives is regulated by the food supply and the means available for obtaining wives.

Adultery. Adultery is sometimes made a matter of complaint, though the cases are rare when this is done, owing to the laws of hospitality and the freedom women enjoy in being able to entertain their husband's friends. Resentment and anger, however, are felt when a wife cohabits with her husband's enemy; the husband will then have the case tried and the man fined if proved to be guilty.

Treatment of women during menses. During her menses a woman is isolated from members of her family; she sits apart during the day and at night she must sleep on the floor. The term used to explain her condition is "Seeking a child." She is not allowed to drink milk nor may she handle milk-vessels. She is given vegetable food and drinks beer, unless she is the wife of a wealthy man who can give her milk from an old cow past bearing.

CHAPTER XII

BIRTH CUSTOMS, SICKNESS, DEATH AND BURIAL

Midwives, their treatment of patients at birth—purificatory ceremony
after childbirth—infant dentition ceremony—ceremony attending
a girl's dentition—education of boys—birth of twins—puberty of
girls—how sickness is accounted for—death, beliefs in transmigration of soul—death customs for king's wives—death customs
among pastoral clans.

Midwives and their treatment of patients. Pregnant women
have no food restrictions because their food consists of milk
only, and a woman takes her usual supplies of milk and continues her ordinary vocations until she is about to be confined.
A few days before her confinement she undergoes a process of
massage to make her bones supple and thus give her an easy
delivery. An elderly woman remains with her some days before
the day of birth, and, when she sees the actual labour pains
begin, she ties a rope to the roof of the hut for the expectant
mother to hold on by while she herself acts as midwife. A
second woman supports the mother and encourages her during
this time. When the child is born, it is placed on the floor on
a small cow-skin, and respiration is set up by the midwife
who rubs the child's eyes, head, face and nose. She puts a
large thorn of an acacia tree into the child's mouth, because it
is said to make the breath sweet. When the placenta comes
away, the umbilical cord is cut with a strip of wood taken
from a drinking-tube. A hole is dug in the doorway of the
hut, lined with sweet smelling grass, and the placenta buried in
it. Mothers dislike a child to be born feet first, because they fear
the child will grow up to be troublesome and unsatisfactory.
The sex of the child is always a matter of interest to the

parents: in the case of a boy, the father digs up the gate-posts of the kraal and puts them on the fire in the hut where the mother lies secluded during the next seven days, during which time the fire is kept burning brightly by day and by night. The mother is given the thong her husband uses for binding the legs of restive cows when milking them; this she wears as a belt until she is quite well again. Should the child be a girl, the mother uses a band taken from her own clothing and the fire is supplied with ordinary firewood and not the gate-posts, while she is secluded.

Purificatory ceremony after childbirth. When the child is a week old and the stump of umbilical cord falls from it, a young sucking bull is brought to the hut, a vein in its neck is opened and a pint of blood is drawn from it; the blood is cooked to form a cake, and sometimes a little milk, with the stump of the umbilical cord cut up finely, is added to it while it is cooking. Young children belonging to the same clan are invited to this ceremony and come in numbers, because the dish is a favourite delicacy. Should the stump of umbilical cord be reserved and not put into the dish, the mother makes a small leather bag and stitches the cord in it and wears it in her girdle. After the meal the children sweep out the hut in which the mother has been secluded; the dust they collect and throw on the kraal dung-heap, and to make quite sure that there is no dust or grass left they sweep the hut out four times. While the children are sweeping out the hut, the mother is undergoing a purificatory ceremony: she washes from head to foot and smears her body with a kind of brown clay which has a sweet smell and is reserved for ceremonial uses. The mother discards all her old clothing, her husband provides her with quite new clothes, she returns to her hut to receive her relatives and friends, who by this time have congregated to see her baby and to congratulate her, and the baby is taken and examined by the women.

Infant dentition. From this time until the child cuts its first two teeth there is no ceremony to observe, but the first two teeth are watched for with great anxiety. When the mother discovers them, she announces the fact to her husband who, if the child is a male, brings a miniature bow and arrows, puts the child to sit on the ground and places the bow and arrows in its hands for a few moments, the mother afterwards putting them away in some place for safety in the hut. It is considered unlucky for a child to cut its upper teeth before the lower teeth, and a mother is relieved when the lower teeth are cut. When these teeth are cast by the child, the mother preserves them with the bow and arrows. The father at this time brings a cow which has only had one calf and that a female; he places the child to sit on its back, and from that time the child is fed upon the milk from that cow alone, no one else being allowed to drink the milk from this particular animal. After the ceremony of sitting on the ground the child's hair is shaved off except a tuft on the crown, and on this tuft beads and cowry-shells are threaded and left. The mother then begins to make a round of visits to her husband's relatives to show the baby, and they make presents of a few beads for the child's arms and legs. When a female child cuts its first teeth, the father places it to sit on the floor and brings an empty gourd such as is used for churning, the child is made to rock it about as is done when churning, and the mother then stows it away. When the teeth are cast they are preserved with the gourd. The mother is more careful to watch over a daughter than over a son and to train her lest she should learn loose habits and grow up impure. When a girl is old enough to learn how to handle and wash up pots, the mother teaches her how to cleanse them and how to fumigate them, and also how to churn and scent butter with the juices of sweet smelling grass. Children are forced by their mother to drink quantities of milk daily; sometimes she punishes a child if it does not drink enough, that is to say the amount she thinks it ought to drink during the day.

Education of boys. At the age of twelve a boy is taken by his father to the head-man of the clan, who instructs him daily in the art of cow-keeping and in the beliefs and customs of the clan. The boy remains some years in the kraal of his instructor until his education is considered complete. He then returns to his father's kraal and takes his place with other herdsmen in tending the cattle. There is no further ceremony until marriage, at which time the son of a chief is given a number of cattle which he manages for his father. Sons of poor people may either assist their father or become independent herdsmen to some wealthy person, receiving in return their food and sufficient cows to enable them to marry.

Birth of twins. There are no ceremonies at the birth of twins except in the *Abatwa* clan whose totem is twins. In that clan the mother and her children are taken to her parents' home and she remains there until the children have cut their first two teeth and the father has performed the ceremony of moving from the old home and building a new kraal, as mentioned above. The husband brings his wife and children to their new home and she goes about her duties as before.

In other clans the husband mounts the hut or stands in the gate-way of the kraal and calls in a loud voice "My wife has twins" until the fact is well known in the vicinity. People are careful what they say about twins, lest a ghost should overhear their remarks and be offended and cause sickness in the clan. Twins sleep in the same hut with their parents, but they have a separate bed curtained off from the rest of the hut.

Puberty of girls. The first time a girl menstruates the fact is kept private by her parents who alone know her condition. The father provides his daughter with milk from an old cow, she may not drink the milk of other cows or handle any milk-vessels and she takes no part in any household duties until she is quite well again[1]. It is thought that should a menstrous woman drink milk from the cows she will cause them injury. Should the daughter be engaged to be married, the relatives and the bridegroom are informed that she is old enough to marry

---

[1] The reason for fearing that a menstrous woman may injure the cows is probably a fear lest she should cause them to become in a like condition and cast their young. Cows are encouraged to conceive again shortly after giving birth, hence the precaution applies to all cows except those too old to bear. This suggestion is only conjecture based on observation and not on any direct information.

when she has recovered, and preparations are made for the marriage to take place.

Sickness, Death and Burial.

How sickness is accounted for.   Sickness is accounted for in four ways:

1. It may be due to the ghost of a departed king who is offended by something done which he disapproves, or he may have been somehow neglected and therefore it is necessary to make an offering. The cause is discovered by divination, and the priest of the temple in the sacred wood where kings are buried is asked to assist by making the offering to the ghost. Paralysis especially is attributed to departed kings, and the priest of the temple of kings alone can assist in these cases; relations bring offerings on behalf of the patient and the priest makes intercession on their behalf and tells what remedies should be used to relieve the patient.

2. Magic is supposed to be the cause of many forms of sickness. A medicine-man is consulted and discovers the person who has caused the illness. Should a man deny the charge, he is tried in open court, and, if he still persists in maintaining his innocence, the case goes to a higher court and finally the king gives judgment; should the man appeal from this decision, he is given the poison ordeal. In most cases a man will confess he has used magic and will state his reason for so doing, and, when he has been pacified, he will remove the spell and allow the patient to recover, and will even find medicine for him. Most complaints and skin diseases are said to be due to magic.

3. Fever is said to be due to climatic influences and during mild attacks common remedies are used. Should a case prove to be obstinate, or should a man grow worse, a medicine-man is consulted to tell by divination whether there is magic underlying the sickness. When a patient becomes delirious, he is said to be under the influence of a malevolent ghost. The medicine-man smokes out such a ghost by burning certain herbs and the tail feathers of a cock and making the patient inhale

the smoke.　Offerings are made to clan-ghosts in order that they may help the patient.

4.　In some cases the illness of a person is attributed to ghostly possession and the ghost has to be exorcised.

A common complaint among these pastoral people is a deep-seated abscess.　The cure for this is to transfer it to some other person.　A bunch of herbs is rubbed over the place and buried in a public road, and the first person who steps over it will catch the sickness and the patient will recover.

Death, the belief in transmigration of the souls of royalty. When a king dies, the knees are drawn up into a squatting posture which is the favourite attitude of men when resting. The body is kept two days in the kraal and is sponged at intervals with milk.　In the evening of the second day a large cow is killed and the raw hide is wrapped around the body and stitched together, and the corpse is taken to a sacred forest called *Ensanzi*.　The ox may not be killed in the ordinary way by having its throat cut, but is thrown down by a number of men who quickly twist its head round and break its neck.　This is the first of many cows which are offered to the spirit of the king; in this case the meat is eaten by the men on the spot, but later offerings are taken to the forest and the meat is given to sacred lions.　The forest is inhabited by sacred lions which are said to be animated by the ghosts of departed kings.　There is a temple in the forest and a priest lives in it with his family.　He has charge of the temple and forest together with the lions; he feeds them and holds communion, when necessary, with the departed kings who are said to animate the beasts.　When a king is brought for burial, the priest receives the body at the temple, removes the cow-hide from it and washes it with milk.　He keeps it several days until it swells and subsides again.　The priest has been busy in the meantime seeking a lion cub, and, when the body subsides, he produces the cub and says this is what the king has brought forth and asserts that it has the spirit of the king.　The body of the king may then be buried in the forest and receives no further attention, because the king is said to live in the lion.　For some days the mourners remain to watch the growth of the cub, which is fed with milk at first and then with meat; when they are satisfied that the animal is going to live, they return home and tell the new king all that has taken place. When the cub has grown big enough to shift for itself, it is turned loose and takes its place among the other lions of the forest. The priest bears the title of Pleader (*Kwegeririra*): he and his family live in this forest and he guards the lions, which are accustomed to be fed regularly on beef and which, though by no means tame, are used to this man and know him. Lions in other parts of the country may be killed with impunity: in this forest only they are sacred.

Death customs among the king's wives. The idea of transmigration is not confined to the king only; the royal family at death pass into animals or reptiles, and the spirits of the king's wives enter into leopards. Princes and princesses go into large snakes; the leopards, that is the king's wives, have a part of the sacred forest in which the kings are buried; and the snakes, that is the princes and princesses, have another part of the same forest. Each class has its own temple and priest who acts as medium to consult the spirits when necessary. The burial rites are the same for each of these groups of spirits as for the king; the leopards are fed with meat and the snakes with milk from cows which are offered to them in sacrifice.

Death customs among pastoral clans. When any other member of these pastoral people dies, his legs are bent up into the favourite squatting position and the body is stitched in a cow-hide and buried in the dung-heap in the kraal. The ghost has no special place of abode. It first goes to the sacred lake Karagwe, but is free to return to its old haunts after a few days. The heir is appointed as soon after death as possible in order to be present at the funeral, it being his duty to stand in the grave to receive the corpse, to place it in position there, and to help in throwing the dung upon it. Mourning continues for three or four months. When it ends, the survivors remove to some new site and build another kraal. The old place falls into decay and is soon overgrown and lost to sight. At the end of the mourning widows shave their heads and undergo a cleansing. It is often necessary to guard widows when a man is about to be buried, because they drink poison and die at the grave in order to go with their husband rather than be left behind with an uncertain future. Should any relative come after the mourning has ceased and wish to know about the dead, the chief widow takes the man a little distance from the kraal and tells him all about the illness, death and burial; they weep together and then return to the kraal. Mourning is not renewed in the kraal when once the survivors have removed, even though some important member of the clan should come to enquire about the dead. Shrines are, however, built at the entrance of the new kraal where the ghost may rest and where offerings may be made to it.

CHAPTER XIII

RELIGIOUS BELIEFS, HUNTING, COUNTING AND DIVISIONS OF TIME, MUSIC AND GAMES

Brief review of beliefs in gods—the war-god—the home of ghosts—
religious ceremony in treating a cow with a newly born calf—
Clan gods—sacred place in the hut for fetishes—magic—belief in
ghosts—cattle sickness and its treatment—taboos against washing
—taboos on the use of milk—taboos on the use of food—people who
are taboo to the king—blood brotherhood—hunting as followed
by pastoral people—counting—division of time—the new year—
music—games.

Review of beliefs in gods. The Bahima are not a very
religious people; the gods do not trouble them and they do
not often trouble the gods except for special reasons. Still
there are occasions when aid is sought from one or other of
their gods through the medium of a priest, for example, in
case of sickness in the family or among the cattle. The chief
deity is named Lugaba. He dwells in the sky and is really
the Creator. The world belongs to him, his smile brings life,
and the result of his displeasure is sickness and death. As in
Uganda so here in Ankole the Creator has no temple and no
priest and therefore no worship; and the common people
make no offerings to him. Still he is well known and acknowledged by all, he is their great benefactor from whom they
receive all the good in life as a matter of course and without
any thought of an offering in return; nor is prayer made to
him.

The war-god. The war-god is named Zoba: he has both a
temple and a priest who is also the medium of the god. Should
an enemy surprise the people in any part of the country, the
women run into hiding in the scrub, and from their hiding
place call upon Zoba to help their husbands and give them

victory.   At such times they often make promises of offerings
on condition of victory being granted them; these offerings they
ask their husbands to pay when they return home.   When the
danger is over, the women return to their homes and place a
pot of milk in the kraal near the spot where the cows stand
to be milked at the fire.   When the men return home they
drink a little of the milk and thank the god for their victory,
which they attribute to him, and ask him to preserve them from
further danger.   In times of peace the deity is left without a
thought.   There is no reason for saying the people are without
religion because of this neglect of their chief gods; there are
other gods whom they may be visiting and consulting for other
purposes, and the multitude of ghosts too call for frequent
attention from individual families.   The king has often to
send to the sacred forest to feed the lions, and through the
priest to make enquiries of his fathers as to the safety of his
country and as to the political state of his land.   In all cases
the priesthood is hereditary, sons being trained by their
fathers in the mystery of caring for the lions and in the art
of calling upon the spirits of the kings.   It is in the gloom
of the hut that the spirit of a king takes possession of a priest
and through him makes known the causes of national trouble
or matters concerning the king especially.

The home of ghosts.   The sacred lake Karagwe is said to
be the peculiar abode of ghosts, but they are not restricted
to it and at times they return to their old haunts where
the cattle are, and therefore each home has its shrine for a
family ghost.   The ghosts take an interest in the affairs of
the family, and hence it is necessary to keep the shrines in order
and to make offerings to them, because they have power to
do good or to cause harm when annoyed.   No ghost will
consent to take up his abode in the shrine of another ghost,
and should his own shrine have fallen into neglect or should
there be no food there, he will turn away offended and send
sickness of some kind into the family.   A medicine-man will
be able to discover which ghost has caused sickness and also
be able to tell how to satisfy the requirements of the ghost.
Sometimes a ghost becomes rich in cattle and slaves, who have

Plate XII

(1) Bead head-dress worn by priests when giving an oracle
(*Banyankole Tribe*)

(2) Weapons of the Banyankole

a large hut built for them to live in.   When the cows belonging
to a ghost are giving milk, the relatives of the ghost choose
the person, usually a child, who shall drink the milk, and use
any butter which comes from their milk.   The child has to
be careful not to drink milk from other cows when he is set
apart for this sacred duty.

**Religious ceremony in treating a cow with a newly born
calf.** When a cow first calves and the stump of the umbilical
cord still hangs to the calf, some person, usually a boy, is
appointed to drink the milk from that cow; he may not drink
milk from any other cow and is careful to avoid eating meat
or salt.   When the cord falls from the calf, the owner of the
cow takes a new pot which must be perfect without any flaw
or chip.   This pot he fills with milk from the cow in question
and carries it to the boy's mother, who drinks as much as she
can and puts it near the fire to keep warm; it is not made to
boil, but to retain the same heat as when newly milked, until
her son comes and drinks all she has left.   The milk from the
cow may then be added to the common supply and is free to
any member of the family to drink.

Clan gods. The Creator and the war-god are common
alike to all clans, but each clan possesses its own particular
god who is supposed to watch over the interests of the clan.
It is to this deity that members resort under ordinary circumstances for advice and help.   The medium is always a member
of the clan.   Members seek this deity for a blessing upon their
marriage, that a wife may become a mother, and they also
ask the aid of this god when the time draws near for a child
to be born, that the wife may be safely delivered.   To this
deity members of a clan go first in cases of sickness and it is
the medium of the clan god who advises them to go to some
particular god, to whom a visit may be necessary, and who
advises them which medicine-man to consult.

Sacred place in a hut for fetishes. In each permanent hut
there is a special place upon which the fetishes of the family
are placed.   In small houses it is almost always a mound of
earth a foot high, two feet wide and three or four feet long,
but it is larger in larger houses.   This mound is beaten hard

and upon it sweet smelling grass is laid neatly, the fetishes being arranged at one end, and the milk-pots at the other, after these have been washed and fumigated and are ready for use.   The fetishes are a heterogeneous collection of objects, the more important being horns or tips of horns of wild animals, especially of the buffalo and antelope.   The hollow of a horn is filled with a sacred compound and the open end corked with wood, the wood often having a small hole the size of a thimble made in it which is used for inserting the drugs prescribed by some medicine-man for a particular disease.   By putting a little of the medicine prescribed into this hole and pouring it back to the rest in the bottle gourd or by giving the medicine direct to the patient from the fetish its potency is increased; the power of the drug is thus conveyed to the sick person with the blessing of the god.   Other fetishes are merely wood decorated with lizard skin or beads, or they may be compositions of clay, claws of animals and what not.   These objects are made by special vendors and are dedicated to particular gods.   Each fetish has its own duty to perform.   A fetish seldom combines two offices, though there are a few which are said to have two duties to perform. Offerings of new milk and small pots of beer are made to these fetishes daily and they are frequently rubbed with butter. The king and important chiefs are able to offer cattle to their fetishes and to smear them with blood of the offerings.   Some fetishes, for example the war fetishes, were on special occasions carried about during hostilities, thus securing the aid of the god through his representative.   In no instance did a man claim that his fetish was his deity, but stated decidedly that it was the representative and contained the essence of the god.   In this sense alone did he possess the power and presence of the deity.   The names of the chief fetishes were: Wamala, Kagoro, Nyekiriro, Lyagombe, Mugasa, Kyomya and Ndahoro.

Magic.   The greatest use to which magic is put is that of taking revenge on some person for an injury received or for any insult real or imaginary.   The injured or aggrieved person seeks to obtain something belonging to the man whom he wishes to hurt by magic; for this purpose he will seek hair, nail-chips,

Plate XIII

(1) Banyankole fetishes

(2) Harp of the Banyankole women

spittle or even a shred from his clothing, in order, by using it in magic, to bring the person under the spell and so cause him a serious illness or even kill him.   One method, when a man had failed to obtain what he wanted and was still determined to carry out his evil design, was to get his sister to make love to the man he wished to injure and lure him to her couch; she would thus obtain some of his semen and pass it on to her brother, who would make the owner impotent so that he would be childless in the future.   In cases of sickness, the chief duty of a medicine-man was to discover the nature of the sickness, and, if it was due to magic, to tell how the spell was to be overcome.   The most common method used by a medicine-man to discover the origin of sickness was by examining the entrails of an animal for markings: he could also tell how to treat the disease at the same time.   In cases where no animal was supplied, the medicine-man resorted to a pot of water into which he cast certain herbs which caused a froth to rise; he next dropped four coffee-berries into the water, watched to see the positions they took, and judged according to their relative positions, the direction to which they pointed, or which side up they floated.   This method of discovering the wishes of a god is also used to discover the kind of medicine to be used after the magic has been overcome.   Few men who are accused of magic deny the charge: they find it easier to give a reason for having recourse to magic than to refute the charge of the medicine-man; they come to terms with the sick man and remove the spell.   Should a man deny the charge of magic, he is almost certain to be called upon to take the poison ordeal in order to clear himself, and that frequently ends in death. When a man is caught in the act of making magic he is deprived of all his property and left in abject poverty.   This is a serious matter because no man will employ him as herdsman, he is an outcast from society and is forced to leave the country, or to find employment among chiefs of another tribe, or to sink to the level of a serf and agriculturalist.

Belief in ghosts.   There is a great fear of ghosts because, while they can do much to help, they can also do much to harm the living.   As a rule ghosts of members of a clan are interested in the welfare of their clans-folk, though they will injure them if they are neglected or annoyed.   Ghostly possession is almost always said to be the act of a ghost from another clan, sent to do harm by some member of that clan who has interceded with his ancestors to cause sickness to an enemy.   A medicine-man is paid to capture the ghost and destroy it: this he does by his magical charms whereby he secures it in a pot, and either burns it to death or drowns it.

Small children are warned to avoid looking at their own shadow, because the shadow may become a ghost and kill them.

When women retire to relieve nature, they are warned to be careful when exposed, lest there should be a ghost hovering about who may enter them.   To guard against this danger a woman carries a small bottle gourd with a long neck to it. The gourd is filled with tobacco-water which she pours over her private parts while she is exposed: this prevents any ghost from coming near her.   Abdominal pains and rumbling noises in the stomach are indications that a ghost has entered a woman, and the sufferer seeks a medicine-man to exorcise it.

Cattle sickness and its treatment.   Sickness among cows is a serious matter: a medicine-man is called in, he comes to the kraal, learns the nature of the sickness and resorts to divination to discover the cause and the remedy.   A favourite method of treatment is to attract the disease to one particular cow; to do this the medicine-man obtains certain herbs and ties them in a bundle.   In the evening when the herd returns from the pasture, an animal is selected to bear the illness of the herd, the bundle of herbs is passed over the other cows and then tied to the neck of the chosen animal, and several fetishes are also tied to its neck.   This animal is taken out and driven several times round the kraal when the herd is inside; it is then left with the herd during the night.   In the early morning the medicine-man again drives it round the kraal several times, and with the aid of the herdsmen he kills it in the gateway by cutting its throat and catching the blood. The blood is sprinkled over the people of the kraal and also over all the cows, and the people file out, jumping over the carcase of the dead cow in the gateway.   After the people the cows are driven out and jump over the carcase as they go. The disease is thus transferred to one cow and the rest escape; the fetishes and herbs are taken from the neck of the dead animal and hung over the gate of the kraal on the outside to prevent the disease from entering the kraal again. The medicine-man takes the meat away; no member of the kraal dare touch it lest the disease should return to the herd.

Taboo against washing. Men and women alike are discouraged from using water, especially for washing themselves. When any person wishes to have a bath, he has to use a kind of clay mixed with butter; he rubs this over his body until he is clean and the clay has been rubbed off. After the clay has been thus used he may rub on butter again. Water applied to his own body is said to injure his cattle and also his family.

Taboos on the use of milk. Milk must not be boiled for food, as the boiling would endanger the health of the herd and might cause some of the cows to die. For ceremonial use it is boiled when the umbilical cord falls from a calf and the milk which has been sacred becomes common. Milk from any cow that has newly calved is taboo for several days, until the umbilical cord falls from the calf; during this time some member of the family is set apart to drink the milk, but he must then be careful to touch no milk from any other cow.

Food taboos. The meat of goats, sheep, fowls, and all kinds of fish is deemed bad and is absolutely forbidden to any member of the tribe; also various kinds of vegetables, such as peas, beans, and sweet potatoes, may not be eaten by any member of the clans unless he fasts from milk for some hours after a meal of vegetables. Should a man be forced by hunger to eat vegetables, he must fast some time after eating them; by preference he will eat plantains, but even then he must fast ten or twelve hours before he again drinks milk. To drink milk while vegetable food is still in the stomach, is believed to endanger the health of the cows.

Men who are taboo to the king. Should the king degrade any chief from his office for some fault and yet spare the man's life, this man is taboo to both the king and people until he has been to the sacred lake at Karagwe and undergone the regular form of cleansing by taking an emetic and a strong purgative, and has also been washed in the lake by the priest; he may afterwards return to his people and seek some means of livelihood.

Blood brotherhood. It sometimes happens that two men of different clans become deeply attached and wish to make a lifelong bond of brotherhood. The ceremony for this purpose is performed in the presence of witnesses, who may be called should there be any cause of disagreement in the future. The two men sit face to face, each pinches up the flesh on his stomach and cuts it sufficiently to draw a little blood, an assistant pours a little milk into the hollow of the hand of the man on his right, who takes a few drops of his own blood on a knife-blade and drips them into the milk, which his friend then drinks from his hand; the second man then takes a little milk in his hand and adds a few drops of his own blood, and the first man drinks it. Each promises to be faithful to the other and to be a brother to him and father to his children, should there be any need. When milk is not to be had, they use a coffee-berry instead and smear it with blood.

It is a sign of great friendship to call another person into the house to drink milk with the family.

Hunting, Counting Time, Music and Games.

Hunting as followed by pastoral people. Hunting is seldom followed because there are few animals which pastoral people may eat, but beasts of prey are hunted down wherever they become troublesome. Other game is left almost entirely to men of agricultural clans who keep a few dogs and hunt game for food.

Counting. The Bahima are accustomed to the use of large numbers owing to their large herds of cattle. They have special terms for units, and from the number of ten onwards they have multiples of ten with the necessary unit, until they reach a hundred. All their herds of cattle are divided into hundreds and each hundred is called a bull for brevity and convenience. In speaking of a number a man not only mentions it but also demonstrates with his hands or fingers the number indicated. Thus:

1. One is indicated by extending the index finger, while keeping the others folded inside the palm.

2. To indicate two the first two fingers are extended while the third and fourth fingers and thumb are kept folded.

3. Three is signified by extending the second, third and fourth fingers, while the index finger is bent beneath the thumb.

4. Four has all the fingers extended, while the thumb is bent into the palm.

5. Five is indicated by folding all the fingers over the thumb and presenting the fist.

6. To demonstrate six the first three fingers are extended while the little finger is bent in and held by the thumb pressing upon it.

7. Seven is shown by bending in the second finger beneath the thumb while the first, third and fourth fingers are extended.

8. To express eight the index finger is placed under the tip of the third and flicked against the second loud enough to make all those in the room hear.

9. Nine is shown by extending all the fingers and bending the second finger and extending it again.

10. To show ten the hand is closed with the thumb placed against the side of the middle joint of the index finger.

Divisions of time. Time is divided into years, months, days, and the day is divided into periods having reference to the cattle. A year consists of periods determined by rains. The longer period is called by the term *Kyanda* and has usually six months, the lesser period is called *Akanda*, and has four months, and there are two months called *Itumba*. During the six months very little rain falls, then come a few days of rain followed by four months of dry weather, and then there are two months of rain. The months are lunar and reckoned from the appearance of one moon to the appearance of the next. When the moon is first seen, the people come out of their houses and clap their hands. Each man lights a fire before his hut and keeps it burning continuously for four days

There are also a number of royal drums brought from their hut into the open and men beat them incessantly for four days. The people speak of a moon as lasting 29 days; 28 it is visible, and for one day it is not seen.   Each day is divided thus:

6 a.m. is milking time, *Kasese*.

9 a.m. *Katamyabosi*.

12 a.m. rest for the cattle, *Baliomubulago*.

1 p.m. is the time to draw water, *Batola masumba*.

2 p.m. is the time for the cattle to drink, *Amasyo ganyuwa*.

3 p.m. cattle leave the watering place to graze, *Amasyo gakuka*.

4 p.m. the sun shows signs of setting, *Ezigoba*.

5 p.m. the cattle return home, *Ente zehiririri*.

6 p.m. the cattle enter the kraal, *Ente zataha*.

7 p.m. milking time.

The new year.   The year begins with the first heavy rains, and the period of a year lasts until the next heavy rains, so that a year may be a few days longer or shorter; it is a matter of no consequence whether it is a week or even three weeks that are taken off or added to the length.   People watch the euphorbia trees to guide them as to the nearness of rain; when these trees begin to shoot out new growth, they know the rains are near.

Music.   The Bahima are not a musical people as regards instrumental music; the only instrument used is a harp which the women have and keep for use in the home for accompanying the love-ditties which they sing to their husbands.   Men have songs which they sing at those times when they have a supply of meat and beer and are abstaining from milk diet. They use no instrument to accompany their songs, but the company join in the choruses.

Games.   The national game is wrestling, and in this men and boys seek to excel.   There are frequent contests when a particular chief will bring his man and defy others to match him.   When such an important event occurs, the men give themselves up to the sport; and chiefs, with their king, come to witness the struggle for the championship.   To attain this glory is a constant aim with them, and youths are always training and striving to surpass their companions in order to become champion wrestler.

High jumping is another game which boys especially love, though this form of sport has few competitors in comparison with wrestling.

Small boys love a game of spinning stones from a fruit very like the damson in shape and size. The stones are dried and each boy brings his stones, and two boys spin together either on a rock or on a plantain leaf; the boy whose stone knocks up against the other and causes it to fall wins and takes the other stone, and they play on until one boy has won the whole lot of stones.

There is a game like nine-pins played by youths, though the game is said to be a boy's game. The pins are long seeds some five inches long; nine of these are set in a line, and those entering the contest stand in a line a few yards away and have a number of stones given them which they throw in order to dislodge the pins from their line. The winner takes forfeits from his beaten competitors.

PART III

THE BAKENE, LAKE DWELLERS

CHAPTER XIV

THE BAKENE, LAKE DWELLERS; SOCIOLOGY, GOVERNMENT, RELIGION, FISHING, BUILDING, DRESS AND ORNAMENTS

Lake Kyoga and Mpologoma river the home of the lake dwellers—the Bakene allied to the Basoga—huts of the Bakene—mode of travelling—description of Lake Palisa—totemic clans of the Bakene —marriage customs—birth of twins—treatment of the placenta of twins—naming twins—headman as chief and ruler—inheritance— belief in the supernatural, in ghosts and in magic—Gasani, the principal god—the god Kibumba—water spirits—methods of fishing—net-making and taboos—hut-building on floating foundations—canoes and rafts—physical appearance of the Bakene— clothing of men—clothing of women.

The district of the Bakene. The district to which the Bakene belong has necessarily a limited area, because their mode of life, together with their staple article of food, restricts them to the few stretches of water in which papyrus-grass grows freely; for that grass forms the foundation for their floating houses, and is also the chief material used in building them, while fresh water fish is their principal article of food. Hence the sources of the Nile and its feeders are the home of these people and their domain is one of water rather than of land. Their houses are to be found either on the floating roots of papyrus on the sunny waters of small lakes or in the forest-like growth of papyrus on the rivers flowing into the Nile.

Floating houses. The Bakene are a small Bantu tribe dwelling in floating huts on the Mpologoma river, on Lake Kyoga, on Lake Salisbury, and I believe also on Lake Rudolf: they cannot exceed three thousand in number.

Lake Kyoga and Mpologoma River the homes of the Bakene. The River Mpologoma rises on Mount Elgon, runs for some miles in a southerly direction, then winds to the west and rapidly widens until it empties itself into Lake Kyoga. The water of the river is held up by the enormous growth of papyrus and spreads over a vast area, in some places several miles wide; the current is sluggish, almost imperceptible, and it is only where the river narrows that the flow is discernible: there is no great depth at any place. It is well named by the natives *Mpologoma*, which means a lion, because of its width and the perfect protective barrier it forms to a population who cannot cross it except with canoes and at established fords. The river has formed a complete line of separation between Bantu people and the Nilotic tribes as far as Lake Kyoga, and the Nile has continued the division to Lake Albert. The river is said to be the original home of the Bakene, for there the tall papyrus forms a perfect shelter for their floating huts and the fish from its waters provides them with ample food.

The Bakene allied to the Basoga. In customs, language and appearance these people are closely allied to the Basoga of the north-east, and there is a tradition that their forefathers came from Busoga[1]. In each tribe both sexes extract the two front lower teeth and many of the women pierce the under lip in order to admit the pointed stone which they wear in their lips; they have no scarifications and do not disfigure themselves in any other way by mutilations.

Huts of the Bakene. On the lakes their huts are exposed to view, though they are always at a safe distance from the shore, which prevents any aggressors from molesting the inmates without the aid of a canoe. The men of the lakes build their huts on papyrus-roots, some of which are mere tufts little more than eight feet in diameter and the hut takes up the whole area of the root with the door opening immediately upon the water; other huts built on larger clumps have small landing-places two feet wide before the door and to these the canoe is secured. On the river the huts are well concealed by tall papyrus and are reached by tortuous water-tracks. When sitting in a canoe, paddled by a man standing to his work, the traveller's mind is carried to Venice and its gondolas; here,

[1] Basoga are the people and Busoga the country.

Plate XIV

Bakene huts built on papyrus roots

however, instead of stately stone walls there are walls of tall papyrus towering fourteen or sixteen feet above the water. Every few moments, as the canoe is paddled along the main water-way, there are side streets passed which lead to the homes of some of the people, these short *cul-de-sac* passages being numerous because, in most cases, each passage has only one family or at most two families living in it, every family preferring the seclusion of its own surroundings.

Modes of travelling. The only means of getting about from house to house is by canoe, but the art of managing a canoe is not confined to men, women and children too being expert in handling the dug-out canoes, many of which are merely wooden shells capable of supporting a child only; even small children of four or five years old have to find their amusement in canoes and get their exercise by paddling about, though at times they play on the banks of the river or shores of the lakes.

Lake Palisa. It was my fortune to reach Lake Palisa, which is a wide open space in the river Mpologoma, in the early morning soon after sunrise. Standing on the shore, awaiting some means of being ferried over the lake, I watched the people engaged in their various duties. Both men and women were busy with their fishing operations, some emptying fish-traps, others fishing with lines in the deeper water, while some women were up to their waists in the water catching fish from walled-in spaces along the shore into which small fish had found their way during the night. Numbers of small children were paddling about from tuft to tuft of papyrus in tiny canoes, enjoying life as much as the happiest of English children could do under more congenial circumstances. In the distance was a huge crocodile floating lazily away into deep water, while some children in a larger canoe were watching it as they fished, and were calling to their companions to notice the monster. On some of the smaller tufts of papyrus-roots were fetish huts and shrines made for the ghosts of some departed relatives, in which offerings of clothing, drink, and so forth, were placed in order to propitiate individual ghosts and thus keep them from troubling the community. It was a pleasant sight, the bright sun shining upon the dazzling water and these busy people, who were occupied with their immediate surroundings and unconscious of the great world stretching away beyond them.

Sociology—Clans, Totems and Marriage.

Totemic clans of the Bakene. There was great difficulty in obtaining much information from the people about themselves, as they were all taken up with their own affairs and distrusted curious questions concerning their social life from a stranger. They were at first unwilling to come to shore to tell about their ancestors and their private life; still, after a little coaxing and gentle persuasion, a few came and were found to be fairly intelligent and communicative. Their clans are:

1. The *Bakene*, who take for their totem the husk of millet, *Bulo*.

2. The *Bagota*, who take for their totem a small animal of the cat family, *Kyachuli*.

3. The *Bagolwa*, who take for their totem the guinea-fowl.

4. The *Babira*, who take for their totem the otter, *Ngonge*.

5. The *Bahugo*; their totem was not discovered.

6. The *Bagule*.

7. The *Bahohanda*.

There may be many other clans and totems in other parts; the above named were given as the chief totems of the limited sphere near the river Mpologoma.

Marriage customs. The tribe is polygamous and the clans exogamous; a man may marry as many women as he can obtain so long as he follows the tribal rule of not marrying into his father's clan or into his mother's clan. They follow paternal descent, the children being reckoned as members of the father's clan and taking his totems as theirs, and his relations being considered theirs, though at the same time their mother's sisters are called mother, and her brothers are called father, and this relationship debars any man from marrying any of his mother's sisters or their children, and a girl is not given in marriage to any man whom her mother calls brother or child. When a youth comes to puberty and wishes to marry, he first builds a hut for his prospective wife. This custom is contrary to that of most Bantu tribes, who do not build a house until the marriage is a completed fact. In this work of building the man may obtain the assistance of his friends and of his father. In the choice of a wife it may be that the man has seen some girl who has taken his fancy, on the other hand he may have thought of no particular woman. Sometimes a man will take all the responsibility upon himself and go boldly to the girl's parents and ask for their daughter, but as a rule he leaves it to his father or to some near relative to make the arrangements for him. In either case the girl has the right to accept or to reject a man's offer; in her choice the girl is invariably guided by her parents and friends, and usually accepts their decision without any questioning. In some cases a youth, after having asked the girl's father for permission to marry his daughter, goes to her house and places a native hoe in the doorway; this the maid understands to be an offer of marriage, and if she takes the hoe, it is a token that she accepts the offer; whereas, if she leaves it, the youth understands that his offer is rejected. When a girl has accepted a man's offer, he returns home and takes a present for each of her parents, a male goat for the father and a female goat for the mother. This present ratifies the engagement and is a pledge between the parents and the youth that his offer for their daughter's hand is accepted; should any difficulty arise between them through some other lover coming upon the scene, he refers to the present as a sign of having done everything in order. Members of the clan decide the amount the man is to bring for the wedding gift; it may be ten goats or more, and a number of barkcloths, or they may ask for other things in addition to those mentioned. Before he can claim his bride a man must procure the amount demanded and present it to appointed representatives who become his witnesses as to the legality of the marriage at any future dispute, should one arise; they also hear the bride's promises to be faithful and obedient to her husband. The bride is taken to her new home by her brother, who is the chief person concerned in the marriage, and has the right to give her away or to refuse to allow her to marry a person he does not like. He takes his sister in his canoe to her new home and is accompanied by numbers of the bride's friends in their canoes. They start from the bride's home in the evening, allowing time to reach the bridegroom's about sunset; on the way the party sing songs and keep time to the music with their paddles. The party stays the night with the bride and are regaled with a good meal consisting of a plentiful supply of fresh meat and such vegetables as they can obtain, the meat being the chief item in the feast with most tribes, and at the close of the meal plaintain beer is handed round. They seldom drink to excess. When dancing takes place they have to find some place on the shore near at hand, where they can dance without being molested. The next morning after the marriage the bridegroom gives each of the guests a small present and they depart to their homes, leaving one girl who is either a sister or some person nearly related to the bride. This girl remains about ten days, when she is sent back with a present of a fowl or a goat, according to the bridegroom's circumstances. The bride is veiled when she is taken to her new home, a large bark-cloth being thrown over her head reaching to her feet. This she retains from four to ten days after she enters her husband's house, and, when she removes it, her husband gives her sister, who has remained with her, a present of a fowl as a thank offering because every-thing has proceeded favourably. The girl must not stay another night with the young couple after she has received her present, but returns home. The bride holds the right to break off the marriage and refuse to remain with the man, should she during these first days discover any reason for disliking him.

Life of a newly married woman. After a few weeks of married life a bride returns to her parents to see them and carries a present of two fowls for them: without this present they would understand she was unhappy and wished to return home. The visit is for one day only, and in the evening the bride returns to her husband, laden with a variety of food which she cooks for him and his special friends; this meal

Plate XV

Man and wife of the Bakene tribe

ends the marriage ceremonies and is the last token which shows that the bride is satisfied with her new home and her husband. After this meal the wife enters upon her full duties as a married woman; she assists her husband in fishing, cooks for him, and attends to all her domestic duties.

Birth customs. No Mukene[1] woman can endure to be childless; the condition is considered to be a disgrace to the home, and a wife who shows no signs of becoming a mother will lose her husband's favour. The husband will assist his wife in every possible way to have a child; he will bear the expense of consulting medicine-men and deities with the greatest cheerfulness, if subsequently the means prove successful; for not only is their home thus happier, but also their future happiness in the spirit-world depends largely upon their children. Should all efforts prove futile, the husband may send his wife back to her parents and they will either give him another wife, if there is a sister to take the place of the former wife, or, failing that, they return the marriage gift. Many a woman who is childless elects to remain with her husband rather than return to her clan, as she realises that there is no longer any chance of marriage for her because no man will knowingly marry a barren woman. Though a wife cannot hope to retain the chief place in her husband's affections without a child, she may yet enjoy some of the privileges of married life, for example, in having a hut of her own, and may be extremely happy if she can hold a place in her husband's affections by being attentive and useful to him.

Women are as a rule strong and healthy, and have children, though few of them ever have more than six, three being the average number for a wife. When a man has more than one wife he builds a hut for each near his own and lives with first one and then another of them. When the time draws near for an expectant mother to be confined, she calls some woman who has had experience in midwifery to come and assist her: the woman called in is from the husband's clan, and a friend also comes to render assistance. At the time of birth the mother

---

[1] Mukene is the singular form, Bakene the plural.

stoops and is supported by the friend while the midwife delivers her. The placenta is awaited before the umbilical cord is cut with a strip of papyrus-grass stem. The mother remains in the house secluded with the midwife for five days after the birth; in the evening of the fifth day she is taken out and bathed, and her hut is cleansed by a woman of her husband's clan. The mother and midwife have a meal together, the husband pays the midwife a sum for her duties and she returns to her home. The husband's mother with a number of members from his clan now come to name the child; they remain the night and on the following day give it the name of some deceased member of the clan: the stump of the umbilical cord, which the mother retains when it falls from the child, is enclosed in a ball of clay and hidden away among the papyrus near the hut.

Birth customs of twins. When twins are born the father announces the fact to all members of the tribe by beating a drum, and the signal is taken up by his neighbours. The rhythm employed at this time is a particular beat which is known to the people as the 'Twin' drum beat. Having made the fact known to the people the father takes two fowls to his parents and two to his wife's parents and presents them without any explanation, as they well understand the meaning. The term 'Twins' is avoided by all members of the clan until the 'Twin' ceremonies are complete. The father's sister's son when he hears of the birth goes and closes the door of the hut in which the mother lies with her children, secures it and makes a new doorway in the hut at the back; this youth is from that time a leading person in all the 'Twin' ceremonies during their seclusion, and it is he who performs most of the ceremonies when the twins are brought out to be named. The parents each wear two cowry-shells on their foreheads which indicate that they are observing the 'Twin' ceremonies. Each child has its own nurse: one is chosen from the father's clan and the other from the mother's clan. The father has to collect food, chiefly animals, for the final ceremonial meal which is given when the twins are brought out from seclusion, receive their names, and are shown to their relatives.

Treatment of the placenta of twins. The afterbirths of twins are put into new cooking-pots, that of each child being kept separate; they are dried over a slow fire, and, when dry, are taken to the shore and left in tall grass near some garden cultivated by a member of the tribe.

Naming twins. When a father has procured all the animals he needs for the final sacred meal, he consults the medicine-man who settles with him the day on which the twins are to be shown publicly and named; the relatives are told the date and come together for the ceremony. Some place on land near the house is selected where the relatives can assemble for the meal, and, after the meal, the twins are brought and named by the father's mother and are shown to the assembled relatives. There follows a day of dancing and singing, while they rejoice together.

Government.

Headman as chief and ruler. There is no person responsible for the government of the whole tribe of Bakene; each clan has its headman to whom members look for advice and redress, should there be any dispute among the members. The headman is chosen by the clan when a vacancy occurs through death. When chosen a man holds office until death, unless he forfeits his right through vice, or in some way shows he is unworthy and incapable of fulfilling the duties. Such cases are rare; still, the clan has power to depose an unworthy chief. There are no taxes levied by the headman, but, when there is a case tried, the parties pay an amount of fish to the headman before the action is commenced; they sometimes pay as much as a goat. The decision given by the headman is final, unless the parties appeal to the ordeal. Theft is most uncommon and there are not many cases of adultery to be tried; should there be such a case and should the man accused be proved guilty, he is punished by a fine. The headman's authority is acknowledged by each household giving him a yearly present of fish or it may be a goat.

Inheritance. The property of a deceased person is divided among the members of the clan who choose the heir and give

him the canoe and fishing tackle of the deceased and some of
the household goods together with the hut.   The wives and
any cattle the man may have are divided amongst the clan-
members.   In some instances the heir is given a wife and some
of the cattle, though this is quite exceptional, the hut, canoe,
fish-traps and nets being the only things he may claim as his
right.

Women do not inherit property.   Widows are taken away
after the mourning ceases and are assigned to their new homes,
the children of a deceased man being taken by some relative
and growing up as his children.

Religion.

Belief in the supernatural, in ghosts, and in magic.   The
religious opinions of the people are akin to those of the Basoga.
There are medicine-men who use divination when a person is
ill, in order to tell whether the sickness is the outcome of magic
or is caused by some ghost ; when the cause has been ascertained,
the spell of magic broken or the ghost appeased, the patient
can be treated for the sickness from which he suffers and which
will now yield to treatment.

Gasani, the principal god.   The chief god they call Gasani
who has power over the sky and water.   This deity has a temple
and a priest officiates in it.   The god Gasani is consulted more
especially in cases of sickness and when an epidemic appears.

The god Kibumba.   Kibumba is a second deity to whom
they go, if they do not obtain the help they need from
Gasani.

Water spirits.   There is a water spirit whom they propitiate
when they go fishing by offering a fowl over the side of the boat.
The fowl is killed in the canoe and the blood allowed to drip
over the side into the water.   The entrails are thrown into
the water, and the flesh is roasted by the occupants of the
canoe, who now expect to be able to take a good haul of fish
after this offering.

Fishing.

Methods of fishing.   The occupation of the Bakene is
fishing, though there may be found a few who till small plots

of land.   The fish they take forms their chief article of diet, but with some of it they obtain other kinds of food from their neighbours.   Various methods are adopted in fishing, though the large traps yield the principal supply.   Men often fish with the rod and line from their canoes, or they place deep-water lines attached to floats, or again they sink traps in deep water. Along the banks of the river and the shores of the lakes they build traps, which are enclosures of wickerwork attached to stakes, an opening with winding inlet leading to the middle of the first part of the enclosure, while another inlet leads into a second enclosure from the first.   Men enter these enclosures and either spear the fish or catch them in hand-nets and throw them into large baskets carried for the purpose.   Some of the fish they smoke over wood fires and carry it to local markets for barter, and in this way they obtain such household pots and vegetables as they need.

Net-making.   When a man is making a new line or net, his father's wives must keep away from him lest they should accidentally step over the materials of his work; such an action would have a disastrous effect, as the line or net would not catch thereafter unless he learned what had happened, and was able to propitiate the spirit of the net by an offering of food which he fastened to the material where the woman had stepped over it.   If this is not done, they say no net over which a woman has stepped will retain fish, they will merely pass through its meshes, unless the spirit is propitiated.

Floating Huts.

Huts built on floating foundations.   The huts, as stated, are built on papyrus-roots which grow in the river or in the lakes. The roots are as a rule firm and strong; in shallow water they strike down into the ground and become fixed to one place, though in deep water they merely hang and are carried about from place to place by the wind.   The method of building is to cut or break down the stems of papyrus on the root to form the foundation for the hut; other stems are laid across the first layer in the opposite direction and layer upon layer is added until there is a strong floor raised above the water line. Stout branches of trees are inserted deeply into this foundation in a circle, according to the size of the hut required; the branches are then bent inwards and their tops bound together with shreds from papyrus stems, thus forming the frame of the hut. Between the branches which form the strong ribs of the hut, papyrus stems are inserted and tied in place; horizontal rows of papyrus are next tied round the frame at intervals from the bottom to the top, and thus a kind of inverted basket is made over which thatch is laid, thus completing the hut. The erection is sometimes fifteen feet high at the apex, though the usual height is ten or twelve feet by twelve feet wide. Inside the hut there are no poles to support the structure, the ribs are strong enough when bent into this dome to carry the thatch. Some huts have a hole left at the apex for smoke to escape. The thatch is gathered from the shore and laid layer overlapping layer from the bottom to the top, a few blades of grass being twisted into the frame at intervals to make it secure. The floor is rough and uneven, and has grass laid upon the papyrus stems for carpeting; and in one place near the centre there is a square of thick mud plastered for a hearth on which the fire is kept smouldering by day and by night. The bedstead is the only furniture in a hut. This is built by placing strong forked stakes in the floor and binding them together by side pieces, and by head and foot pieces. This frame is laced together by rope of papyrus fibre, or, it may be, a cow-hide is tied on it which forms the spring mattress. As a rule a bedstead is five feet high in huts built on the river, because the water often rises quickly and, should the house be flooded before the papyrus platform on which the hut is built can rise, the inmates are thus by the height rendered safe, if in bed, from immersion. Again, some huts are fixed so that they cannot rise when the river is in flood and, as the water often rises three feet in a short time, the doorway becomes impassable and a new exit has to be made to reach the canoe, should the flood occur during the night when the inmates are asleep. There is no need to make a door, nor to close the huts by night, the inhabitants being safe from the approach of wild animals and also from their enemies who cannot reach them without canoes. As a rule the doorway opens immediately upon the water so that the owner steps out of his hut into his canoe, but some of the better finished houses have a small landing in front and a path leading from one hut to another, if the owner has more than one wife. The paths are made by cutting the papyrus down and throwing other stems across the first layer until there is a structure strong enough to walk upon.

Canoes and rafts. All the canoes used are of the dug-out kind, some of them being merely slabs of wood upon which the people can sit and paddle about. The larger canoes are some twenty feet long and two feet wide and are made from one tree, some of the smaller being not more than six feet long. The paddles are often four feet long with leaf-shaped blades. Rafts made of papyrus stems tied together several layers deep are used on the lake in shallow water for fishing purposes. When paddling, both men and women stand in the canoe and paddle first on one side and then on the other, as they guide their crafts about at will. For years the Bakene have held the ferries on the river and charge a small fee to convey passengers from one side to the other. Sometimes they ferry cows over the river in these canoes.

Dress and Ornaments.

Physical appearance. In appearance and build the Bakene are like the Basoga. The nose is inclined to be flat and broad, though there is no mark of the protruding jaw of the negro. They are straight in the back with a good carriage and well developed limbs having little spare flesh. They have short curly hair, and pleasing features always ready to smile. They are from five feet eight to a little over six feet in height; the women in most cases are about five feet seven or eight inches in height. They are naturally better developed in the arm than in the leg owing to their living always in canoes with little opportunity for walking. Both men and women extract the two lower incisors, and the women also pierce the lower lip to insert the lip stone.

Clothing of men.   When engaged in their work in the canoe, the men wear merely a strip of bark-cloth fastened to a waist-band in front, passed between the legs and secured to the waist-belt at the back.   When idle, they throw a bark-cloth over the left shoulder and pass it under the left arm, and the end is also thrown over the right shoulder, the left arm being thus uncovered while the right is covered.

Clothing of women.   Women wear short girdles of bark-cloth round their loins and also wear belts decorated with cowry-shells ;   those who can afford it wear bracelets and anklets made from brass and iron wire.   Both men and women wear their hair short and shave their heads from time to time.

PART IV

THE BAGESU A CANNIBAL TRIBE

CHAPTER XV

THE BAGESU, CULTIVATION, FOOD AND GOVERNMENT

The Bagesu one of the most primitive of Bantu tribes—the higher
slopes of Mount Elgon the original home of the people—type
of people—staple food, method of cultivation—increasing arable
land—first-fruits offered to the deity—cattle rearing followed on a
limited scale—custom of bleeding young bulls—the chief of the clan
the paramount chief—taxation—punishment for theft—punishment for murder—punishment for manslaughter—punishment for
adultery.

The Bagesu one of the most primitive of Bantu tribes. The
Bagesu are a Bantu tribe living upon the eastern and south-
eastern slopes of Mount Elgon. They are a numerous people
when judged by the numerical standard of other African
tribes, being estimated at not less than a million souls. They
are a very primitive race and stand low in the human scale,
though it is somewhat difficult to understand why they should
be so intellectually inferior, surrounded as they are by other
Bantu tribes much more highly cultivated and civilised than
themselves. They are treacherous and unreliable to persons
outside their own clan, even members of their own tribe being
unable safely to walk about alone among other clans, except
at certain periods of the year when a truce is proclaimed in
order to fulfil certain tribal customs and ceremonies. The
land may truly be called a land without graves, because the
dead are not buried but cast out of the villages in the evening,
and during the night portions are cut from the corpse for a
ceremonial meal, the rest being left for wild animals.

**The higher slopes of Mount Elgon the original homes of
the people.** The part of the country visited by me was the
south-east end of the mountain. The people have their villages

on the ridges, which stand out like the ribs of some monster running up the sides of the mountain and leaving deep valleys between them with streams of water which drain the mountain and country. It is in these villages and on the mountain sides that the people grow most of their crops. The natives say that it is only during recent years they have ventured to live on the lower slopes of the mountain; within the memory of man they lived much higher for safety from foes, and there was a time when they only ventured down from the heights to cultivate their crops during the daytime and climbed back to their homes in the evening. As years passed they followed the richer land to the lower slopes, where they found the warmth more congenial and better suited to their labours. New sites for villages were then occupied and the old heights were abandoned, though certain caves were still kept provisioned as refuges to which they could flee, should any powerful foe appear. The paths to these caves are difficult to climb, and in many places they only afford room for persons to walk in single file; hence they can be guarded with comparative ease by a few men. In their descent from their old homes the clans appear to have followed ridges or ribs of the mountain which have thus formed land-marks, indicating divisions of territory. By this means clans have been kept from infringing upon the agricultural possessions of other clans, this method of reclaiming land serving to delimit the clans and to preserve them from intermingling, so that clan is shut off from clan and has no reason for invading the district of any other. During the few years that the British have been in residence in that part of the country and the people have felt safe from the incursions of foes, they have descended lower into the plains and have thus extended far from their original homes. The cultivated tracts of land are regarded by members of a clan as freehold property and are jealously guarded against any encroachment by fellow tribesmen. The sides of the mountain have many natural terraces which afford ample space for a village, with land for cultivation both in the valleys and up the sides of the ridges. Copious streams of excellent water, gushing from springs on the mountain, supply the needs of the people and irrigate the land through which they flow. Many of these streams have their origin in beautiful waterfalls which dash down hundreds of feet of sheer precipitous rock. Down the faces of these rocky walls lovely ferns, maiden-hair and many other kinds, grow in profusion, while exquisite tropical and semi-tropical plants also flourish in the moisture and spray from the falling water, which affords the necessary humidity. Most of these waterfalls, if not all, are sacred and are supposed to possess healing powers of which the natives seek to avail themselves when necessity arises. The streams from these falls rapidly drain into the great Mpologoma river which empties itself into the Nile.

The physical appearance of the people. In appearance the Bagesu are of the common negroid type: they are of medium height, have broad noses lacking any pretensions to a bridge, and are brachy-cephalic with short woolly hair curling into tufts. The features on the whole have a pleasing character, there being nothing repulsive about them as is the case in some cannibal tribes met with nearer the West Coast. The people are well formed and developed, though they cannot be said to be of a heavy build. Few have any spare flesh, yet they are strong for the work they follow, that is cultivation of their fields of millet and plantains; but they are not suited for heavy work such as lifting and carrying, or for that of general porters. The women of this tribe are much more independent and more inclined to assert themselves than is usual among Bantu tribes; there are instances related where women are said to have resented the treatment meted out to them by their husbands and have made stout resistance, even returning their blows. The tribe is agricultural, though there are traces that they were once more dependent on their cattle and have since passed from that stage to the present state of agriculture They still retain small herds of cattle and a few goats and sheep, and each village has its fowls. These herds and flocks are left to children to guard as they graze on the mountain sides, their elders being thus set free to labour in the fields.

The tribe and its clans. The tribe is divided into a number of clans which are exogamous, that is, no man may marry a woman of his own clan: children belong to the clan of their father, not of their mother. Each clan keeps separate from its neighbour and retains an entire independence in regard to mutual intercourse and common action, except when some person has special reason to visit another clan, *e.g.* when it is necessary to make matrimonial arrangements and also during the annual feasts of wine-drinking. The clans bear the following names:

1. Babesi	2. Banyuwaka	3. Baukoki
4. Baholasi	5. Bahuku	6. Baduda
7. Basukuye	8. Baliyenda	9. Baluke
10. Balage	11. Bakike	12. Bapete
13. Bakikaye	14. Baheva	15. Bakumunya
16. Basihu	17. Bamasiki	18. Bakonde
19. Bayobe	20. Basave	21. Balusekya
22. Balukulu	23. Bamoni	24. Batunduye
25. Babangobe	26. Batiru	27. Bambobi
28. Bakumana	29. Bafumbe	

Though the men of the clans are commonly hostile to each other yet women are free to go about as they choose, and no woman would be molested by any man of any other clan; and thus it is largely through women that intercourse between the clans is maintained.

Only a limited number of people wear clothing. Both boys and girls go nude until initiation ceremonies take place. This period may be said to be the most important in the life of a man or of a woman. It is the time of decision whether the person is to be admitted into full membership of the clan and undertake the promises of membership or not. The ceremony will be described later; here it is sufficient to say that a man wears the regulation goat-skin round his neck, with the right arm through the loop of the skin which keeps it in place, and hanging down the right side to the thigh. Young women at the time of initiation often begin to wear a waist-band of plantain fibre. To this band at the back long threads of twisted plantain fibre are woven by married women, the lower ends of these strings being bound together, and the owner is most particular to tie the ends herself, no other woman may do this for her. These strands may only be worn by women when they are married. This fringe is frequently eighteen inches long and is passed between the legs from the back to the front and secured by passing it under the band.

Ornaments and scarifications. Many young unmarried women may be found wearing a bead apron in front six inches wide and three inches deep as their only garment, while others wear a similar apron of plaited grass. These aprons seem to have been recently introduced from their neighbours, the Bateso. The two incisors of the lower jaw are extracted, and round the edge of the ear small holes are pierced in which straws or iron rings are stuck. The lower lip is also pierced for inserting the lip-stone. This is a tapering stone half an inch in diameter and two inches long. Iron finger-rings and bracelets are commonly worn by all classes and by both sexes. Women are fond of wearing several coils of wire round the upper arms, such ornaments being indications of wealth. Women scarify their bodies freely, from the breasts to the pit of the stomach and also on the forehead, thus forming rows of small almond-shaped swellings. These are produced before initiation and their production is a painful and often prolonged operation. Those on the stomach a girl usually makes herself, while those on the forehead are made for her. The instrument used for making the scarifications is an iron hook some four inches long, a quarter of an inch thick and bent to a crescent. One end is beaten fine to a needle point, the other end has a ring to slip on the finger to carry it on the back of the hand when not in use. The flesh is pinched up between the thumb and finger and the hook run through it. This is done in several places at a time and fine wood-ashes are rubbed over to stop the bleeding; the wounds heal, leaving raised flesh. It is also a common custom for a woman to wear rings on her toes.

Cultivation and Food.

The staple food and methods of cultivation. Plantains are grown freely, but they are not so prolific nor is their quality so good as in Busoga or Uganda; doubtless this is due to the cold nights and the altitude. Plantains like warmth with moisture, whereas the nights in the Elgon district are decidedly cold, and often there is little moisture in the air. It is perhaps well that the people do not rely entirely upon these trees but also grow small millet and sweet potatoes, which enable them to have a supply of grain to fall back upon when their plantains fail them. Men work side by side with the women, hoeing the fields ready for sowing, and they share also in the toils of sowing. Seed-sowing is done by two persons; one goes in front with a hoe making holes for the grain while the second person, following, drops in the seed and covers it with the side of the foot. A few more energetic people sow sesame, beans and maize, though the majority only grow plantains, millet and sweet potatoes.

Increasing arable land. When a man wishes to increase the amount of his land for cultivation, he asks permission from the headman of the village, who makes sure that the required plot does not belong to any other person before he grants the request; for, should it have been cultivated in the past by another person, he will be sure to claim it, and occupation by some other member of the clan would cause friction. When breaking up new land, a wife does the initial digging and her husband follows to prepare it for seed. This is the reverse order to that of most tribes. A portion of seed to be sown on new land is taken to a medicine-man, who mixes herbs with it and pronounces a formula over it which ensures its growing. This pot of seed is mixed with the whole seed necessary for the new plot of land and imparts blessing to the whole. A pot of beer is poured over a new field to secure the favour of the earth-spirit before the sowing takes place. The task of weeding young plants is left to men, though women assist in weeding the plantain groves. At harvest men again help in reaping the corn. The heads of millet are cut off, put into baskets and carried to the threshing floor, where the corn is stored in large baskets until it is threshed, the straw being left standing in the field until the next digging-time, when it is burned. The method of threshing and of winnowing is of the most primitive and laborious kind: the heads of corn are held up and the grain is beaten out with a short stick, the grain being then swept up from the floor and put into baskets ready for winnowing. A dry windy day is selected for winnowing. Small baskets of grain are held high and the grain is slowly poured out into a basket on the floor, the wind carrying off the dust and chaff. This action is repeated until the grain is quite clean, when it is carried away to the village and stored in the granary. Each house has its own store, and most of the granaries are built on stakes, though some rest on stones. They are large baskets varying in size from two feet in diameter and from four to five feet deep. The inside is smeared over with clay and cow-dung and the baskets are thus made weather-proof. The roof is a conical structure which hangs well over the sides and can be raised to allow the owner to look in and take any grain required.

Sweet potatoes are grown in large quantities to meet any emergency, so that, should a crop of millet fail, the people are not left with insufficient food. Their staple food is porridge and plantain boiled and mashed. Millet is ground between two stones and in consequence the flour contains a certain amount of grit. The chief meal of the family is in the evening. Other meals are merely aids to enable a person to go on comfortably through the day until the real meal in the evening. The family dines together, husband, wife and children sitting in a circle round a common vessel from which each person takes the food until it is finished. Here, as in most parts of Africa, animal food is highly prized and is a luxury only provided on special occasions; at other times edible weeds, such as common spinach which grows wild in every garden, form a relish to the vegetable food. This relish is especially welcome if there is salt to season it. When spinach is not to be had, a little sesame may be pounded into a cake and handed round in small quantities to each member at the meal.

First-fruits offered to the deity. At harvest, before any of the new corn is used for food, some of the first-fruits are gathered and sent with a little of the last year's corn and a fowl to the medicine-man, who offers them to the special deity before any one in the village may partake of the new corn. Such an

offering frees the village from taboo and enables its members
to begin eating the new crops of the year.

Cattle-rearing followed on a small scale. Cattle-rearing is
not a great feature in the life of the Bagesu or a great aim
with them. The more wealthy people keep a few cows, and a
village may have from ten to twenty in it, though it seldom
has fifty. The cows are a small breed and are herded on
the mountain, together with flocks of goats and sheep, by
boys and girls who play together while they herd. The
principal use of cows is to obtain wives, though elders of
villages like to have their small herds. Girls are permitted
to herd cattle with boys until they attain the age of puberty,
and at times a married woman may be found herding cattle
when her husband has gone to the field and they have no
child or servant who can undertake the duty. Cows are
milked by either men or women in this tribe, there being no
restrictions placed upon women dealing with the animals.
It is also a singular fact that milk is boiled, with grain
added as it boils, to make a kind of porridge; it is seldom
drunk fresh, and in almost every instance it is cooked in
earthen pots, which are the common vessels used for milk,
whether for milking into or for holding the milk set aside for
future use. Should it be necessary for a woman to herd cows,
her husband will relieve her as early as possible. If he has
work to do in the field, he goes early and returns about ten
o'clock to enable her to go to her household duties. Women
churn and also wash the milk-vessels, though the vessels are not
in any wise considered sacred. When a cow calves, the calf
has the milk on the first day; on the second day the cow is
milked and the milk is slowly boiled until it forms a cake,
and the owner of the cow with his wife and a few relatives
eat this cake. The day after this ceremony the cow is milked
at the ordinary milking-times, and the milk is added to the
common supply.

Custom of using blood of young bulls. Young bulls are
frequently bled, and the blood is baked for a special dish with
salt added to it. This is considered a great delicacy. The
animal from which the blood is to be drawn has a cord tied

around its neck to make the artery swell, and a man takes an arrow with a guard on it, which prevents it from penetrating too deeply into the flesh, and shoots it into the artery. From two to three pints of blood are drawn, and the bleeding is then stopped. The animal soon recovers from the loss of blood, and it is said to be none the worse after a day or two.

Government.

The chief of the clan the paramount ruler. The great source of weakness in this large tribe of Bagesu is their lack of a leader to bring together all the clans and form a united nation. Each clan keeps aloof from its neighbour and jealously strives to maintain its own rights and independence. An elder in each village holds the place of chief and manages the affairs of his small circle. This man is the magistrate and is assisted by one or two of the senior members of the village. In any serious question affecting the clan there is a senior member of the clan who presides in council, but every initiated man and youth has a voice in the meeting. There are not many serious questions arising in a village. Should any member of another village wish to accuse a person, he pays the elder a goat as a fee, or even a cow, if the matter is at all serious, in order to have his case tried. Should the litigants be dissatisfied with the decision, they can appeal to the órdeal test. A medicine-man administers this test, and is paid a fowl by each of the men concerned to come and conduct the trial. His favourite test is that of taking an iron hoe, heating it and applying it to the thigh of first one and then the other litigant. He then examines each to see which of them is burned, and the man who bears any marks of burn is judged to be in fault; should both suffer, they are judged to be equally guilty and the case is dismissed.

Taxation. There are no taxes paid to elders or chiefs, though it is customary for members of a village to acknowledge the position of their elder by giving him presents of corn during harvest; sometimes a man gives a goat or even a cow, but these gifts are made for some special reason such as boons conferred. The only compulsory payment is the court-fee which must be paid before a person can accuse another and have his case tried.

Punishment for theft.   Theft committed by day is punishable by a fine.   A medicine-man is asked to divine in cases where the thief has not been caught in the act, or when the culprit cannot be discovered; the punishment for theft is usually the fine of a cow.   Theft committed by night or housebreaking, which is done by digging under the walls of the house and thus entering it by a tunnel, is a more serious matter. If the inmates are roused by the thief, the householder takes his spear and silently awaits the appearance of the head of the thief, and all who are in the house remain silent as though asleep until the head appears, when it is speared and the alarm raised. Neighbours run to the help of their companion and the thief if not dead already is despatched without mercy.   In the morning the body is taken to the nearest waste land and burned.

Murder.   It seldom happens that a man murders another of the same clan, for he stands to him in the relationship of brother.   But it is a frequent occurrence for a man to lie in wait for and kill a member of another clan.   Such murders are the outcome of old feuds passed on from generation to generation.   They are cases of blood revenge, where the members of a clan wait for years to appease the ghost for some murder in the past, the perpetrator of which has escaped, while a son perhaps or a grandson of the murderer is being watched and waited for until he attains manhood.   A man who has had the charge laid upon him to avenge the death of some relative will wait for years, and, should he be unable to carry out the deed of expiation, will charge his son to do so, and he in turn may have to wait some years before he can effect it.   Such murders are the causes of clan wars which at times end in bloodshed and severe wounds, though fortunately seldom in deaths.   When two clans thus contending wish to make peace, the chiefs of the clans come together to some spot away from their villages, where they discuss the matter and fix the terms.   To ratify these a dog is brought, and one chief holds the head while the other takes the hind legs and a third man at one stroke with a large knife cuts the animal in two.   The body is then thrown away in the bush and left.   The members of the two clans may after this ceremony freely intermingle without any fear of trouble or danger.

Manslaughter.   Should there be a case of manslaughter, the chief of the clan tries the guilty man and arranges the fine, if the case is proved to be manslaughter.   It is always necessary to prove that there was no previous bitterness, and that there is no cause for thinking there was design and intention in the deed.   When a guilty person belongs to the same clan and village as the slain man, he has to leave it and to find some new home, even though the case is settled amicably.   The smallest fine ever imposed for manslaughter is the amount needed to procure another wife, and this is paid to the father of the slain man, who is expected to have by her another son in the place of the dead man.   The guilty man has to take a goat, kill it, smear his chest with the contents of the stomach, take the remainder and throw it upon the roof of the house of the murdered man to appease the ghost.

Adultery.   Any man who is caught in adultery, or proved to be guilty of adultery, is heavily fined, and the fine is paid to the injured man.   Cases of adultery are rare, for married women are seldom tempted to do wrong, and the idea of appropriating another man's wife is contrary to public feeling. If an unmarried girl is discovered to be with child, she is compelled to confess her lover's name, and he is asked to bring the dowry-money and marry the woman.   Should he refuse to do so, the woman is given in marriage to some other man who also takes the child, and the real father loses all claim to it.   Few men are willing to allow a child to pass from their own clan into another.   It is no disgrace to a young woman to become a mother before marriage, nor does it prevent her from obtaining a husband; indeed men like to know that a woman can bear children, and her fault thus rather adds to her value than detracts from it.

CHAPTER XVI

MARRIAGE, BIRTH, SICKNESS AND DEATH

Marriage customs—polygamy practised—birth ceremonies—taboos observed by husband and wife before child-birth—ceremony of naming a child—birth of twins—the cause and treatment of sickness—transferring sickness to others—ghostly possession—death and treatment of the dead.

Marriage customs. Marriage among the Bagesu is a matter of expediency rather than of love, because children are the means of assisting the ghost after death; during life it is an investment, because a wife materially helps to make a man happy and comfortable and married life gives him a better position among his clansmen. There is no such thing as love-making before marriage and there is seldom a marriage from love. The man realises the advantages of married life with a family, and a woman gains by having a home of her own and loves to have children who look to her for sympathy and help during infancy and youth, who protect her when they attain to years of discretion, and provide for her in her old age. The man without doubt reaps greater benefits from marriage than the wife, but an unmarried and childless woman finds no place in social life among primitive people, for woman's principal function is child-bearing and in the second place that of making a home for some man. With the male section of a clan the marriage of a woman belonging to it is of importance because of the marriage fee they receive. There are no arrangements made for marriage between couples until adolescence and until after the initiation ceremonies have taken place; then it is a man seeks a wife. She must be from some clan other than his own, and he avoids women from his mother's clan. The young man's father has the right to arrange the matrimonial affairs

Plate XVI

(1) Married women
(Bagesu Tribe)

(2) Sick woman standing by fetish hut
(Bagesu Tribe)

of his son and to see that the bride is in no wise related to him. A high price is usually asked as the marriage fee: as much as six cows and a number of goats, from six to twelve, and a few fowls is a common price. This is a large sum for a man to obtain and it often takes eighteen months or even two years to realise the amount, and during this time he trades in various ways, or begs and borrows when possible. When the man pays the sum demanded, the day for the marriage is arranged, which is usually a month later to enable the bride to undergo the special treatment for her marriage and to make her final preparations. She has to be fed upon the best food in order that she may grow fat, she is washed and oil is rubbed on her body daily to make her skin smooth and soft and free from any eruptions or skin disease. On the day of the marriage the bride is taken from her village to that of her husband by a few relations and friends, chiefly women. The women friends remain with the bride three days and go each morning to the bridegroom's field and dig until nearly noon. The more land they can dig and prepare for seed the greater honour is given the bride. The bridegroom's mother cooks daily for these guests and invites them to have their meal with her; custom, however, forbids them from complying with this invitation, and they have to take the food prepared for them and eat it secretly when other women are absent from the house. On the fourth day they return home to the bride's parents, taking the bride with them. A substantial meal awaits them and after the meal they spend the day and night dancing, and disperse to their homes in the early morning. The bride remains a full month with her parents, who during the time brew large pots of beer, which are taken to the bridegroom with a goat by the bride on her return to her husband. She takes only one relative to stay the night with her and the maid returns to her home the next day. The marriage is thus completed and married life commences, the bride hereafter going about her daily duties as an ordinary woman.

Polygamy. The tribe is polygamous, though men generally find it difficult to obtain the means to procure more than two wives and many men are satisfied with one. There is no restriction against marrying sisters and a wife never objects to her husband marrying as many wives as he can afford to secure, whether they be her sisters or other women, the one stipulation she makes being that she insists upon having her own house and field.

Birth ceremonies. In this tribe, as in most primitive tribes, a childless wife is of no value. A wife soon realises whether she is going to become a mother or not, and, if the signs are not forthcoming within the first few months, she begins to call for assistance from gods and fetishes and spares no pains to bring about the longed-for condition. A husband will also help his wife in every possible way; no pains are spared and fees are paid ungrudgingly to medicine-men, and every detail of their advice is followed to secure a child. Should all efforts fail, the wife's value in the eyes of her husband is gone; he returns her to her parents, who supply him with a sister or with some other woman from the clan, or, failing that, they refund the marriage fee.

Taboos observed by husband and wife before child-birth. An expectant mother has great freedom in her choice of food and also in her actions: there are no food taboos for her to follow, though she is careful as to the kind of food she eats, but more attention is paid to the amount of work she undertakes, lest she should over-tire herself and so injure her unborn child. The husband is also restricted in his doings; he must not work too hard nor may he take violent exercise, such as hunting, he must avoid climbing trees, rocks, or even mounting a house, lest he should slip and thus injure his wife and cause untimely birth. At the time of the confinement an elderly woman comes and remains with the expectant mother. Should the woman be of a nervous disposition a second woman comes in at the time of delivery to hold her and to cheer her, thus leaving the midwife free to attend to her duty of delivering the woman. Everything is simple at a birth: there are no elaborate ceremonies, the afterbirth is awaited before the cord is cut, and, when it appears, the cord is cut quite short with any knife and the placenta is buried near the fire-place in the hut. The mother remains in the house three days secluded from her friends and is attended by the midwife. On the fourth day she is purified by washing from head to foot, and the hut is carefully swept up; the mother then resumes her ordinary duties.

Naming a child. A mother nurses her child without any ceremony taking place until it is old enough and strong enough to sit alone unsupported, when the father puts it to sit on the floor and names it after a deceased ancestor, the particular ghost thus invoked being supposed to have charge of the child. Should the child be illegitimate, the ghost will kill it because it does not belong to the husband. Instances are recorded of women having changed the names of illegitimate children and given them names of ancestors of the real fathers, calling upon their ghosts to protect the children against the ghosts of their husbands' ancestors.

Should a child appear sickly and delicate after it has been named, the parents consult a medicine-man who divines the cause. Sometimes he attributes the cause of illness to the child having been given a wrong name of an ancestor and the guardian spirit resenting the name. The parents, therefore, change the name and thus please the spirit, and the child recovers and thrives.

Birth of twins. The birth of twins is a solemn event, though it is a joyful occasion. There are so many risks to be feared and taboos to be observed that the parents are full of apprehension lest they should offend the god of plenty, the giver of twins. The event is heralded by special drum-beatings. These not only acquaint the relatives with the event, but also summon them to the spot. A new hut is hastily built into which both parents and children are put and the entrance is built up, leaving only a small hole through which food and firewood can be handed to the inmates. On the third day a male relative comes and cuts a doorway into the hut, and both parents come out bringing the children with them. It is a day of rejoicing, feasting, music, and dancing which continues throughout the night. The parents bathe and are thus purified, and are then permitted to see their friends and also to visit friends and members of the clan in other villages.

During this period of visiting friends and relatives, dances are held and the parents are careful to take their meals together, as they fear that one may eat something which may give an advantage to the child he or she represents and thus cause the god to be angry on account of the other child which has suffered neglect, and to take it away in displeasure. Each child is said to be connected with a parent in a special way according to their sex; the mother represents and is attached to a girl and the father to a boy. Should both children be of one sex, they are both attached to the parent whose sex they follow; and, should this happen, the parents realise that one of them is in favour with the god and the other parent in displeasure. Hence parents like twins to be of different sexes. The parent of whose sex the twins are not makes special offerings to propitiate the god and remove the supposed disfavour.

Sickness and Death.

The cause and treatment of sickness. The chief cause of sickness is said to be magic, and, to discover its source, the relatives of the sick person seek a medicine-man and from him obtain a verdict by divination. He may discover some object hidden in the thatch or buried near the house which he pronounces to have been the cause. It has, he informs the relatives, been hidden there by some ill disposed person and the magical spell has to be broken and the object in question destroyed before the sickness will yield to treatment. When once the spell of magic has been broken, the medicine-man finds no difficulty in dealing with the sickness. At times counter-magic has to be used to heal a sick person, because a ghost has seized him. In such cases the medicine-man is supplied with a fowl which he divides into four parts, placing them in four shallow holes made on a plot of waste land. Having thus divided the fowl he goes through a form of incantation in which he commands the ghost to leave the sick person and trouble him no more. He then removes the meat from three of the holes; one piece is taken, cooked and given to the sick man, a second is taken to the deity of the clan, a third

Plate XVII

(1) Sick child standing by fetish hut
(Bagesu Tribe)

(2) Bagesu huts

piece the medicine-man himself takes, cooks and eats, while the fourth piece is left in the hole on the waste land for the ghost.

Transferring sickness. At other times, it may be, the illness has to be transferred to some other person by means of herbs. The medicine-man chooses his bunch of herbs from an uninhabited part of the country, ties them neatly into a bunch, brushes them over the patient and then carries them to a distant path where, by night, he buries them, covering the spot in such a manner as not to attract attention. The first unsuspecting person who passes contracts the disease and the patient recovers.

Ghostly possession. A medicine-man sometimes attributes sickness to ghostly possession, which he says must be cured by propitiating the ghost. He will probably tell the attendants of the sick person that it is the ghost of some relative who has been offended in some way and has therefore sent sickness. Should the person be a rich man, a hut is built as a shrine in honour of the ghost, with a long pole standing through the centre of the thatch at the apex. The patient gives the medicine-man a goat or an ox to offer to the ghost; the animal is killed near the shrine, the blood is caught in a vessel and put into the shrine with a portion of the meat. The people assemble in numbers to take part in this ceremony. The medicine-man climbs the hut after making the offering of blood, spikes a large piece of meat on the pole and proceeds to cut it into small pieces which he throws among the crowd, who eagerly scramble for them and eat them. The sickness is supposed to be widely scattered by this ceremony and thus rendered harmless, and the patient quickly regains his usual health. Any meat that is left the medicine-man takes away with him for his own use.

When a case of sickness proves fatal, the relatives again appeal to the medicine-man to discover who has caused the death that they may seek the accused person in order to put him to death. When discovered he is tried, but sometimes he may succeed in escaping death by paying a heavy fine.

Death and treatment of the dead. When a person dies, the body is only kept a few hours in the house. The relatives have previously been summoned when it was seen that the patient was dying, and they are present when death takes place. There are no ceremonies to be performed such as washing the dead, taking leave of him or preparing a grave. There is a short period of wailing near the body during the day of death until a little after dusk, when the body is carried from the village and deposited on the nearest waste land. Soon after the relatives. have returned from casting out the dead, certain old women proceed stealthily to the spot, cut up the body and carry back portions to the village. These they cook for a sacred meal. This meal is restricted to relatives who have been fully initiated and are now invited to partake of it in secret during the night. The rest of the body is left for wild animals, especially for hyaenas which are numerous, and it is usually devoured before daybreak. Mourning continues during the following three days. On the fourth day the mourners shave their heads and the majority of them return to their homes and regular duties. The near relations and widows continue to mourn in the house of the deceased for the following three months. When mourning ends, an ox is killed and the mourners have a sacred meal with the principal members of the clan. At this feast the heir is announced, the property and the widows of the dead man are divided among the clan, the heir taking a share with the members of the clan. He is also given the hut and the utensils in it.

CHAPTER XVII

RELIGIOUS BELIEFS

Primitive condition of religion—snake-worship—belief in ghosts—rock-spirits—waterfall-spirits—rain-making—initiation of boys—initiation of girls—purificatory ceremony at the end of initiation—dancing and drinking to celebrate the membership of the young people.

Primitive condition of religion. Bagesu religion is in a primitive state. There are no permanent temples, nor are there any objects of veneration which represent gods, though there are fetishes and amulets. There are no priests, the medicine-men being the repositories of wisdom and skill, with the elders of the village, and acting as mediums for the gods. When occasion requires, a shrine, which is a rude hut, is built in the place the medicine-man indicates, and offerings according to his directions are made; but as soon as the cause of anxiety passes and the danger is gone, the shrine is neglected and soon falls into ruin, and the god is forgotten until a new cause of trouble necessitates building a new shrine.

Snake-worship. The people have great faith in snake-worship, the serpent being worshipped under the name of *Mwanga* and having a special hill to which the devotees resort. There is a particular medicine-man attached to this worship whose official title is *Namwangala*, and he is the priest and medium of the deity. This god has power over disease, makes known the cause of sickness when an ordinary medicine-man has failed, and he also prescribes for the patient. Childless women seek his aid when all other efforts have failed to bring about the desired motherhood. In each case a suppliant takes an offering of a goat or, should the person be very poor, a fowl is accepted.

Belief in ghosts. In each clan ghosts of members who have passed away have special provision made for them, these disembodied spirits being regarded as the particular guardians of children. There is no fear attached to the presence of ghosts. They are supposed to dwell in their old haunts and large stones are frequently placed near the doorway of a house in which a person has passed away in order that the ghost may rest there under the projecting roof, sheltered from rain or the fierce rays of the noonday sun. Any wants a ghost may have are made known by dreams to the inmates of the house, as it is thought that ghosts hold communication with the spirit of a sleeping man. It behoves the man, when he wakes and recalls his dream, to act at once and supply the things he heard the ghost say it wanted. The necessary things are then placed by the stones near the door. Food and drink are regularly placed beside these stones, and, when the person puts them out, he addresses the ghost saying, "Be kind to the children, do them no harm." Ghostly possession is believed to be due to hatred or enmity on the part of some person of another clan who has prevailed on a ghost of his own clan to seize the person and, if necessary, kill him or her. Hence such ghosts are captured, and are destroyed when exorcised. An offended ghost of a clan may cause sickness to a member, but it rarely enters a person and there is no exorcism used, but rather propitiation.

Rock-spirits. Almost every rock is supposed to be animated by a spirit which is capable of rendering service in the neighbourhood or of causing trouble, should it be offended. Rock-spirits use the elder of the village as their priest and make their wishes known to him by dreams. When a spirit appears to an elder he announces the fact to his village and orders a shrine to be built at the base of some rock and offerings to be made. The wealthier people take goats, others take fowls, and the children carry plantains or sweet potatoes. The animals are offered and killed, the blood is caught in a vessel and left in the shrine for the spirit, and the meat and food are cooked and eaten by the people on the spot. After one of these visions the elder of the village takes two fowls to the rock and dedicates them to the spirit. One fowl he kills and eats on the spot, the other he takes home to breed, the eggs from the fowl being saved and hatched, and the chickens reared and cared for until there are enough to exchange for a female goat. The goat is then kept, together with any young it has, until the elder is able to exchange them for a cow, when this and any calves it has are kept for the spirit by the elder, though he may use the milk, and the animals continue to breed and form a herd of cows.

Mothers frequently betake themselves to a rock-spirit when a child falls sick, or when it does not make the progress it should. An offering is made at the base of some rock and she calls to the spirit to have pity on her child and make it well and strong. A man or a woman who is in delicate health will also go to a rock, make an offering and ask the spirit to make them well.

Waterfall-spirits. Each waterfall is supposed to have a spirit, and these spirits are thought to be of the greatest help to mothers to make their children thrive. A mother will take her water-pot and climb the steep side of the mountain, get between the rock and the falling water, fill a pot with it and carry it home. It is a dangerous and a difficult task, calling for a cool head and strong nerves. The water is used to sprinkle over the head of the child and is said to give it health and to make it thrive.

Rain-making. The most gifted men in the art of rain-making are medicine-men. This body of men approach the nearest of all primitive people to what we should term educated persons. They are men who have inherited a certain amount of information from their predecessors, to which store of knowledge they have been able to add by personal experiments and observations. Their unbounded faith in their art works upon their fellow-men, inducing them to accept what they say and inspiring confidence in their abilities. They are able to hold their tongues, when anything said would be harmful, and they are astute enough to make careful study of human nature and make use of their knowledge, when occasion arises. Such are the chief characteristics of a rain-maker.

By constantly using their magical arts and seeking to influence others, and by their effort to regulate the supply of sun-shine and rain, they have come to believe that they can bring about what is wanted, and the people have the utmost faith in their powers. These men have not always the happiest existence. There are days which for them are decidedly unpleasant, anxious days, full of evil omens. Rain does not always fall at the right moment, and crops suffer in conse-quence. The people then betake themselves to the rain-maker, carrying offerings and making requests for immediate showers of rain. If the rain comes in a day or two, all is well; but should weeks pass without a shower, then the crops wither up and the people become angry and remonstrate with the rain-maker for not exerting himself and giving them what they require. Should the rain still be delayed, they attack him, rob him, burn down his house, and roughly handle him, even to doing him bodily injury.

The usual procedure of a rain-maker is to take two fowls which some suppliant has brought. One fowl he kills by hitting it on the head with a sacred stick; he then cuts it open from the underside of the beak to the tail, removes the entrails and examines them for marks, these markings being the signs which enable him to give the oracle when the rains may be expected. Some markings cause him to replace the entrails in the fowl and expose it to the heat of the sun; after a time he shakes the fowl about and, if the entrails make a noise, he announces that there will be a strong wind which will destroy the crops. The second fowl is killed after the manner of the first, and is intended to confirm the inferences drawn from the former. Should the rain still delay, the people threaten the man and, unless it comes then, they carry out their threats and punish him because they are convinced he has the ability to help them and is not using his influence. In most instances, after making an attack upon the rain-maker, the people restore his property, thinking that otherwise the god will be angry with them for their doings, and make special offerings to the man for the damage they have done. The rain-maker may consent to take the extreme measure of climbing the mountain and paying a visit to the deity on the top, a step which he asserts is fraught with danger to him and may cost him his life. A black ox is brought and a quantity of beer, which are taken up the mountain by several village elders who accompany the rain-maker to a plateau near the mountain top. Here the ox is killed and eaten by the company, with the exception of one leg, at a sacred meal at which the blood is offered to the god. The leg is carried up the mountain to a priest who lives near a sacred pool in which is said to be a large snake which is the god. This pool is the spring which supplies many of the water-falls upon the mountain. The priest takes the meat and hears the request of the rain-maker. The priest and rain-maker now make a trough of clay near the pool and pour the beer into it. The priest then stands near the trough and puts a long beer-tube into the spring in order to suck a little water through it. The snake resents this, for it guards the spring against any person drawing water from the pool. It is said to capture any man who rashly attempts to do so. When, therefore, the priest attempts to draw water, the snake darts forth and winds its deadly coils round him, but the odour of the beer saves him, for the reptile smells it, hastily uncoils itself, drinks the beer and is soon helplessly drunk. As soon as the men see it is helpless they break its fangs and proceed rapidly to fill a number of water-pots from the sacred spring, arranging them round the pool. The water thus drawn and set on the top of the mountain will without fail bring rain which will continue to fall daily until the priest takes steps to stop it by emptying the pots again. The rain-maker descends the mountain with the elders who have waited for him on the upper plateau and in a short time rain begins to pour down. The rain-maker now waits, knowing that the people will soon come with offer-ings and requests to have the rain stopped. When the people have had enough rain and see that their crops will spoil for want of sunshine, they go in a body to the rain-maker to beg for sunshine. The rain-maker has now to make a second visit to the serpent-god with an offering of beer, and has to go with the priest through a similar performance to that above de-scribed in order to make the god drunk, after which he empties the pots and turns them bottom upwards to ensure sunshine. Thus the harvest is assured, the seasons are readjusted and the year proceeds in its proper course.

Initiation ceremony of boys. Initiation ceremonies are a vital part of the religion of these primitive people; hence they are placed here under the head of religious observances rather than before marriage customs. Both sexes have a prescribed form to follow, and undergo a course of instruction, before the rite of circumcision is administered to boys and a corresponding rite is administered to girls. Among primitive people no person keeps a register of his age; some event which happens about the time of his birth is all they require to mark the period and this is handed down to fix his approximate age. Hence boys and girls are judged to have attained the right age to be admitted to the rite by their physical development. Boys about fourteen years old are expected to present themselves for training and circumcision, and girls may be a little younger. The vows and compulsory observances of the ritual, with all the mysteries of the clan and the solemn traditional oaths to redress wrong and to avenge blood, often have a greater weight of awe and fear and cause boys to hesitate more than the actual physical suffering. The preparations for the ceremonies are made after harvest, when there is an abundance of food and a supply of beer can be obtained. A fortnight before the operation of circumcision boys meet at some house in a village where an elder is appointed to give them daily instruction; their bodies, hands and faces are smeared with white clay leaving only their hair black, and in this guise they parade the villages of their own clan. A boy from any village of the clan may present himself for instruction, and these youths decorated and parading about, singing and dancing, impress the young people with their importance and inspire in them the desire to join the band. When their term of instruction is ended, the day is arranged for the operation of circumcision; it is usually fixed to fall near full moon, rather before the full moon than after it. In the morning of this particular day the boys are smeared from head to foot with black clay and each of them proceeds to his village to beg for animals and fowls

Plate XVIII

(1) Youths ready for the initiation ceremony
(*Bagesu Tribe*)

(2) Dancing at the initiation ceremony
(*Bagesu Tribe*)

for the feast which precedes circumcision; and in addition to these animals the chief in whose village the ceremony takes place kills an ox for the occasion. A large joint of meat is put upon the pinnacle of the hut in which the boys live, and this is reserved for the end of the ceremony. When the boys have gone their round begging, they return together to the village in which they are to undergo the operation. Before entering the village they collect stones and other missiles which they take with them and, as they enter the village, they commence an attack upon an unseen foe, shouting and rushing about, beating the air and throwing stones until the foe, which is said to be hostile ghosts, is driven out from the village. A special meal is provided, and after it the elder of the village comes and draws up the boys in a line facing an admiring crowd of people composed of both sexes and all ages, who stand to watch the performance. In front of each boy a pad of grass is laid on the ground with an egg on it, after which an old man walks along the line and gives to each boy a small piece of root to chew, which is said to possess a medicinal property which stops bleeding. As the boys stand with their toes to the grass pad the elder of the village comes and gives them a charge concerning customs, history, marriage, and other things they have been taught during the weeks of residence: he tells them they will be expected to be faithful to friends and unrelenting to enemies of the clan, and above all he impresses upon them the necessity of being brave in war and ready to fight on behalf of the clan. After this charge is delivered, another man comes and smears each boy on his chest with a mixture of undigested food taken from the stomach of a newly killed goat. The old man next stands in front of each boy and recites a formula which the boy repeats after him word for word to the end, and, when he has said it, he jumps into the air three times alighting twice with his legs astride of the grass pad and the egg, but the third time he leaps he comes down on the egg breaking it into pieces. Each boy performs this ceremony until they have all made their public profession and given the sign of faithfulness by breaking the egg. Another village elder now steps forward and examines each boy and pulls forward the foreskin as he passes along the line. While these matters have been going forward, the surgeon has kept out of sight in one of the huts near; he has sharpened his knives for the operation and is quite ready to perform his part when the elder has completed his investigation along the line of waiting boys. When all is declared satisfactory, the surgeon steps out quickly to the first boy, seizes the foreskin, pulls it well forward and cuts it off, throwing it over his shoulder. Having looked to see that the operation is correctly done, he passes rapidly to the next boy and thus circumcises each of them before they fully realise what has happened. Should any boy require further attention after the first sharp cut, the surgeon's examination detects the fault, he quickly corrects it and passes on along the line. It is seldom that the man requires to make a second cut on a boy and, when his work is done, he hurries away as quickly as he came and passes into a house out of sight until all the people have dispersed. Old women follow the surgeon to see that the operation has been correctly performed and make sure everything is satisfactory. Other friends and relatives carry plantain stems and place them behind the boys for them to sit upon in case they are faint and need to sit down. Another elder advances along the line, takes a little blood from the wound and rubs it on the chest of each boy as he stands rigid with his legs apart on either side of the grass pad waiting until the bleeding ceases.

The foreskins are collected and buried near the chief's hut and, when these have been buried, a man mounts the hut on which the meat is spiked, cuts it into small pieces and throws it among the people, who struggle to obtain it and eat it. This meat is supposed to bring good fortune to the man or woman who can secure it. When the bleeding ceases, the boys are conducted to their house and remain in it until they are quite healed.

Initiation of girls. During the time boys are undergoing their period of instruction previous to circumcision, a number of girls who for some months, seldom less than twelve, have been preparing for their ceremony and have scarified their bodies with special clan-markings, are set apart in some hut where an elderly woman instructs them in their duties as wives and mothers. The final ceremony is to cut away some portion of the genital organs and to correct the scarifications on their bodies or to complete what is lacking. Both boys and girls have two teeth in the lower jaw extracted and girls have the lower lip pierced for the lip-stone. Sometimes men too have their lip pierced for this stone, though it is usually regarded as the proper ornamentation of the women.

Purificatory ceremony at the close of initiation. When the wounds of both groups are healed, a period of general drinking and feasting ensues. It seldom happens that a boy or girl dies at this time in consequence, though some have died afterwards from excessive bleeding due to the operation. The elder in whose village the young people are assembled goes through another ceremony with a companion, when he knows that all the boys and girls are well: they take a goat and a fowl to a sacred tree in the early morning, the goat and fowl are killed at the root of the tree and blood is made to flow upon the root, the meat of the goat is then cooked and eaten near the tree, but the fowl is laid on the root and left as an offering to the spirit of the tree. After the meal they proceed to a sacred pool in the neighbourhood which is said to be guarded by a snake. They go armed with a pot of strong beer which they place on the bank of the pool and wait until the snake has been attracted by the smell and has drunk itself helplessly drunk, when they break its fangs and leave it harmless. While the snake is in this condition, the young people who have been circumcised follow the two men to the pool and bathe. Sons of chiefs first enter the water and wash, followed by the other boys, and afterwards by the girls. This bath is supposed to make them strong and well, and above all it makes the young women able to have children.

Dancing and drinking to celebrate the close of initiation ceremonies. In the evening public dancing begins when members from other clans come and join. No weapons are brought but only bamboo rods in which are their long beer-tubes, and drinking and dancing continue for several days. At this time the fullest license is given to both sexes, marriage

ties are disregarded and men and women live together promis-
cuously without any restraint. When the beer is ended in one
village, they move on to another where it has been prepared,
and continue the festivities from village to village until all the
beer is drunk in the district. These dances end the initiation
rites. Initiated youths are no longer boys but men, and hence-
forth take part in the affairs of state, having the right to sit
in councils and to speak on important subjects and also to
wear the regulation goat-skin dress strung round the neck
and hanging low enough to cover the circumcised organ as
they stand. Young people are now able to marry, for, until
these ceremonies are performed, no woman will marry a man
and no man will marry a woman. Should a couple who have
not fulfilled the customs and have not been circumcised marry,
they are ignored by the clan and their children are outcasts,
they are outside the sphere of the gods' protection and are cut
off from all rights as members.

Plate XIX

(2) A warrior of the Bagesu Tribe

(1) . Man wearing the regulation dress after initiation
(*Bagesu Tribe*)

CHAPTER XVIII

MUSIC, DANCING, WARFARE, BUILDING, AMUSEMENTS AND HUNTING

Musical instruments—dancing and the use of thigh bells—warfare—ceremony to cleanse a warrior who has killed one of the foe—villages and huts—furniture of huts—amusements—hunting customs.

Musical instruments. These people are fond of music: they have a primitive harp, and also a rude kind of drum which accompanies songs and dances. The harp is used to accompany songs in the house, but is not used in public songs and dances. In dances the drum only is used, and bells, attached to the thighs and to the ankles, are made to clang by stamping the feet to the rhythm of the drum. Songs are sung during the dances, which take place almost monthly when the moon is nearing the full and the evenings are light. Girls make a small instrument of reeds after the pattern of a zither. This instrument is used by a girl as she sings her love ditties.

Dancing and the use of the thigh bells. In dances both men and women take part and form sides, the men use the thigh bells and stamp with their feet to make the bells sound and produce a thud from the stamp; the women only sing as they dance. The parties move in circles as they dance, or march from opposite sides of a square to meet in the middle and retreat. The season most devoted to dances is after harvest when each village is able to make its brew of beer and contribute to the village supply for the dancing. It is at this time, when all feuds are dropped and members of clans can intermingle without fear, when weapons are put away and there is nothing but

the most cordial relations, that men seek wives and make their
matrimonial arrangements.

Warfare. Only on rare occasions are there wars. These
are, ordinarily, wars within the tribe and are due to some case
of murder or bloodshed; the more serious wars take place when
some other tribe makes a raid and the clans combine to resist
the common foe. In the more frequent fights between clans
warriors arm and meet at some place near. The weapons
used are bows and arrows—the latter with roughly made iron
tips—spears, shields, and stones. There is no order in the
army: it is an unorganised mass, any man may rush out and
attack or he may hold back as he wishes. The combatants
shoot arrows and sling stones, they seek cover and strive to
get within shooting-range unobserved, and again at times one
or two men from either side will rush out and engage in a
hand to hand fight while the armies look on, till possibly one
man is seriously wounded or perhaps killed. Such a combat
of champions will end the battle, and the winning side will
dictate the terms of peace.

Ceremony to cleanse a warrior who has killed one of the foe.
A warrior who has killed another in battle does not return
home the same day; he returns to his village, but spends the
night in the house of a friend. In the evening he kills a goat
or sheep and takes the contents of the stomach in a pot and
with them he smears his head, chest and arms. If he has any
children, they too are brought and smeared in like manner,
and return home. After having thus fortified himself and his
children, the man proceeds to his house and paints each door-
post with the mixture, throwing the remainder on the roof of
the house. For a day the man does not touch food with his
hands, but conveys it to his mouth with two sticks cut for
the purpose. On the second day he is free to return home and
to his ordinary life. These restrictions do not extend to a
wife of the slayer: she is not only free from them but may go,
if she wishes, to mourn over the slain man and take part
in the ceremonies of the dead.

Building.

Villages and huts. Villages of the Bagesu are clusters of huts built on fairly level ground on the slopes of the mountain. From some prominence on a mountain ridge numbers of villages may be seen, some high up the mountain sides, others on lower slopes little removed from the great plains which stretch away to the far distance. Some of the villages have only two or three huts, whereas others have fully forty, a number which betokens some competent leader who commands respect through bravery or other such personal power to attract. With few exceptions villages are open on all sides, the few have growing fences round them, the chief protection being their position. Each clan may have many such villages dotted about in the district it claims as its property. As a rule at marriage a man builds his hut near his father's house, and he seeks help from his parents both to collect the materials for the hut and also to build it. The elder of a village is consulted about the site on which to build, and, having obtained his consent, the man levels the place and traces a circle on the ground the size he wishes to build his hut. The walls are composed of short stakes about four feet long above the ground. He digs holes a few inches deep for each stake and puts them side by side. They are bound together at the top and at the bottom by creepers and form a strong wall. A stout pole is erected in the centre of this circular wall; the top is tapered and a few feet down it is notched. Rafters are tied to this pole and extend to the wall. The pitch of the roof is determined by the builder, it is usually acute. The rafters are secured to the wall and rows of strong twigs are tied on to the rafters at intervals from the wall until the apex is reached. This roof is thatched with common grass which abounds in the neighbourhood, the grass being fully two feet long and forming good thatch. The centre pole stands out three feet above the thatch. The roof projects some eighteen inches or two feet beyond the walls and carries off rain to a safe distance from the hut. The walls are plastered on the inside with clay which is thrown with force against the stakes and smoothed with the flat of the hand. As the clay dries, all cracks are filled until there is a smooth surface. The floor is made by digging up the earth and adding, if necessary, more earth of clay composition and beating it hard with short sticks while it is still damp.

Furniture in a hut. The furniture in a house and kitchen is scanty; in fact furniture does not exist, though in one or two huts a stool may be found. There is seldom any attempt to make a bed: the family lie down on the floor round the fire without any clothing or even grass to lie upon, and contact with one another is the only means of warmth apart from the fire. The door is closed soon after sunset to keep out the cold wind and to make the room warm and cheerful. The door consists of either reeds or twigs laid side by side upon cross-bars and bound together, and is held in position over the door-way by a post on either side, behind which it slides when opened. The fire burns in the middle of the room on the floor and the smoke finds its way out as best it can through the roof, as there is no chimney. While the family is absent during the day, the hut is closed but not secured in any way: few people attempt to rob a neighbour. To make a house doubly secure during the day when the owner is absent, if he thinks it is likely to be entered, a man will lay his stick along the step. Any person who crosses that stick may be dealt with as a thief; it also carries with it a magical power which will affect the thief.

There are no attempts made to secure sanitary conditions in any village: the grass and scrub round the village are left to grow as they will, and hither members of the community retire to relieve nature. Atmospheric action alone keeps the place from becoming too offensive for people to endure the smell, and it alone prevents the spread of disease.

Amusements. The chief amusement is dancing: each new moon is celebrated by the beating of drums, and dancing then takes place. The moon is watched for by all and the first person who sees it calls attention to it; men and women dance, and mothers carry out their infants to see it because it is said to make them thrive. Often, a few nights before full moon, village dances are performed by the young people.

Among youths and boys wrestling is a never-failing source of interest: one village will challenge another and competitions are often going forward. Small boys have a game of kicking which affords great amusement: they choose sides and pit one boy against another, the combatants stand on one leg and with the other foot try to kick their opponent with the sole of the foot on the thigh, knock him down and then claim him as their man. This is a game of agility rather than of strength, the art being to avoid a kick and then to kick out quickly and overthrow the other before he has time to recover his balance.

Hunting. Beasts of prey, especially leopards, are hunted down when there is special danger from them, when for example an animal has attacked a man in the daylight, or has entered a house or village by night and carried off some one. The men from several villages then assemble and track the animal to its lair, when they surround the thicket beating down the grass with heavy clubs, shouting and singing at the topmost pitch of their voices. Each man carries a shield on his left arm which he presents should the animal spring before he can club it. The beast seldom escapes and rarely injures any of the beaters. The noise seems to bewilder the animal and it is clubbed and killed before it knows which way to turn to flee. It is speared after being clubbed to ensure death.

Hyaenas are usually left to wander about as they will; but, should one of them take a goat from a herd, it is followed and clubbed to death. Hyaenas are useful scavengers to clear off the remains of the dead and all offal, and are respected as connected with the dead.

Elephants are hunted at times, the method of hunting being for two or three men to hide in trees while others go out as beaters and turn the animals to the trees. The men in hiding choose an animal with large tusks and spear it as it passes under them. A wounded animal invariably seeks its foe, and, should one of the beaters be discovered, it will give chase and, if it captures him, it will crush him to death by kneeling on him. The man who first spears an animal claims the tusks, the other men share the meat, which is eaten by the tribe. A wounded animal is followed sometimes for several days before it can be surrounded and killed.

Antelopes and small game are hunted with the spear and club. Several men combine and run an animal down by turning it first to one and then to another of their party until it is breathless and tired, when they club it. The division of meat is a frequent source of angry words and at times the cause of a fight.

Boys are fond of trapping herbivorous rats which they eat and consider a delicacy; even their elders are fond of a share of the spoil.

PART V

THE BASOGA

CHAPTER XIX

NORTH-WESTERN DISTRICT, CENTRAL DISTRICT AND THE SOUTHERN DISTRICT

The country with its divisions—the North-western District—the Central District—the Southern District—physical features of the country —the people and their occupation—list of chiefs in the Northern District—a chief's successor—death of a chief, appointing his successor—mourning for a chief—arrival of the heir—how mourning is ended—ceremony to ensure a new chief's health and prosperity—disposal of widows of a deceased chief—removing the jaw-bone of a dead chief—list of chiefs in the Central District—appointing a new chief—clans in the Northern District—clans in the Central District.

The country with its divisions. Busoga, which to-day forms part of the Eastern Province of the Uganda Protectorate, has from time immemorial been tributary to one or other of the surrounding nations. For many years the Baganda have governed the whole of Busoga, but formerly the country was divided among and governed by three nations: the North-western District was governed by the Banyoro, the Central District was under the rule of the Bateso chiefs, while the Southern District was governed by the Baganda. The whole area of Busoga is small: it falls between the equator and the first degree north of it, and its longitude lies between 33 and 34 degrees east of Greenwich.

The North-western District. The North-western District is commonly called Nadiope's country or Kamuli after the chief's capital, and has had a young chief governing it for some years. He has recently died and the district is now under the management of regents until the young son of Nadiope shall be old enough to take control under the British Resident. The original chief of this country is said to have been a man named Kitembo to whom the Banyoro gave the country[1]. The people claim, through this man, affinity with the Banyoro royal family, for they say Kitembo was a Munyoro prince. When the Banyoro were still the overlords of this part of Busoga, it was customary for the chief to send his son to be servant to the king of Bunyoro; but, when the Baganda wrested the country from Bunyoro, the chief's son was sent to the Uganda court. Even to the present time there is a link of affection with the Banyoro, and the people still look upon the Banyoro as their friends.

The Central District. In the Central District, Zibondo's country, or Kaliro as it is called, the people claim to have come in the first instance from Bukedi; and, though for many years they have been under the rule of the Baganda and have had their representatives in the court of Uganda, they still lean to the Bakedi as their friends. This district is much smaller than either the North-western District or the Southern District.

The Southern District. The Southern District, commonly known as Luba's country, has been under the rule of the kings of Uganda for many years; its previous history is unknown. It is bounded on the south side by Lake Victoria, while Kavirondo winds round it from the south and along its eastern side; on the west the river Nile is the boundary for all Busoga and divides it from Uganda. It has been the custom for many years for the chief's sons of the Southern District to be sent as pages to the Uganda king; and the language of the country is purely Luganda, though it is spoken with a foreign accent. With these three important divisions in the country it can readily be understood that the language, though asserted in some parts to be an independent language, has always been influenced by that of the ruling sovereign and is of a mixed character, and that for many years the language of Uganda has been the dominant language spoken. There are two or three other small chiefs, but, as they belong to one or other

---

[1] *Banyoro*, the people in the plural; *Munyoro*, singular; *Bunyoro*, the country—similarly *Baganda*, *Muganda*, *Buganda* or *Uganda*.

of the three divisions already mentioned, the reader need not be troubled by having them enumerated.

Physical features of the country.   The chief physical feature of the country is its fertility; the vast amount of arable land, with extensive groves of plantains and plots of sweet potatoes and millet interspersed, has always been a matter of comment among travellers.   The atmosphere of Busoga is much moister than that of Uganda.   There are a few clumps of forest which supply the people with building materials and firewood, and there is a limited amount of uncultivated land which affords pasture for their herds.   The country is undulating and has one or two good rivers beside the Nile, which, as stated above, flows along the western side.

The people and their occupation.   The population is large for the area of the country, and women preponderate, though this has been a fruitful field for slave raiding and for years the Baganda looked to Busoga[1] especially for their supply of domestic women-slaves.   The temperament of the Basoga is much more submissive than either that of the Baganda or that of the Banyoro, and they dislike warfare though they have had their intertribal battles, chiefly due to cult and taboo which often involved bloodshed for their settlement and caused retaliation on the part of the injured tribe.   The features of the Basoga are those generally known as negroid; the nose is almost bridgeless and flat, the face round with thickish lips which do not as a rule protrude.   Both men and women are of a medium height, from five feet six inches to five feet ten inches.   In each district the chief industry is agriculture, though cows, goats and sheep are reared and almost every peasant breeds a few fowls; many peasants keep one or two cows and take them into their huts by night to protect them from wild animals.   The flocks of goats and sheep are the chief means by which the people obtain meat; the peasants are almost vegetarians owing to the difficulty of procuring the money to buy meat.   Goats and sheep are the chief means by which a man purchases his wife and pays his taxes, so that he

[1] *Busoga*, the country, *Basoga* the people.

cannot afford to eat his animals freely. In Busoga is to be
found the long-haired goat which thrives here, though in other
countries it deteriorates rapidly and loses its hairy coat. Here
also may be found the sheep with the extraordinary fat
tail, reaching to and at times trailing on the ground. There
are considerable differences in the customs of the several
districts which will need to be noted, and this may lead at
times to some repetition. Where there are no differences, the
story will run as that of the North-western District, because
it has been possible to get fuller notes from thence than from
other places. From Southern Busoga no notes are given
because famine was too severe there to allow men to come and
give the necessary information.

The North-western District.

List of chiefs in the North-western District. The first great
chief recorded was Kitembo, who was said to be a Munyoro
prince and who came to rule Busoga with his brother Muzaya.

2. Mawevu, the son of Kitembo	3. Nadiope
4. Kagoda	5. Gabula
6. Kajumbula	7. Mutimbwa
8. Naika, deposed by the British	9. Nadiope

This list is incomplete, but it is the best that could be
obtained during the short time available when I was passing
through the country.

A chief and his successor. The heir to the chief is always
the son of his principal wife; or, if she happens to be childless,
she adopts a child of her sister whom she has induced to become
a wife of her husband. It is a common custom for a wife to
entice her sisters to become wives of her husband; they
stipulate, however, that they shall each have their own house.
Should the chief wife have children who are all girls, or should
she be childless, she adopts a son of one of her sisters and brings
him up to be the heir. Such a child, when old enough to leave
home and enter the service of the king, was sent to the court
of Bunyoro to be trained as a page. As the king had numbers
of boys who were pages, the duties of each were light and

consisted chiefly in running errands, laying the king's mats in
the court-house and carrying them from one place to another,
or spreading other mats in the path for the king to walk upon
as he went from one house to another, or playing flutes before
his majesty as he went from one court to another. Such were
the duties of pages. The son of a Busoga chief usually remained
in Bunyoro until his father died, when he was sent back by
the king with a responsible escort to establish him in the chieftainship of his father. He was given a shield and two spears,
a wooden dish and a stool which he afterwards used as his
seat of office.

Death of a chief and appointment of his successor. When
the chief dies, the people send messengers to Bunyoro to tell
the king and to ask him to appoint the successor. The body of
the chief is not buried until the heir comes and covers it with
a bark-cloth. This ceremony can only be performed by the
heir. The grave is in the house in which the chief died, and is
a large pit dug in the middle of the floor. A bedstead is built in
the grave and numbers of bark-cloths are put in it and under it,
and upon this bedstead the body is laid to await the heir who
has to cover it with a specially prepared bark-cloth. A large
house is built near the tomb and is surrounded by a fence
of reeds hung over with dry plantain-fibre. When the heir
arrives, he enters the house and remains there mourning three
months or more. No woman is permitted to enter this house,
but the sisters and relatives of the heir have small huts built
round the tomb and strictly observe the rules of chastity.
All mourners are forbidden to leave the precincts of the tomb.
Should they do so, or should they break any mourning taboo,
such as that of chastity or the abstaining from cutting nails
and hair, they must leave the place of mourning at once. When
the heir arrives, the sub-chiefs gather and build huts at a
distance from the tomb; they may eat and drink freely, as
they are not restricted from the usages of ordinary life by any
mourning taboos.

Mourning for a chief. Each morning at daybreak the
mourners gather at the tomb to mourn and continue wailing
some three hours; first one and then another throws himself

or herself upon the grave, calling to the dead to return and asking him how they are to live without him. At the close of the morning's wailing the mourners return to their huts and remain about, idly talking and gleaning any gossip they can, for they are good talkers and seldom lack a subject for conversation. Mourners do not wash, they never trim their nails or hair, but allow them to grow until they cease mourning; when about to have a meal, they sponge their hands with plantain sponges, this being the only washing they may indulge in, even when the period of mourning lasts six months.

Arrival of the heir. When the heir arrives from Bunyoro, he takes the bracelet from his father's right arm and wears it on his own right arm, this being the token of office and passing from chief to chief. A second son of the deceased chief is chosen by the members of the chief's clan to take charge of his younger brothers and sisters, to be their representative in any dispute among them; he is given his father's waist-band to wear as his badge of office. Each Musoga wears a string waist-band; under this band, it is usual to put a strip of bark-cloth some six inches wide and to pass it from back to front between the legs. This is looked upon as an important item of clothing and is in fact the only article which to the Musoga mind is essential to decency, for without it a man is said to be naked.

How mourning is ended. To end mourning the chief calls upon his sub-chiefs to bring a number of oxen and pots of beer. When these arrive, one of the finest oxen is selected and taken to the door of the tomb, the heir is presented with a spear and kills the animal with one sharp thrust; should he fail to kill it by the one thrust, it is a token that he will not prosper in his office. The deceased chief's sister's son takes charge of the meat of the animal and presides over the meal which follows. The meat is cooked on the spot, and only relatives and friends who have observed all the mourning taboos are allowed to partake. Should any man or woman have yielded to sexual desires, which is a serious fault and is the worst form of infringement of the taboos, he or she is excluded from the meal; if any guilty person presumes to eat, it is believed he will die—the ghost will kill him.   The next morning after this meal the new chief shaves his head and puts aside his mourning garments, and all the people follow his example.

Ceremony to ensure a chief's health and prosperity.   The chief's hair which was shaved off is made up into a small ball, wrapped in bark-cloth, and taken the following day by two or three warriors into the next district of Busoga.   Here they lie in wait for some man to come along the road; they first greet the man and then seize him, thrust the ball of hair into his mouth and strangle him; the body is left in the road and the warriors escape back to their own chief.   When the body of the murdered man is discovered by the relatives, they hasten to acquaint their chief with the outrage.   This outrage leads to a tribal war, for the meaning of the ball in the man's mouth is well understood: it contains any evil which otherwise might befall the new chief, but which has now been transferred to the murdered man.   The two chiefs meet in battle and for a few days there are petty skirmishes.   Peace is made after blood has been shed, but it does not follow that there has been a death, it being enough to spill blood; though of course some one may have been killed or seriously wounded and may die of his wounds.   The new chief gives the first man who has wounded one of the enemy in battle a wife, and others who have distinguished themselves receive a cow each.   The new chief's brother after this war appoints one of his sisters to be the principal sister to the chief.   This is an office much coveted among women because of the wealth and privileges it carries. The sister is to all intents and purposes a wife, but is not ex- pected to have children and takes precautions that there are none born.   One of the daughters of the late chief boils a pot of butter and smears the grave with it in the early morning of the day when the meal is given which ends the period of mourning.

The fence enclosing the chief's house is rebuilt and all signs of mourning are removed, care being taken when the new fence is built to make the gateway opposite the tomb of the chief's grandfather and not in front of his father's tomb.

Disposal of widows of a deceased chief. The widows of the deceased chief become wives of the new chief; but, should any of them prefer to go to some of his brothers as wives they may do so. Should any widow have children by her late husband, it does not debar her from becoming a wife of the new chief; he only avoids his own mother or a woman of her clan.

Removing the jaw-bone of a dead chief. At the end of six months the grave of the late chief is opened and the jaw-bone removed. This is cleansed and put into a shrine, situated some distance from the chief's residence, wherein are the jaw-bones of all former chiefs, which are preserved and guarded by a man appointed for this office. Attached to the shrine is an estate which provides food for the guardian and his assistants.

The Central and North-western Districts.

List of chiefs of the Central District. The chiefs of the Central District claim affinity with the Bateso. They say that their first chief came from Bukedi. The names of the chiefs, in so far as they are known, are:

1. Lubogo
2. Soba
3. Mukenya Bwainda
4. Wako Kibondo
5. Kisira
6. Wambuzi, deposed by the
7. Zibondo (Ezekieri)   British

Appointing a chief. The heir is appointed to succeed a deceased chief by the principal medicine-man who lives at a place called Kaduweri. The usual custom is to choose the eldest son of the deceased chief, unless the medicine-man says he is unsuited to rule. Should this son die before his father, one of his brothers is chosen, unless there is a grandson, that is a son of the deceased eldest son, who is old enough to rule, in which case he is chosen to inherit in the place of his grandfather. The heir is given a spear and a shield as his insignia of office.

Clans of the North-western District. The North-western District is divided between fifty-seven families, which are indeed small clans. Each clan is known by a particular name and

has its own totems.   In most cases it was impossible to obtain
the names of the second totem of each clan, though there
is no doubt that they exist.

The names of the clans are as follows:

1.   *Bulondo*, whose totem is a Monkey.

2.   *Basekwe*, whose totem is the Mushroom and the second
is a vegetable, *Tabutantyo*.

3.   *Senkwanga*, whose totem is the Elephant and the second
is an Antelope, *Kongone*.

4.   *Semwayo*, whose totem is Birds, *Akasende*.

5.   *Ngobe*, whose totem is an Antelope, *Mpongo*.

6.   *Basubo*, whose totem is Birds, *Kamyali*.

7.   *Magamba*, whose totem is Yams, *Ziriamiri*.

8.   *Gaga*, whose totem is Husks of Millet.

9.   *Sensolya*, whose totem is the Otter, *Ngonge*.

10.   *Bakike*, whose totem is Buffalo.

11.   *Njene*.

12.   *Banangwe*, whose totem is a Sheep that has cast its
young, *Mbuzi akasowole*.

13.   *Bakoyo*, whose totem is Lung-fish, *Nabibalu*.

14.   *Semugaya*, whose totem is a large Water-lizard,
Mubulu.

15.   *Bagaya*, whose totem is the Crocodile, *Ngonyi*.

16.   *Mwasi*, whose totem is an Antelope, *Njazi*.

17.   *Basekula*, whose totem is the Wild-pig, *Mbizi*.

18.   *Kitamwe*, whose totem is Guinea-fowl, *Nkofu*.

19.   *Mwangu*, whose totem is an Antelope, *Ngabi*.

20.   *Nono*, whose totem is Cooked Plantain, *Nfuka*.

21.   *Senyulya*, whose totem is a Bird, *Kasenke*.

22.   *Tambe*.

23.   *Mabiro*, whose totem is Dry Slices of Vegetable Mar-
row, *Bikukuju*.

24.   *Katuma*, whose totem is the Flea, *Nkukunyi*.

25.   *Mulinda*, whose totem is Swallows, *Katai*.

26.   *Nyana*, whose totem is the small Calves.

27.   *Muluta*, whose totem is Colobus Monkeys.

28.   *Muyombo*, whose totem is a Bird, *Kasusima*.

29.   *Musere*, whose totem is Overflowing Rivers, *Miga-*

ejude. The clan may not draw water from such rivers nor attempt to cross them.

30. *Mugwano.*

31. *Sendasi,* whose totem is an Antelope, *Ngabi.*

32. *Mutediba.*

33. *Bango,* whose totem is a Bird, *Sosolyo.*

34. *Toli,* whose totem is an Antelope, *Mpongo.*

35. *Bere.*

36. *Mayanja.*

37. *Kisuwi,* whose totem is the Leopard, *Mpara.*

38. *Basuswe,* whose totem is the Hyaena, *Mpisi.*

39. *Mwebya,* whose totem is a kind of Grass, *Buyanja.*

40. *Semagoba,* whose totem is the Hippopotamus, *Nvubu.*

41. *Wenzu,* whose totem is a kind of Monkey, *Kamununya.*

42. *Busigisigi,* whose totem is Doves, *Emba.*

43. *Baego,* whose totem is an Antelope, *Nfume.*

44. *Sekijugu,* whose totem is Lung-fish, *Nakibala.*

45. *Bakose,* whose totem is Chaff of Sesame.

46. *Umbwe,* whose totem is White-ants, *Nswa.*

47. *Basoko,* whose totem is an Antelope, *Mpongo.*

48. *Bambade,* whose totem is Husks of corn, *Musisi.*

49. *Eboka,* whose totem is the Snail, *Kovwa.*

50. *Sango,* whose totem is Guinea-fowl, *Nkofu.*

51. *Kaima,* whose totem is an Antelope, *Njaza.*

52. *Gulu,* whose totem is the mouth of an old water pot. The clan may not touch it nor have it in their presence.

53. *Kiembwa,* whose totem is *Lusambya* posts. The clan may not use such posts in building their houses or fences.

54. *Kaibare,* whose totem is Dogs, *Mbwa.*

55. *Kigoma,* whose totem is that they may not eat during the day of full-moon.

56. *Lubanga.*

57 *Sabwiri,* whose totem is Lung-fish, *Nabibalu.*

Clans of the Central District. In the Central District there are thirty-one clans. Here also only the principal totem was obtainable, the second having fallen almost entirely out of use.

The names of the clans are:

1. *Ngobe*, whose totem is an Antelope, *Mpongo*. This is the chief's clan.

2. *Baigage*, whose totem is Chaff of Millet.

3. *Bahoya*.

4. *Kwanga*, whose totem is the Elephant, *Njovu*.

5. *Soswa*, whose totem is the Hyaena, *Mpisi*.

6. *Baisonga*, whose totem is Civet Cat, *Mondo*.

7. *Mulondo*, whose totem is a Monkey, *Nkima*.

8. *Lemu*, whose totem is the Leopard, *Mpala*.

9. *Wiro*, whose totem is Female organs. A man of the clan may not approach a woman for sexual purposes during the daytime.

10. *Ruba*, whose totem is Gazelle, *Kasiri*.

11. *Mucwa*, whose totem is Female Antelopes, *Mpongo*.

12. *Mpanzira*, whose totem is Water-buck, *Ngobe*.

13. *Mwanga*.

14. *Mugonya*, whose totem is Mushrooms, *Butiko*.

15. *Kiminya*, whose totem is Hyaena, *Mpisi*.

16. *Kitengya*, whose totem is Wild-pig, *Mbizi*.

17. *Mukose*, whose totem is Chaff of Millet.

18. *Mulamya*.

19. *Segaga*, whose totem is Chaff of Millet.

20. *Miyangwa*.

21. *Mwoya*, whose totem is an Antelope, *Ngabi*.

22. *Kadodo*, whose totem is the Frog, *Kikere*.

23. *Banyakatamya*, whose totem is Water-buck, *Ngobe*.

24. *Mulandya*.

25. *Nsanga*, whose totem is Birds, *Kamonyi*.

26. *Nyanzi*.

27. *Nsubo*, whose totem is Birds, *Kamonyi*.

28. *Nsweza*, whose totem is Mushroom, *Butiko*.

29. *Mbala*, whose totem is Rats, *Mpube*.

30. *Semasoza*, whose totem is an Antelope, *Njaza*.

31. *Sempunda*, whose totem is a small bird which builds in plantains, *Kasanki*.

The clans are exogamous, that is, no man may marry a woman of his own clan. The children belong to the clan of their father, not of their mother.

CHAPTER XX

MARRIAGE AND BIRTH CUSTOMS

Methods of choosing a wife—cousin marriage—the marriage-fee—elopement—marriage customs in the North-western District—ending the period of marriage seclusion—marriage customs in the Central District—differences in marriage customs in the North-western District and the Central District—birth customs in the North-western District—tonic given to a pregnant woman—acknowledging a child as a clan-member—children kept at home until marriage—birth customs in the Central District—disposal of the umbilical cord—proving the legitimacy of a child—customs concerned with the birth of twins in the North-western District—preparing for the ceremony of naming twins—birth of twins in the Central District—announcing the birth of twins to the chief—the mother's period of seclusion—purificatory rites after the period of seclusion.

Methods of choosing a wife. A youth is considered fully grown at about the age of seventeen and begins to think of marriage. No record of age is kept and it is only by his physical appearance and actions that it is decided whether he is old enough or not to have a wife. In the north-western part of Busoga a youth has much to say on the question as to whom he is to marry. He will tell his father or his father's brother that he wishes to marry and also name the woman he desires to have to wife. It then becomes the duty of the father to investigate the matter and to find out whether the woman is a desirable person, whether she is eligible and outside the forbidden circle of relationship, and whether she is free to marry. Should all prove to be satisfactory, he will arrange the matter and settle with the woman's relatives the amount to be paid as the marriage-fee. The regular rules of exogamy must be followed; a man must refrain from marrying a woman from his father's clan, nor may he marry a woman from his mother's clan, and, should a couple marry and afterwards discover that there was a mistake and that they are too closely related, they part at once and make an offering to the gods to atone for the offence. Such cases are rare; it is almost impossible to make such a mistake, though it has been known to happen.

Cousin marriage. The marriage of first cousins is forbidden, that is, the children of a brother and sister are forbidden to marry, though they have different totems, but second cousins may marry each other, if they are the grandchildren of the brother and sister respectively, and if the father of one of them was a son of that brother, and if the mother of one of them was a daughter of that sister.

The marriage-fee. When a father has approached a woman's relatives and they consent to the match, the youth is told the amount he has to pay as the marriage-fee, and the two are considered an engaged couple. The amount for the marriage-fee varies according to the circumstances of the man: chiefs are expected to pay more than peasants, the payment in their case being from two to five cows, whereas a peasant is not expected to pay more than ten or twelve goats and sheep, which are equal in value to one cow. Women are fond of making their intended husbands pay large sums for the marriage-fee: it is a form their pride takes, as they can afterwards boast of the sum that was paid for them and its amount gives them honour in the eyes of their companions.

Elopement. Sometimes young people arrange their own matrimonial affairs and the bridegroom elopes with his bride and carries her off to his father's house or to the house of a brother of his father or to that of some friend. The bride's relations have to hunt for her and, when she is discovered, the bridegroom is told the amount he has to pay as the marriage-fee. In such cases the bride remains with her husband and the fee is paid as soon as he can find the money. There is no punishment for this runaway marriage. The time it will take to obtain the marriage-fee sometimes makes a young couple impatient, and so they run away and marry, for it may be fully a year before the man can obtain the amount demanded, and during this time the young people may not meet or see each other.

Marriage customs. When the marriage-fee is paid, the bride's relations assemble at her parents' house in the evening and escort the bride to her new home. They sleep in the house with the bride the first night, and on the following day the bridegroom's relatives entertain them at a grand meal which is always well provided with such things as the natives consider dainties, especially with butcher's meat. The bride is present at this meal but is fed by a sister; and from this time on to the end of her period of seclusion she is not allowed to touch food with her hands, but is fed by her sister. She is fed like a child, her sister smearing the food over her mouth exactly as a mother does with her baby. The marriage day is a day of music and dancing and of general rejoicing. After this day and night of festivities the relatives return to their homes, leaving the sister to remain with the bride and minister to her. At the time the bride leaves her home her parents admonish her to be faithful to her husband, to cook well, to be obedient to him, to treat his guests with courtesy and to give them of her best cooking. She is warned that, if she neglects to follow these instructions and incurs her husband's anger, they will not help her nor intercede for her and it will be useless for her to come to them for help. The bridegroom's father also admonishes his son to care for his wife and never to be rough or unkind to her. When a bride arrives at her new home, she stands outside until her husband comes out and welcomes her and gives her a small present. A new bark-cloth is spread on the floor for the bride to sit on, and this becomes the property of the bride's aunt. The sister, who remains with the bride during her period of seclusion and attends to her wants, often becomes a second wife to the bridegroom and does not return home, but allows the man to find another marriage-fee for her and lives with him as his wife. In the case of such a wife the preparatory ceremonies for marriage are dispensed with, and she falls into her place as a wife at once. The husband avoids his mother-in-law; should he wish to hold any communication with her he does so when she is in another room.

Ending the period of marriage seclusion. At the end of the month the bride begins her normal life, goes to dig her field and undertakes her household duties. When three months are completed, a bride returns home to her parents, is entertained by them for one night and tells them all about her life, and how she likes her husband; on the following day, when she leaves for home, she is given a large supply of food which is carried for her by relatives. This food she cooks and prepares a special meal for her husband, who invites his friends to join him and give their opinion of his wife's cooking abilities. This meal is the ratification of the marriage, because it is a voluntary act on the part of the wife and testifies that she is satisfied with her new life. Should a wife be dissatisfied with her husband, she goes home at the end of three months and refuses to return to him. The relatives who were witnesses at the engagement try to settle any misunderstanding; but should the cause of disagreement be of such a nature as to justify the breaking off of marriage relations, they return the marriage-fee and the marriage is dissolved.

Marriage customs in the Central District. In the Central District a youth is at times given an opportunity of choosing his own wife and, when he has found the woman and possibly spoken to her about marriage, he will tell his father whom he wishes to marry. Another method which gives to the youth, and also to the woman, an opportunity of deciding the question of marriage for themselves is as follows: the father makes a round of visits to parents who have daughters of a marriageable age and invites the women to assemble at some particular house on a stated day at a fixed time. At the time appointed the young women sit together in front of the house and the youth walks out and sits before them. After greeting them and talking to them for a short while, during which time they scrutinise each other, the youth asks for a little water to drink and the woman who rises to give it to him is the person who agrees to become his wife. If he does not like the appearance of the women, he does not ask for water; and, if they do not like his appearance, no one responds to his invitation to give it. When everything is satisfactory, arrangements are made for the marriage, the amount for the fee is decided and the young people are engaged.

Another method by which a youth discovers whether a woman will marry him is by taking a hoe which he places by the door, and, after a short talk with the young woman, he leaves her for a time and returns to see if she has taken the hoe. If she has removed it, he accepts the token that she consents to become his wife; should she have left it, he knows she refuses to marry him.

It is a serious offence for a youth to try to get a woman who is already betrothed to another to change her mind and accept him. The relatives of the first suitor insist upon the case being tried in court, and the guilty man is fined and loses any gifts he may have given the woman or her parents with a view to marrying their daughter.

Difference in marriage customs between the North-western and Central Districts. Another difference in custom from the North-western District is in the actual marriage, when the bride is taken by her relatives to the bridegroom's house. In the Central District a house is set apart for the bride and her party and they reside in it for several days. Each morning the party goes forth to dig the field which is to be the bride's and they work hard until noon. During four days they continue to dig, the bridegroom not being seen but providing the best possible food for these workers. On the fourth day he sends a messenger to them with a present of fowls and food and says he wishes to claim his bride in the evening; the bride's party thereupon make ready in the afternoon and await the bridegroom, who goes at dusk to the house in which they are assembled and scatters cowry-shells from the door of the house to his own house, and the party follow picking up the cowry-shells as they go. A public meal takes place and the bride enters upon the period of seclusion, but before she goes into her house, she is taken to visit any female relatives of her husband who live near and is introduced to them and to any wives the man may have, if he is already married.

Birth.

Birth customs in the North-western District.   After marriage the husband and wife are anxious that there should soon be signs of maternity; there can be no true home-life for them where there are no children, and the husband seeks to divorce a barren wife.   A husband does not abandon his wife at once, but, should she not have a child within her first year of marriage, he becomes anxious and spares no pains to help her to obtain the remedies and advice from medicine-men and gods.   He will take his wife to a god and ask help, and there are times when the god tells the suppliant to go to some greater deity. Walumba is the greatest god; and should the local god advise the couple to go to Walumba, he also tells them what offering to take and instructs them how to approach the god and secure his favour.   Should there be no signs of birth after two years, the wife is returned to her clan and another woman is given in her place.   Sometimes such a woman may elect to remain with her husband, but her life is not happy without children. Should a wife become a mother after seeking the aid of the god, she makes a thank-offering to the god at the temple and very probably calls the child after the name of the deity.

Tonic given to a pregnant woman.   An expectant mother is given various kinds of herbs to mix with water to drink daily. The object of these herbs is twofold; they are expected to assist the mother by giving her an easy delivery, and also they make her offspring strong and healthy.   During her period of pregnancy the mother eats little salt and in many instances none at all, because it is likely to give the child skin-disease. Parents like their first child to be a girl, because the mother will live longer and have more children, whereas, should the child be a boy, the mother is likely to die without having any more children.   At birth, when the midwife has ascertained the sex of the infant, she cuts the navel cord accordingly: that of a boy is cut on a weeding-stick with a strip of reed taken from the ceiling near the right side of the door; that of a girl is cut upon the mother's hoe handle with a strip of reed taken from the ceiling on the left hand of the door.   The strip of reed used to cut the cord is tied to the middle pole of the house and preserved until the child is received into the clan. When the stump of cord falls from the child, the mother preserves it, wraps it in plantain-fibre, and wears it in her belt. The placenta is buried at the root of a plantain-tree, the tree being chosen according to the sex of the child: the tree chosen for the placenta of a girl is the kind used as a vegetable, and that for a boy's is the kind used for making beer. In each case the trees must have their flower-stem pointing to Bunyoro. Some clans bury the afterbirth near the door of the house, on the right side if the child is a boy, and on the left if it is a girl. When the time comes for the child to be named, the mother sits outside the house on the left of the doorway and the midwife on the right side. The relatives place a pot of water before the midwife and she washes the child, singing as she does so. This ceremony is said to strengthen the child, and they say that it lengthens its life. Children of wealthy parents are washed in a pot of milk which is mixed with beer.

Acknowledging a child in a clan. The mother takes the stump of umbilical cord and throws it on the floor on one side of the house. The child is then received into the clan as a full member. Some days later the father takes the child to his father who gives it the name of some ancestor; a child is never given the name of a living grandparent. The mother continues to nurse her child until it is at least three years old, and sometimes for a longer time. Names are chosen of people who were known to have been fond of children. Should a child die in infancy, the ghost after whom it was called is said to have been the cause; and, should two children die, who have been named after that particular ghost, the name is dropped and no child is called by it afterwards.

Children kept at home until marriage. Both boys and girls live at home with their parents; but boys have a small house built for them near their father's house and live in it until marriage, while girls live in the house with their parents until they grow up. When a girl grows up and has her first menses, she is taken to reside with a married brother with whom she remains until marriage.   Every woman during her periods of menstruation is separated from men especially, and usually from all members of her family, nor does she cook for her husband or touch anything belonging to him.

Birth customs in the Central District. In the Central District, when a woman finds the months passing after her marriage without any signs of maternity appearing, she seeks the aid of the god Gasani: this is not done by going to any temple, but rather by going to some spot where there is a large ant-hillock which she climbs and faces first one quarter and then another, calling upon the god to help her. She also vows that an offering of a goat or of a fowl, according to her circumstances, shall be made when the child is born. After this visit to the god a medicine-man gives the woman a mixture of herbs to drink daily, and also tells her how she is to diet herself   she may be called upon to eat alone and to use special drinking cups, while salt and some other kinds of food, especially certain vegetables, are forbidden until the child is born.   Should all go well and a child be born, the parents with a few relatives take a goat and a fowl to the ant-hillock upon which the woman stood when she called to the god, build a shrine at the base of the hillock, and kill both the goat and fowl; the blood of them is then offered to the god and placed in a vessel in the shrine, the meat being cooked and eaten near the shrine in the presence of the god.   They thank the god for hearing and answering their request and ask for a blessing upon the child.

Disposal of the umbilical cord. At childbirth a woman, besides undergoing similar rites to those performed in the North-western District, pays more attention to the stump of the umbilical cord. When it falls from the child, she goes with the midwife into the plantation and seeks a tree about to bear fruit which is of the same sex as the child and buries the stump of the cord at the roots of the tree. The fruit, when ripe, is given to the midwife who eats it alone, and the plantain-tree from that time belongs to her, the parents never eating the fruit from it.

Proving the legitimacy of a child. There is a much more severe test of legitimacy in this part than in the North-western District. After the week of separation the midwife and her assistant have a meal at which a small kind of fish and goat-mutton are supplied. At this meal the midwife is given some uncooked beans and sesame to eat; and, if the child sickens, it is said to be illegitimate, whereas, if the wife has been faithful, this ceremony makes the child stronger than before.

If it should happen that a child is proved to be illegitimate either at the ceremony of naming it or at that of testing it at the sacred meal, the mother is tied up to a post in the house until she confesses who is the father of the child. The accused man is brought to confront the woman and is charged with adultery. They are then taken out of the house; both the man and woman are stripped entirely naked and a wild gourd vine is tied round the waist of each of them. The woman thereupon stands with her legs apart and the man creeps through them; he then rises and comes to the woman, and possibly confesses his guilt. Should he deny the charge of adultery he takes hold of the woman's breast and asks her, "Shall I suck?" She knows that, if she is telling a lie in accusing him, then, if she consents to his tasting her milk, she will die; consequently she will not permit him to taste it. Whereas if she is speaking the truth and the man is telling a lie in denying the charge, she believes that he will die if he dares to taste her milk. When, therefore, a woman consents to a man's sucking her breast, he is condemned by the judges and is not often given time for the milk to work his death; he is at once believed to be guilty and the people kill him. In recent years the sentence of death has been remitted and the fine of a cow and five goats is now imposed.

When a child is three years old, vows are made by the parents to the god on behalf of the child, if the god will protect it. They go to the ant-hillock upon which the mother stood before its birth, offer a white goat and a white fowl, and ask the god Gasani to care for it. They then eat a meal and offer the blood to the god. A medicine-man is called who shaves off the hair of the mother and child, and takes the hair away with him. For his services he is paid a goat.

Should a child cut its upper teeth before the lower, the parents fear it will come to a bad end and they give a dance to the gods to preserve it from evil, because such a child will cause the death of its parents, if it is allowed to live without this ceremony being performed to avert the evil.

A woman who becomes the mother of several children is commended by members of her own clan, who send and claim every second child, that is to say half the number; the father has to redeem them with the assistance of his clan.

Birth of twins in North-western District. The birth of twins is a joyous event. If the birth takes place in the open, as most births do when children are born during the day, the mother is taken into a small enclosure at the back of the house, until a special house can be prepared for her and her children. When the house is ready, the mother and children enter and the door is closed and secured, a fresh doorway being cut through the thatch at the back. The house itself is divided into two parts, and the mother and her children use one room which is kept private for her use alone. The mother remains in her house for a period varying from one to six months according to the medicine-man's decision, while her husband obtains food for a sacred meal to be given when the children are brought out. During the day-time the mother is not allowed to come out into the open, unless she covers her head and keeps her eyes cast down to the ground. When the twins and their mother have been secluded, the father goes to his parents carrying a creeper of a wild gourd which he drops upon the doorstep and departs quickly without a word; he does the same at the house of his wife's parents and then returns home. The grandparents choose representatives to go and live in the house with the twins, the paternal grandparents sending a boy and the maternal grandparents sending a girl. These representatives remain in the house until the twin ceremonies are completed.

Preparations for naming the twins. The afterbirths are buried but the stumps of the umbilical cords are preserved by the mother. The father goes about during his wife's period of seclusion paying visits to his relatives and friends, and obtains presents of food and animals for the final meal when the ceremonies end. While the father is going about paying these visits he may not eat food with any member of his clan unless the person first pays him a few cowry-shells which are kept for decorating the stumps of the umbilical cords; he is always welcomed by those he visits because he is supposed to carry blessing wherever he goes. He reserves a little food from each meal and carries it to his wife. The persons of both husband and wife are sacred, and no man would dare speak a sharp word to either of them at this time because they are believed to be under divine protection. The father names the day when the period of seclusion shall end, arranging the time with the priest. Any member of his clan who has had a child born during the period of twin-seclusion brings it to the house in which these twins live to go through the ceremony of naming it with the twins. In the morning of the day chosen to show the twins to the relatives the mother makes a tour round the nearer houses, singing and dancing, and food is given to her which she carries home for the feast. While she is absent from home, her husband sits by the door outside the house with the thumb of his right hand bent into the palm of the hand and the fingers closed over it; he may not speak nor open his hand until his wife returns. The remainder of the day is spent in showing the children to friends, naming them, and in dancing and rejoicing. In the early morning before daybreak the boy who is the representative from the father's clan and has lived in the house with the mother of the twins is brought into the room in which the mother of the twins is dwelling, a rope is tied round his waist and they lie on the bed a little distance apart. The rope is held by two or three men who stand outside. A lighted torch being held high to give light to them, the boy works himself nearer to the woman, who welcomes him and also draws near him. When he is about to embrace her, the men pull the rope and drag him away. The woman immediately rushes out of the room into the next room where she meets her husband, and he has sexual relations with her. The door of the house which has been closed during the time of seclusion is now opened and the man and his wife come out, the man by the original door and the wife by the door at the back, and they run round the house naked in opposite directions. They next dress and the twin-ceremonies are ended; the relatives and friends have an early meal and leave for their homes. The boy from the father's clan and the girl from the mother's clan are each given a goat and return to their homes. After this the parents pay visits to relatives and friends as they wish, with their children.

Birth of twins in the Central District. In the Central District the birth of twins, though it brings a time of rejoicing, is also a cause of fear: the children are considered to be of divine origin and any mistake in the ceremonies or in treating them may be visited with divine displeasure, perhaps with death. When twins are born, the midwife and her attendant raise a shrill cry such as women raise to give the alarm when they are in danger. All who hear this cry refrain from eating any food until evening. This danger-call always causes considerable excitement; every person who hears it runs to find out whether he is wanted and if he can be of assistance to those in trouble or in danger. When the hearers of the cry learn the cause, that it is the birth of twins, they have to fast until evening. The newly-born children must not be removed, nor may the umbilical cords be cut until a medicine-man has come and sanctioned their removal. Most mothers are confined out-of-doors, and the children are kept in the open until the arrival of the medicine-man. This sage is summoned with all haste and, after seeing the twins and giving advice, he orders the midwife to remove them and to care for them. The umbilical cords are cut with a knife which is only used as a razor, and each afterbirth is put into a new cooking-pot and kept in the house until the ceremonies end When the twins are a boy and a girl, each child has its medicine-man to care for it, and both of these men, as also the parents of the twins, wear two cowry-shells on their foreheads to mark them as connected with twins.

Announcing the birth of twins to the chief. The husband's sister's son takes a bark-cloth to the district chief and drops it at the door saying, "I have brought the children," and then turns and flees. The people of the place try to catch him, and should they do so, his relatives have to pay the ransom of a goat for his release in order that he may continue his duties in connection with the twins. This youth has to go both to the father's and to the mother's parents; he takes a hoe to each house, drops it by the door, and flees back to the house in which the twins live. A representative is sent from the clan of each of the grandparents of the children, a boy from the paternal grandparents and a girl from the maternal grand-parents. These two representatives are directly responsible for the welfare of the twins, whom they must not leave by day or by night until all the ceremonies of birth are fulfilled.

The mother's period of seclusion. The door of the house in which the mother and children live is closed and a new door-way is cut at the back of the house and enclosed by a fence to prevent outside friends from approaching it. Thus the mother and her children can move about without risk of being seen. The mother, however, is not allowed outside the house during the day time. Should circumstances compel her to go out, she covers her head with a bark-cloth and keeps her eyes fixed on the ground lest she should see the sun, because this would cause the death of the twins. The father of the twins is free to go about when the representatives have arrived and taken charge of the children It is his duty to pay visits to his relatives and to those of his wife and to obtain goats and fowls for the final meal which takes place when the ceremonies end. During the time of preparation for the final ceremonies the parents are not allowed to see blood, and the father is expected to return each night to sleep at home. Should he find this impossible, he may not sleep in any house without first paying the woman to allow him to stay there. When the husband has collected sufficient goats and fowls for the final meal, he announces to the relatives the day for this special meal at which the naming of the twins is to take place, and he calls upon them to brew beer and prepare vegetable food for the occasion.

Purificatory rites at the end of the seclusion period. Early in the morning the parents, accompanied by the two medicine-

men and the father's sister's son, take the two pots containing
the afterbirths to some ant-hillock near and deposit them at
the base of it.   The hut is swept out during their absence and
on their return a goat, a sheep and a fowl are killed in the house
in the presence of the parents and the blood is made to flow
into the fireplace on to the ashes.   The skins of these animals
are made up into two bags and the stump of each child's umbilical cord is put into them and preserved.   A bark-cloth is
spread before the door of the house and the father of the twins
sits on it; the two medicine-men come and beg from him and
he gives a present to each of them.   The twins are then
brought out and the midwife washes them in a mixture of
beer and water.   The father's sister's son shaves the heads
of the children and of the parents and, as he does so, each of
them receives five cowry-shells.

Any child born during the time the twin-ceremonies have
been in performance is brought and washed in the bowl of
beer and water in which the twins have been washed.   He is
then named and receives a blessing.   On the following morning
the mother and boy go through the ceremonies as in the North-
western District.

CHAPTER XXI

SICKNESS, DEATH AND BURIAL

The causes of sickness. Methods of diagnosing sickness. Sickness is rarely if ever attributed to natural causes, but is generally said to be the result of magic or of ghostly possession; a medicine-man is required to discover the cause of sickness and inform the relatives who is its author; he also destroys the magic and prescribes remedies for the sick person after the spell has been removed. There are various tests used to discover whether it is magic which is causing the sickness and if so who the guilty person is who has worked it. A favourite method used to discover magic is to fill a pot with water and place the pot in a sling used for carrying milk-pots; the medicine-man swings it round his head and, as he does so, he mentions the name of the man supposed to have been guilty of magic-making. If, after swinging the pot round several times, no water is spilled, the man is declared to be innocent, whereas, if some of it spills, he is pronounced to be guilty; should no water spill another name is repeated and the medicine-man again performs the ceremony and goes on with name after name until the guilty person is discovered. The intestines of a goat or fowl are often used to discover the origin of sickness, when people can afford to supply the medicine-man with a goat or fowl. Some men prefer to cast nine leather slips, and, according to the position they take, the case is judged. Sometimes, when the sickness is pronounced to be due to magic, a fetish, *Nakalondo*, is asked to help to discover the person guilty of working magic. The god comes by night and calls through the closed door the name of the person and also describes what he has done. Any person thus accused by a medicine-man is brought before the local authority and asked to explain why he has worked magic. The chief is thus able to settle the case, if it is due to some dispute; the spell is removed and the medicine-man can treat and cure the patient. In certain cases a medicine-man will decide to transfer the illness to a goat or fowl or a bunch of herbs, after consulting his oracle. The animal is brought into the sick man's presence and tied to him; if it is a fowl or bunch of herbs, the patient is brushed over with it and the sickness is commanded to leave him. The animal, bird, or bunch of herbs is taken to waste land, and is killed and left there, unless, in the case of an animal, the medicine-man takes the meat and eats it himself.

At other times an oracle may declare sickness to be due to ghostly possession and the medicine-man has to exorcise the ghost; after capturing it, he takes it away and destroys it. Pain, such as headache or any other ache, the oracle may declare to be due to a bone or to some insect having got into the body, and the medicine-man has to extract it. Medicine is given to cause the object to come to the surface and poultices of herbs are made and applied to the place until the object is said to have been brought to the surface, when the medicine-man makes an incision and a bone or an insect is produced and pronounced to have been the cause of the pain.

Death.

Treatment of the dead. Should all the skill of the medicine-man fail and death ensue, the faithful watchers who have been caring for the sick person give no sign to cause others to suspect that death has taken place until they have removed as much of the patient's wealth from the house as is possible without incriminating themselves to some place of safety. When all is safe, wailing begins and members of the clan assemble to take part in the mourning and burial, and to appoint the heir;

leading members of the clan now remove everything of value
left in the house of the dead and place the property in some place
ready for distribution, and commence the funeral preparations.
The body is washed by the widows, but the deceased man's
sister's son has to carry the water and make the sponges for
washing the body; the legs are straightened, the arms are
crossed on the breast, and the corpse, wrapped in a bark-
cloth, is carried out of the house until the grave is dug.

The grave in the house. A deep pit is dug in the house
in which death took place; if the deceased was a chief, the pit
is dug much larger than is necessary to receive the body.
This is lined with bark-cloths, a bed is made in the middle of
the pit and the corpse is laid on it, after the members of the
clan have taken leave of the dead in the open where the body
lay. After the body is laid in the grave, it is covered with
bark-cloths and is guarded until the heir arrives. The leading
members of the clan choose the heir, they also accompany
him to the house and announce him to the mourners. When
the heir arrives, an ox is brought to the door and he spears it
and rushes away to a house prepared for him to live in during
the season of mourning; he thus seeks to escape the poor
members of the clan who try to capture him and beat him with
sticks to extort promises of presents and beer from him. Those
who remain in the house of the dead take the ox and cut it up
and divide the meat for a meal in the presence of the dead.
A portion of the meat is cooked for the ghost of the corpse:
this is placed in the grave at his feet, the remainder being
eaten by the assembled mourners. The meat for the dead is
put into a wooden vessel and covered with bark-cloths, while
another empty vessel is put under the head of the dead man,
intended to catch the skull when it drops from the body.
Every member of the clan brings one or more bark-cloths
according to his circumstances and these are spread in the
grave and almost fill it, leaving only a little room for earth.
Two young men or boys, sons of the deceased man's sister,
go into the garden and break off two leaves from a plantain
tree, cut out the midrib and come and stand one at the head
and the other at the foot of the grave holding the midribs in

the grave as the earth is thrown in; when a quantity of earth has been thrown in upon them, they draw them out, carry them away and hide them in the garden.

Setting the ghost of the dead free.   When all is ready for the earth to be thrown into the grave, the chief widow steps into the grave and catches two handfuls of earth as it is thrown. That in her right hand is from the first spadeful of earth and that in her left hand is from the second.   She steps from the grave, rolls the earth into a ball and carries it to the nearest bush or small tree and throws it over it saying, "If they have caught you, fly free."   This precaution is taken because it is said that the person who caused the death may also have captured the ghost with the object of tormenting it and of killing it.   This ball of earth from a grave is said to have greater efficacy than the strongest magic and can therefore release a captive ghost.   The grave is filled with earth and the floor is made level, and the widows now occupy the house during the season of mourning.   It is the office of the heir to regulate the daily mourning and he states when it is to end. Should the heir be a chief of importance, his sub-chiefs build temporary huts in the vicinity and await their new chief's instructions, but they take no part in the mourning, their duties being purely concerned with matters of state.   They therefore eat and drink freely and indulge themselves in every respect.

Mourning for the dead.   On the day of the funeral the mourners sleep round the grave and on the following day they build huts around the tomb, in which they live until the mourning ends.   Each mourner wears a girdle of dried plantain leaves round the waist, the knot by which the girdle is tied being made at the back, this is a distinctive feature of mourning; they also wear a band of plantain fibre round the head.   At dawn of each day the mourners prostrate themselves on the grave and wail, calling upon the dead to return, asking why he has left them, and what they are to do without him: they remain at the grave wailing from two to three hours, taking turns to prostrate themselves and utter their cry.   At the end of three weeks a quantity of beer is brought by relatives

who have not been able to take part in the mourning; those
mourners who feel unable to continue mourning, or who are
disinclined to remain longer, drink the beer and return to
their ordinary occupations. Some of the beer is poured on
the ground at the head of the grave before any is drunk, the
remainder is drunk and those who drink it must retire, as must
also any who have not kept the strict rule of sexual avoidance
or who have broken any other taboo of mourning. No married
woman may return home alone; her husband must come for
her, and he must redeem her by bringing a pot of beer and a goat,
for unless he does this she must remain in the neighbourhood
with members of her clan even when the mourning ends. A
wife is not allowed to drink beer with the others who wish to
retire at the end of three weeks, unless her husband has come
for her. Mourners are always members of one clan and are
so related that there is seldom any danger of their yielding to
sexual desires; and the widows live apart in the tomb itself
and are thus safe from temptation. It is believed that the
earth on the grave will crack and that the couple who do wrong
will be killed by the ghost, should any mourner yield to such
desires during the period of mourning. When therefore any
man or woman is guilty of any breach of continence, he or she
flees away in order to be safe from the ghost.

Ceremony to end mourning. When the heir announces
that the mourning is to end, the clan and friends bring pots of
beer to the grave. The mourners open the grave, removing all
the earth from the uppermost bark-cloths and spreading a
number of new bark-cloths over the old ones. The earth is
replaced and beer is poured on it for the dead, as it is thrown
in; this binds it together, and a small mound is made over
the grave, beaten hard, and rubbed smooth. In the morning
the sisters of the deceased man boil butter and smear the
mound over the grave with it and make the clay perfectly
smooth; after this ceremony the mourners shave their heads
and bathe in some stream and return for a meal which is eaten
together. They are then free to return to their homes. Before
the mourning ends the lower jaw-bone of a chief is removed,
cleansed and wrapped in a skin well decorated with cowry-

shells. It is then taken to a temple in a remote part of the
district where the jaw-bones of all former chiefs have been
placed and are preserved. The guardian is a priest and
medium; he holds converse with the ghost and conveys any
message to the ruling chief

During the time of mourning the door of the house is
thrown into the open space before the gateway and is left
there as a sign to other people not to enter the enclosure
because of the mourning. When the rites end and the mourning ceases, the house is deserted and never repaired; no
person may live in it, though the chief's house is built near
the site.

Burial customs in the Central District. In the Central
District, after a chief has been buried some months, his ghost
appears to one of the relatives and tells him, "I wish to
move." The new chief is told and at once orders the grave
to be opened and the skull, which has by this time dropped
into the wooden bowl mentioned above, is taken out of
the grave, and the earth is filled in again. The skull is
cleansed and three skins are made ready to enclose it, one
being that of a cow, the second that of a sheep, and the third
that of a gazelle; the beads the chief wore round his neck
are used to fill in the eye-sockets. Before the first skin is
wrapped around the skull, it is damped and stretched tightly
round the skull and stitched; when it dries, it becomes very
tight. The second skin is treated in the same manner and,
when it is dry, the last skin is added in the same way. The
outside is then decorated with cowry-shells.

Disposal of the skull of a chief. A woman is sought from the
clan to which the nurse of the deceased chief belonged and she is
taken to the new chief, who explains to her the duty of guarding
the skull and how she is to become the medium of the ghost
and attend to its wants. She is furnished with a female goat,
a cow and a hen, which are intended to provide food for the
ghost. A special escort conducts the woman to a place called
Nakazungu, which is on the Mpologoma river, where a large
house is built for her. The skull is put into a shrine, which is
more of the nature of a temple; it is the house of the ghost.

In this temple the skull of the last chief is always kept in state until another chief dies, when his skull takes the place of the former.   The skull which is removed is taken to a forest on an island in the river Mpologoma, where it is deposited in the open with the skulls of former chiefs; a spear is also taken from the temple and is stuck into the ground beside the skull.   The woman who was guardian of the skull and medium of the ghost of the previous chief goes to live in the forest, there to continue her duties as medium to the ghost which she still represents, though few people ever seek any oracle from this chief when there is the new ghost in the temple.   This sacred forest has a special guardian who has general charge of the skulls and mediums.   When a skull is removed from the temple and added to the number in the forest, special offerings are made: a cow, a sheep and a goat are offered, which must be white, the offering being made in the forest and the meat being left with the guardian, who is also given a woman to wife.   When the escort returns to the chief and gives him the account of their journey and all they have done, how the skull is installed and the other taken to the forest, he kills an ox and they have a special meal with a free supply of beer.   The new chief sends offerings to the ghost of his father, and the medium becomes possessed by the ghost and reveals the wishes of the deceased.

Treatment of dead peasants.   When a peasant dies, the death-wail begins as soon as the man is known to be dead and the funeral rites take place at once.   The grave is dug in the house while the body, after being washed and prepared for the funeral, lies outside for the final farewell ceremony, when the relatives file past and gaze on the features.   The burial takes place the same day, when the grave is filled in and the earth beaten hard over it; the main posts of the house are removed and the roof is allowed to fall down upon the grave.

Burial of women, unmarried men and children.   Women, young unmarried men and children are buried in the gardens near the house in which they lived, because they have no house of their own.   Ornaments are frequently put upon the dead

to enrich them in the ghost-world.   When a man's wife dies,
her relatives supply her husband with another wife to become
heir to the dead woman.   The husband makes a present to
the clan, but pays no marriage-fee.   At harvest time shrines
are usually rebuilt near graves, and offerings to the dead are
made to secure their blessing upon the harvest and full enjoy-
ment of the crops.

CHAPTER XXII

GOVERNMENT, INDUSTRIES, PLEASURES, BUILDING AND WARFARE

The chief the owner of the land—sub-chiefs and their powers—inheritance—disposal of property in the Central District—adultery—fornication condoned—magistrates—theft—agriculture the chief pursuit—sowing seed and harvest customs—blessing of twins sought when sowing seed—cow-keeping—cow-keeping in the Central District—breeding sheep and goats—women forbidden to eat fowls and eggs in the Central District—hunting customs—hunting the hippopotamus—hunting small game—building methods—building customs in the Central District—dress and ornaments—scarifications—causes of war—weapons and methods of fighting—making peace in the Central District—insecurity of life—blood feuds.

The chief the owner of the land. Each of these three districts of Busoga is governed by a paramount chief who is said to be the owner of the land. His family has for many generations been the head of the tribe and his relatives have been the undisputed rulers. For many years the chief of a district has been under the suzerainty of another country: for some time this has been Uganda, though all the details of government of each district have been left with the paramount chief and there has been no appeal to Uganda, except in the question of a man taking his place as heir to a deceased chief when there have usually been several claimants for possession. Each district has numbers of sub-chiefs; indeed a peasant may become a chief at any time, if he can so advance himself as to be able to provide enough cattle to pay the paramount chief a handsome present, and if he also has a few men at his command. Once a sub-chief is established in office, he pays no taxes because there are no taxes levied in the country by any chief; still, a peasant acknowledges his over-chief by giving him presents of goats, sheep and, sometimes, a cow, and by making him gifts of beer and food, and especially at harvest by sending to him quantities of grain. The paramount chief appoints sub-chiefs, and has the power to depose them if he wishes to do so, but he seldom deposes a man except for some flagrant fault. Chiefs who purchase their land regard it as freehold and cannot be deposed.

Sub-chiefs and their powers. These sub-chiefs have little power over their peasants and it is only in disputes, when they act as magistrates, that the majority of peasants look up to them for any guidance. Should a man wish to have the freehold rights of a plot of land, he first consults the medicineman, who divines whether the place is free from ghosts and ascertains that it will be a healthy spot for the man and his family and also likely to yield good crops. Having received satisfactory accounts of a site the man pays the District chief a sum for the land; the next thing is to dig a portion of his ground and in the cultivated plot to dig a pit. He then calls a few friends and members of his clan to come and witness a ceremony and assist him in it. He kills a goat over the pit as an offering to the earth-god and lets the blood of his victim run into the pit. The animal's head is laid in the pit together with the head of a tortoise, and he then cooks the meat of the goat and eats a meal with his friends by the pit, afterwards filling in the earth and burying the heads of the goat and tortoise. He may then plant his field with plantains and sow his seeds and the earth-god gives his blessing. He also knows that no man can ever turn him off that plot of land: it is his and his children's after him.

Inheritance. At death a man's property passes to the possession of the clan; it is the duty of the leading members of the clan to decide who shall be the successor to any deceased person. A son of the deceased is given the first consideration, but the members do not feel obliged to make a son heir because, by the laws of the tribe, all men of the clan are related and therefore have an equal right to any property a man may leave at his death. If, therefore, the responsible members of the clan consider another man better qualified to become the heir than one of the real sons, they do not hesitate to appoint him. The sons feel no grievance, if they are overlooked in the disposal of their father's property; they hope they may be chosen to inherit the goods of some other person in the near future. When a man dies having a large herd of cattle, it is usual to give some to each of his children; if there are only a few beasts, they are given to the heir, who is responsible for the debts of the deceased and has to settle them, if the claims are made within a reasonable time after the death of the debtor. One ox is set aside to be speared by the heir at the funeral. The clan-bracelet is taken from the wrist of the dead man and is put on the wrist of the heir. Household property is usually divided among the children. Widows are given the choice to go to the heir, to go to the sons, or to return to their own clan. Should they decide to go to their own clan, their relatives are requested to restore the sum that was paid them at the time of marriage. There are times when a widow elects to go to some member of the clan of her deceased husband other than a son, and this is permissible. It is permissible for a man to marry any of his father's widows provided they are not from the same clan as his own mother.

Disposal of property in the Central District. In the Central District it is the custom when any man dies, having grown-up sons, for these young men to try to remove all their father's property and leave the clan and heir the land only. The bailiff tries to rescue the property and often has to resort to force of arms to preserve it, especially to secure any cattle there may be.

Adultery. Men are much more lenient with their wives in Busoga when they have yielded to sexual desires than in Uganda. A husband will pardon his wife for two or three offences, if she promises to be faithful in the future; should she continue her evil course, after being warned, the husband divorces her and demands the marriage-fee from her clan. If the woman returns to her clan, they refund the money; but, if she goes to live with her lover, he has to pay the amount. This plan of divorce and repayment is the usual and common form of law for settling cases of adultery.

In the Central District when a man is proved to be guilty of adultery, he is fined a cow.

Fornication condoned. An unmarried woman is not condemned for unchastity, unless she becomes with child. Should a man discover his sister in this condition, he questions her as to her lover; the man is then questioned and asked to marry the woman and told the amount he is expected to pay. If he does not pay this fee and take the woman to wife, the brother turns her adrift in disgrace and she has to find a home with some member of another clan. Such outcasts are welcomed by other clans who take care of the woman and, when her child is born, they provide for her and her infant until she marries, when they claim the marriage-fee. When a sister is thus turned out by her brother, he calls in a medicine-man who kills a goat and cooks a meal for the inmates, thus purifying the house from any taint and propitiating the god of the family; the skin of the sacrificial animal, with any food that is over, the medicine-man carries away with him and thus removes all evil from the family.

Treatment of fornication in the Central District. In the Central District when an unmarried woman is found with child she must not eat with her parents or any member of her family, she has her meals alone. When she confesses the name of her seducer, he is tried and if proved guilty, the woman is sent to live with him as his wife. When the child is born, the man takes a sheep and a goat as a peace-offering to the woman's parents, a medicine-man comes and purifies the guilty couple, the animals are killed and all eat a meal together in the open air. The man then brings the marriage-fee and the woman is his legitimate wife.

Magistrates. Each chief is a magistrate in his neighbourhood; to him any man may go, if he has a complaint to make. He pays his fee of a fowl or a goat or, it may be, only a few cowry-shells, and the chief summons the accused to appear and account for his doings. The case is tried and the punishment inflicted according to the offence. The judge is paid a goat by the man who wins the case.

Theft. Theft is common in Busoga; the people bear the

name throughout this part of Africa of being the greatest adepts at thieving. When a man is accused of theft, he may appeal to some test; a favourite test is for a medicine-man to flick a glass-bead into the accused man's eye, and, should it stick, he is guilty but if it falls out he is innocent. Another test is to heat an ordinary earthen pot with fire and apply it to the stomach of the accused man: if it sticks to the flesh, the man is guilty but, if it comes away leaving no mark, he is innocent. The punishment for theft is to deprive the guilty person of all his property.

Industries.

Agriculture the chief pursuit. Agriculture is the chief pursuit of these people; every household has its field and the house is built on or adjoining the field or arable land, whether the householder be a tenant or the owner. Chiefs generally build a high fence round their houses with only one gateway leading through it which can be shut and guarded against intrusion. In this enclosure the chief may have several wives and some slaves in addition to his retainers: sometimes they number over a hundred in all. To keep these wives and retainers supplied with food he has extensive groves of plantains; each wife has her plot of land and has room on one side or other to reclaim more land, should she desire to do so. As the man adds to the number of his wives he also increases the land under cultivation. A man assists his wife or wives in their work in the fields and does the heavier work in the plantain groves. The chief food is plantain supplemented by sweet potatoes. Millet is grown for brewing beer; few people ever grow it for flour, the majority use it for making malt for fermenting their beer, the kind usually grown being a bitter kind unfit for flour. Many women have a plot of sesame and yams, and a few grow beans and peas with a little maize, but these are all luxuries and not necessaries of life. Before grain is sown the owner carries a little seed to the medicine-man, who powders certain herbs over it to cause it to grow and also to keep off insects and birds; the owner also carries back some herbs to spread over the field. When the seed grows and is in ear and the people are afraid of birds robbing it, they obtain powdered herbs from the medicine-man and scatter this powder over the field; the workers must remain quiet for some time after scattering the powder as otherwise it will lose its efficacy. Should any person passing salute the workers, they must not reply but ignore the greeting; the period for which silence is enjoined is the day on which the herb-powder is scattered.

When a newly-married couple begin housekeeping and cultivate their first crop of millet, they take a little of the first-fruits to the husband's father before they use any of the harvest themselves.

Sowing and harvest customs. At the beginning of each season, before sowing, a medicine-man is consulted and gives his blessing to the land and seed; and, when the harvest is reaped, the people take a few grains of corn in each hand and throw them over their shoulders, first the right and then the left, saying, "Give us blessing in eating." A few grains are then thrown in front and the words are repeated.

The blessing of twins sought at sowing seed in the Central District. In the Central District, when a woman has twins, the people to whose clan she belongs do not sow any seed until the twins have been brought to the field. A pot of cooked grain is set before the children with a cake of sesame and all the seed that is to be sown. The food is eaten by the people assembled and afterwards the field is sown in the presence of the twins; the plot is then said to be the field of the twins. The mother of twins must sow her seed before any person of her clan will sow theirs. The medicine-man sends special herbs to mix with the seed which is to be sown. When the harvest is ripe, the people take a little of each kind of food from the field and put it in the road to be walked on by all passers. This action is said to ensure safety in eating the food.

When a woman is about to sow beans, she adds a little butter to the basket of seeds and stirs them up until all the seed is well greased, and in this greasy state they are put into a bag generally used for keeping salt. This seed is said to be certain to grow with the butter and any salt that may cling to it from the sides of the bag. It is also customary for a woman to smear butter on her body when she goes to weed and hoe her plot of beans, because it is said to impart powers of fertilization to the beans.

Cow-keeping. The tribe of Basoga are fond of cows; even a peasant strives to have his cow. The kind of cow commonly known as the Busoga cow is a smaller breed than either the Uganda or the Ankole breeds and is mostly black or black and white, with an inclination to a hump. Chiefs keep their cows in a small kraal and the cattle are always in the open by night, whereas peasants keep their animals in the house with the family, the cow having its special place near the door. When a cow has a calf, its milk is taboo for general use, and some male member of the family is set apart to drink it during the first few days until the navel-cord falls from the calf. The boy or man who drinks the milk observes certain restrictions such as not drinking milk from any other cow, and he eats no salt. When the stump of cord falls from the calf, a number of relatives come together and drink the first lot of milk, and after the ceremony the milk becomes common to all members of the family. Women are strictly excluded from milking or herding or from having anything to do with the cows; they must not come into contact with the animals, they may churn, wash the milk-vessels and smoke them only. Butter is chiefly used for anointing the body, but it is also used as food with their plantains when desired.

Cow-keeping in the Central District. In the Central District, when a cow calves, it is milked, but the milk is boiled and set aside until the stump of the umbilical cord falls from the calf. When this takes place, the owner of the cow calls his friends together and provides each of them with a small cup made of plantain-leaf, and they drink the milk. The cow is tied near by during the ceremony and, when the milk is drunk the men pass the cow and tap it on the head between the horns with the cups, as they pass. The calf is next brought out of the house into the open for all to see, this being the first time that it comes out of the house from the time of its birth. After this ceremony the milk is common to all and women may also drink it.

Sheep and goats. Few sheep are kept in comparison with goats, though there is no special reason why they should not be more commonly bred, except that the people find that goats are more prolific and they have moreover come to like the flesh better than that of sheep. Busoga is noted for a kind of long-haired goat which seems to thrive there, whereas in other parts of the country its coat is not nearly so good. The hair is often ten and sometimes twelve inches long and is used for decorative purposes: head-dresses, shields, drums and trumpets are frequently decorated with this beautiful hair. Some chiefs also wear aprons of this skin, when going to war. Women are forbidden to eat mutton and fowls, though they may freely eat goat's flesh. Sheep are said to be much hardier than goats, and lambs go out to pasture at birth with the mother, though kids are kept at home until about a month old. The Busoga sheep is much larger and finer than the sheep of Uganda and has an enormous tail which trails on the ground. Sheep are clubbed to death, as in Uganda; it is thought to be a sure token of some misfortune, should a sheep see the man who comes forward to kill it. Goats are kept in large flocks and are bred chiefly for paying off debts and for purchasing wives. Every peasant has a number of goats which sleep in the houses of his wives, tethered by a foot to a peg in the ground near the wall. Children herd the flocks in the vicinity of their houses. Few people will kill and eat goats, except they be chiefs or wealthy men. The common people, though very fond of butcher's meat, live almost entirely upon vegetable food.

Women forbidden to eat fowls and eggs. In the Central District women may eat the flesh of either sheep or goats. There are no restrictions forbidding mutton, as in so many parts of Africa among Bantu tribes; fowls only are forbidden and their eggs are also forbidden to women.

Fishing. Along the banks of the river Nile, and also along the shores of the Lake Victoria, there are fishermen who give their time to this industry and, though they have fields and grow plantains, still their principal occupation is fishing, agriculture being left to their wives. Basket-traps and lines let down in deep water with the end of the rope attached to floats are the chief means of fishing on the Lake, though the rod and line are also used. On the river Nile basket-traps form the principal method of fishing. A large quantity of the fish caught is smoked over wood fires so that it will keep several weeks. Smoked fish is carried many miles to inland markets where it is bartered for food, or for things such as household utensils, salt, iron and clothing.

Hunting customs. The country does not furnish extensive hunting-grounds, and is too small in area and too thickly populated to be a home for wild animals. Herds of elephants, however, at times cross the country when passing from one feeding-ground to another; and there are men who are ever ready to risk their lives in the hope of obtaining a tusk of ivory and meat which they can turn to profit. Before going out on an expedition a hunter pays a visit to the god of the chase. The god is supposed to inhabit uncultivated land, and thither the hunter with some of his followers repairs, taking with him a goat and a fowl. These victims are killed and their blood, with the heads, is offered to the god. The meat is then cooked and eaten by the worshippers, who ask the god to give them success and to protect them from danger. After this meal the man collects his beaters, of whom he likes to have a large number, even a hundred when possible. The only weapon they use when going out to hunt elephants is the spear. The elephant-spear is a special kind, the blade of it is of the usual leaf-shape pattern; but it has a long iron shank, some eighteen inches long, with a socket into which a short heavy wooden shaft is fitted. The end of the shaft has a large knob to make the spear heavy, and to it a long cord is attached, the other end being tied to the tree where the hunter hides. He selects a tree with branches hanging over the path, and upon this he takes his stand and throws his spear as the animal passes under him. Several huntsmen climb trees and hide, while the beaters surround the herd of animals and drive them under the trees, the chief huntsman being given time to choose and strike his animal before the others attempt to spear any of them. When an animal is speared, it usually stops and trumpets and looks for its foe, which enables the other huntsmen to discover it. One of them now calls to it and, as it rushes forward to the place whence the sound comes, it is again speared The rope attached to the spear tears it out of the flesh, as the animal flees away, and gives the man time to recover his weapon and use it again, when possible. By calling to an animal, huntsmen can usually detain and kill it, though at times they have to follow a wounded beast for several days before they can come up with it. One tusk of an animal becomes the property of the chief huntsman, and the second belongs to the chief in whose district the beast is killed. The meat is cut up and dried for sale. The men usually build huts where the animal drops and cut up the flesh, dry it upon frames over wood fires and then carry it off for sale. After a successful hunt an offering is taken to the god of the chase. During their expedition huntsmen are careful to abstain from washing and from any contact with women.

Hunting the hippopotamus. Preparations for hunting the hippopotamus are much the same as those for elephant hunting. Weapons are taken to the god of the chase for his blessing and are sharpened. The weapon used in this case is a harpoon attached to a float. The men go out in canoes to a place known to be frequented by hippopotamuses and wait for an animal to rise in the water. The hunter throws his harpoon with sufficient force to drive it home and the men paddle away to some place of safety. When an animal is thus harpooned, it tries to escape by diving, unless it sees the canoe, when it will make an effort to come up with it and, if successful, it will destroy it and possibly kill some of the men; or they may be drowned, as few canoe-men can swim. A speared animal is awaited until it has to rise to breathe, when it is again harpooned and possibly killed. When dead it is towed to the shore and its flesh is cut up and dried in the sun. The meat is very fat and only a few people care to eat it.

Small game. Small game is hunted into nets which are

stretched to enclose some yards of scrub, and beaters drive the animals into them with clubs and dogs. Beaters go armed with clubs and spears and also have a number of dogs, two or three of which have bells tied round their bodies to indicate where they are; the people also say that bells protect dogs from the attacks of snakes. These men drive game into the nets, and other men are stationed beside the net, hidden behind some bush where they await the animals and spear them down when they become entangled in the net. Before going to hunt the chief huntsman goes into the bush, taking a fowl with him, and calls upon the god of the chase to help them and to give them success. He kills the fowl and pours the blood on the ground and afterwards burns the fowl to dust which he scatters in all directions, as he calls upon the god for success. Meat taken in a hunt is divided before the men leave the spot where it was taken, the entrails of the animal being given to the dogs, a leg reserved for the chief of the district, and the remainder divided equally among all who took part in the hunt. During an expedition no hunter may wash his hands or body.

Building. The style of architecture is similar to that of Uganda. A dome framework of reeds or thin canes, resting upon pillars of stout trees and thatched thickly, is the Busoga house. When about to build, a man measures out the site he wants for his house and levels it; he then plants his poles, which are to support the frame, in lines ranging in height from the central poles to those near the sides. The roof always comes down to the ground on all sides and the doorway is cut into this dome, and a porch is built over it. Thatching begins at the ground and ends with a pinnacle at the top. The poles are always the most difficult part of the work and often have to be carried long distances, and frequently twenty-nine or more men are necessary to carry each tree to make a pole. The reeds and grass are brought by each workman as he goes to his work daily. Men go to work about seven o'clock in the morning and leave at about two o'clock in the afternoon. The floor is of clay beaten hard and smeared over with cow-dung. Each house is divided into two rooms, the back room being used as the sleeping apartment. Often, in peasants' houses, the division is made by a bark-cloth only; in good houses the division is a reed-wall. The fire is made in the middle of the floor, where a log of wood smoulders by day and is made to blaze by night. There are no sanitary arrangements in connection with a house; the garden is the usual place to relieve nature, and the excretions are covered with a little earth, thus keeping the place from becoming foul. When a man enters a new hut, his wife cooks a special meal, and a few friends are called in to share it and thus give the house its warming.

Building customs in the Central District. In the Central District, when a man is building a new house, he must live with his first wife only, during the time the building is proceeding; should he fail to observe this restriction, it is believed that mishap will befall the house. It is customary with wealthy people to have their special sleeping-house and to invite first one wife and then another to come and share it; but in the case of poorer men, with only one or at most three wives, the husband goes to live in the house of first one wife and then another.

Dress. The universal dress is a bark-cloth dyed black or a dark-grey, nearly black. The dye is a black clay frequently found in swamps. In earlier times skins of animals were commonly worn as loin-cloths, but the introduction of bark-cloth has entirely superseded the skin-garment and the latter is seldom seen. Almost every man wears a waist-belt with a piece of bark-cloth threaded under it and passed between the legs from back to front. This is the essential dress and without it men are said to be naked; it is the only dress worn by men when at work. The larger bark-cloth is thrown over the left shoulder and passes under the right arm with the end thrown over the left shoulder again, thus leaving the right arm free for use. Women wear their bark-cloth wrapped round the body, passing under the arms and secured round the waist by a girdle of the same material. They thus have both arms free for use, without discarding the bark-cloth when they wish to work, as is done by men. The upper part of the body is mostly naked when women are at work and their bark-cloth falls down to the waist. Most boys have only the strip of bark-cloth passed between the legs secured under their waist-band, girls frequently go naked until grown up, when they wear bark-cloth loin-cloths. Among poor people the bark-cloth worn by day is their only bedclothing by night. This is due to idleness and want of the application needed to make more cloth rather than to any other cause, for each man grows the trees in his field and can himself make the cloth, if he wishes to do so.

Ornaments. There are no special tribal markings by mutilation beyond the extraction of the two front lower incisors. The loss of these teeth has a marked effect upon the pronunciation which gives the Basoga a peculiar dialect. Both men and women wear bracelets of brass and iron, and are fond of carrying one or two on each wrist. Each clan has its large heavy bracelet which is passed down from chief to chief as a valuable possession to be guarded for the clan.

Warfare.

Causes of war, weapons and methods of fighting. The Basoga are a peaceful people. There have never been any prolonged wars of a serious nature, the only wars they have to record being tribal conflicts when, owing to some ceremonial customs, a man of another tribe has been captured and killed to end a taboo and thus has been the means of interrupting friendly relations and embroiling the two tribes; or again, when there has been a disagreement, perhaps through theft or infringement of their rights by members of another tribe, and, it being impossible to obtain redress, they have resorted to arms. The call to war is by the sounding of a special rhythm on large drums. Immediately men, old and young, arm themselves with shields, spears and slings, assemble at the residence of their overchief and march to the paramount chief, who leads the army in person to some place on the border where they are sure to meet a force of the other tribe. The opposing armies face each other until some braver and bolder warriors rush out of the ranks and meet one or two of their opponents, when a hand-to-hand fight takes place and one or more may be wounded or killed. The men with slings often do the most damage by slinging stones which injure the heads of their enemies and frequently cause ugly wounds which at times result in death. Three or four days may be spent in this peculiar kind of fighting; each night the armies withdraw and sleep in peace, and begin operations again in the morning. After two or three days, when one or two men have been killed and a number wounded, peace is declared, the chiefs settle the dispute, and the armies return home.

Warfare in the Central District. When peace is declared after any war, in the Central District, the party desiring peace plant young plantain-trees in the sight of their enemies, which betokens the desire for an armistice and for the opening of peace negotiations.

Insecurity of life. It is never safe for a man to walk about alone on the frontier of a district, as he is always liable to be caught by people wanting to end some sacred ceremony with the life-blood of another person. When men from different tribes attend a beer-drinking feast, they go armed, and, should a quarrel ensue over their cups, they will fight it out. At times it happens that one or two of the party may be killed. Such deaths cause feuds and lay on the clans the task of avenging the blood, unless the matter can be settled amicably. The clan whose member has been killed will seek to capture a man from the offending clan and kill him. Sometimes they succeed in capturing one of its members, most often a youth in the road. The captive is dragged away to the grave of the man who was killed and has his throat cut over the grave, the body being left near it in order to make atonement to the ghost. Women are never caught or punished for the offences of the men. They are exempt, and sometimes a woman will marry into a clan which is hostile to her own, even though the members cannot meet to make any marriage arrangements. In such cases she will go forth, fully understanding that she is breaking with her own clan in marrying the man of her choice who belongs to its sworn foes.

Blood feuds. In the Central District the blood-feud may

last for months and even for years, and several people may be killed before the question can be settled. The injured party will capture some person from the murderer's clan and kill him, whereupon the other party will retaliate by capturing and killing some one else, and this state of things will continue for months, first one party killing a man and then the other, until at length they decide to come to terms and settle the question by arbitration.

CHAPTER XXIII

RELIGIOUS BELIEFS

Worship of the dead and worship of the gods—the goddess Nalongo—the
goddess Nawandyo—the god Ingo—the gods Male and Luhanga—
the goddess Nakiwulo who detects thieves—the god of plague—
religious beliefs in the Central District—the god of death—Mukama
the Creator—Gasani, the giver of children—tree-spirits—tree-
spirits in the Central District—rock-spirits—the earth god of the
Central District—Kumbya the rock-spirit—fetishes—the fetish
Nakalondo—the fetish Nambaga—Gomba, the fetish of women—
fetishes of the Central District—rain-making—human sacrifices in
rain-making—statistics from the North-western District.

Worship of the dead and worship of the gods. In all parts
of Busoga worship of the dead forms a most important part
of the religion of the people, and the belief in ghosts and the
propitiation of them are the chief features of their most constant
and regular acts of worship. The gods, with fetishes and amulets,
are able to do great things for the living; but, after all, it is the
ghost that is most feared and obtains the most marked attention
In childbirth, in sickness, in prosperity, and in death, ghosts
materially help or hinder matters; hence it behoves the living
to keep on good terms with them. It is because of this
belief that people frequently make sacrifices of fowls and
other animals to the dead and constantly seek their help.
First and foremost, it is because of the firm conviction of the
presence of ghosts that the elaborate funeral ceremonies are
performed which have been noted above. In the beliefs of
these primitive people we must relegate gods to a secondary
place after the worship of the dead. It will be noticed that no
god is believed to influence the future life of man nor do they
think of ghosts as dwelling with the gods.

There are a few temples in which are priests and mediums, but the worship is not developed to any great extent; the chief gods are given below with brief accounts of their worship and their special functions.

The goddess Nalongo. Nalongo is a goddess and receives the greatest honour in the North-western District. Her temple is kept in good repair by the state and there is a portion of land attached to her temple sufficient to provide food for her following of priests and servants. Any man or woman in the country with a large navel is sent to this temple as a servant to the goddess. The aid of this goddess is sought when any epidemic, such as small-pox, plague, or fever, attacks the inhabitants of the district. The people offer cows, sheep, and fowls when they make their requests at her temple.

The goddess Nawandyo. Nawandyo is another goddess who is provided for by the state, has a portion of land attached to her temple, and has offerings made to her of servants, cows, sheep, goats, fowls, and beer. Her aid is sought for in any private case of sickness or when any trouble comes upon a family. The suppliants never go empty-handed when they seek her aid.

The god Ingo. Ingo is also a public god who attends to the general needs of the people. His temple is built by the state and he possesses land and slaves. The principal feature in his worship is that only members of the chief families and aristocracy may provide grass for carpeting the temple. When offerings of cows, sheep or goats are taken to him they have garlands of wild creepers festooned round their necks.

The gods Male and Luhanga. Male is another god of great power. He never accepts any women-slaves or servants; men only are allowed to come near him. Luhanga is also an important god to whom supplications may be made on ordinary occasions.

The goddess Nakiwulo, who detects thieves. Nakiwulo is a goddess who detects thieves and is able to trace lost property and missing cattle. When a suppliant goes to this deity he takes his offering of a sheep or a fowl, and makes his statement of the lost property. The priest then resorts to the medium, who seeks the desired information from the deity, becomes possessed by the goddess and tells where the lost property is and who has stolen it. The matter then becomes a question for the magistrate, who will send and capture the thief, obtain the missing property, and punish the thief.

The god of plague. Bijungo is the god of plague and is a rock-spirit. He is greatly feared, though he has no temple nor indeed any permanent shrine, nor has he any regular priest or medium. When the god wishes to make his desires known, he takes possession of some person, it may be a man or a woman; the person mounts a rock and calls out to the people, who assemble to hear what the god has to say. They are told that plague is imminent and are informed what offering they ought to make and when a sacred meal should be held at the base of the rock to avert plague. Should the plague have already begun, and should there be any patients, they are told the remedies to use in order to restore them to health. Offerings may be of sheep or goats and the meal is eaten at the base of the rock where the blood is offered to the god.

Other gods are Kabaganya, Nende and Kagulu, whose worship is much the same as those mentioned above.

Religious beliefs in the Central District. In the Central District worship is more highly developed than in the North-western District; there are more temples and a higher and more elaborate cult is followed.

The god of death. The god of death is known by the name Semuganda. He is a python, having five sons whose names are Kintu, Kiwanuka, Bijingo, Kabamba and Meru, and each of whom is a god. Offerings of black cows, goats, sheep and fowls are made to the deity. Women seek the aid of this god to give children. When a woman has asked such a favour and she gives birth to a child, she dedicates the child to the god in recognition of the boon granted. Men seek the assistance of this god when they wish to become wealthy and important land owners. Should one of these pythons die or be accidentally killed when it has left the temple and is wandering about, the people beat drums and wail as they carry it to a place of burial. It is buried in some place near the temple,

where it is covered with creepers of wild gourd. After the
burial another python is appointed to take the place of the
dead reptile.

Mukama, the creator. Mukama is the great creator who
made man and beast. At one period he is said to have lived
in a deep hole on Mount Elgon, where, with his sons, he worked
iron and forged all the hoes which were first introduced into
the land. He is also the creator of all rivers, which are said
to have their source at his home. Should a child be born
with teeth already cut, it is said to be a reincarnation of
Mukama; a hut is built for the child and a high fence built
around it, and the mother with the infant is placed there
during her seclusion. When this period ends, the child is
shown to relatives and friends. A vessel of water is brought
from Lake Kyoga and also a reed from the papyrus-grass
by the husband's sister's son, who has to go secretly to the
lake; he must not be seen by any person, neither as he goes
nor as he returns. He takes with him four coffee-berries which
he offers to the water-spirit of the lake, as he draws the water.
Two houses are built for the reception of the child when the
period of seclusion ends; one is intended for a sleeping-house
and the other for a living-house. The mother with her child
is conducted to this new home with great ceremony. In front
walks the sister's son, carrying the papyrus-reed as a spear,
and behind him follow a number of medicine-men. Next
comes a woman carrying a native iron hoe which she brandishes
as she walks. She utters a shrill cry as women do when in
danger, in order to warn people of their approach. Behind
this woman come members of the parents' clan, and, last of
all, the parents with the child. The mother is escorted into
the living-room where a sacred meal is eaten, and after
the meal the child is brought out and has its head shaved,
the water brought from the lake being used to wet the head
for shaving and to wash it after the shaving has taken place.
After the ceremony of shaving is ended, the father gives his
shield to the child. The company remain three days with
the mother and her child. On the third day the papyrus-reed
is handed to the child who is appointed governor over a

portion of land. The mother remains with her child, her husband giving her up to this duty, and her clan presents him with another wife instead of the mother of Mukama. The child is now regarded as a god, and people come to him to make requests for any purpose. When he dies, a medium is appointed to hold converse with him and to give his replies to suppliants.

Gasani, the giver of children. Gasani is the god who has control over the births of children in general; twins are always ascribed to him. When twins are born and the medicine-men have been appointed to take care of them, they go to a place where two roads cross and dig up some of the earth from the path; the earth is put into a basket with a few beans, a little sesame and a little millet, two fowls are also brought with the basket to the house in which the mother with her children is secluded. The man who carries the basket sings special songs at the highest pitch of his voice as he carries the earth, a shrine is built near the house in which the twins live and the basket with its contents and the fowls are deposited in it after being solemnly offered to the god Gasani. This shrine is the place to which barren women go to make offerings to the god, to ask his blessing and seek the gift of children.

Tree-spirits. Every large tree has a resident spirit, and this makes a man careful not to cut down any tree unless proper precautions are taken. There is one kind of large tree from which drums are made which is an exception to the rule; this tree may be felled without any ceremony being performed. When a large tree is wanted for building or for a canoe, the man who is going to fell it takes a goat or a fowl for an offering, kills it by the roots of the tree and pours out the blood on the roots. He cooks the meat and eats it with his companions who are going to work with him. After the meal he strikes one sharp cut into the tree with his axe and waits until the sap begins to flow, when he stoops and drinks some of it from the incision and thus becomes a brother of the tree. He may then fell the tree and use the timber as he wishes without any danger to himself or to his family.

Tree-spirits in the Central District. In the Central District there is a large sacred tree named *Kaliro*, which gives its name to the district. This tree receives all offerings made for permission to cut down any tree in the district; it is the father of all the trees in this part of the country. There is a medicineman connected with the tree who lives near it. When any person wishes to get timber he comes to the medicine-man and asks him to ascertain by oracle whether the particular tree he wants may be cut down or not. The suppliant who wishes to have the timber of the tree takes with him either a goat or a fowl when seeking permission to cut it down. The medicine-man makes the offering to the tree-spirit and as medium declares the wishes of the spirit. If all is well, the suppliant eats a meal near the tree with the medicine-man and any followers who may be present. Should a tree be cut down without seeking the spirit's permission or contrary to the spirit's wishes, the chief or one of his people will die in consequence.

Rock-spirits. Each piece of rock and large stone is said to have its spirit, which is always active in a district either for good or for evil. Various kinds of diseases, especially plague, are attributed to the malevolence of rock-spirits. When sickness or plague breaks out, the spirit invariably takes possession of some person of the place, either a man or a woman; and, under the influence of the spirit, the person mounts the rock and calls from it to the people. The chief and the medicine-men assemble the people, make an offering of a goat or a fowl to the spirit, and are then told how to act in order to stay the disease. After making known its wishes to the people, the spirit leaves the person and returns to the rock, and the medium goes home to his or her ordinary pursuits and may possibly never be used again by the spirit.

The earth god of the Central District. In the Central District Kitaka is the god of earthquakes; he is regarded as present in the form of a great stone or rock. A shrine is built beside this rock to receive offerings and is the place to which people go to pray to the god. Sometimes men disappear from the district and are said to have been spirited away by the god. Fowls and goats are offered at the rock, the blood is poured on the ground by the shrine, and the head of the goat or fowl sacrificed is buried by it.   The meat is cooked and eaten in the vicinity of the rock.

Sometimes the god is said to journey through the land and to cause the earth to quake, as he passes on his way.   He is always followed by another god, Kibaho, who is greatly feared because plague or sickness of some kind will almost be sure to happen, unless it can be averted.   When, therefore, Kitaka passes, medicine-men set to work to avert the evil which his follower will cause.   He passes, they say, from Mount Elgon to Lake Kyoga, and they call upon the people to cut a path for the god Kibaho that he may pass as rapidly as possible. In each sub-district the people cut down the grass and shrubs and smooth a road some ten feet wide, while others bring food and place it at the border of their territory to be carried on by those in the next sub-district.   This road is said to expedite the god and to carry him through to Lake Kyoga without doing any harm.   The people of the next region take up the work and pass on the food to their boundary; and in this manner the path is made and the food carried on with the additions from each sub-district, until Lake Kyoga is reached. There a canoe is ready, and the food is put into it and rowed to an island where a priest takes the food and offers it to the god by scattering it upon the water.   This offering averts plague and death.

Kumbya, the rock-spirit.   Kumbya is a large rock which gives the name to the Central District.   From this rock a spring flows, and prayers and offerings are made there to avert sickness.   Should any sickness appear in the district, the god is asked to heal the sick and to remove the cause of illness.

There are many rocks and large stones which are sacred in this part of the country, and are called *Misambwc*.   They are, indeed, local deities; and to them the people go under all manner of circumstances to pray for help.

Fetishes.   There is an extensive use of fetishes throughout Busoga.   Here, as in Uganda, the object of veneration is supposed to have the powers of the god it represents, by whose name it is called.   In many instances peasants say the fetish is the embodiment of the god, so that to have a fetish is to them the assurance of the presence of the god and they speak and act in its presence with the greatest reverence. Only skilled medicine-men are able to make fetishes, and they keep their knowledge secret and pass it on to men whom they train as their assistants and successors. These men use various stones, herbs, clay, and so on, which they pound and mix with the blood of fowls and goats to bind the compound together. Sometimes horns of various animals are the receptacles into which the compound is put; at other times it is moulded, dried, and stitched in leather cases. The medicine-men have the skins of various wild animals in which the compound is put, when horns are not used. These fetishes are sold to the people at high prices and the large amount asked for them keeps them from becoming common. The one on the accompanying plate cost a woman; the man who purchased it paid a slave-woman for it, and at his death passed it on to his son.

The fetish Nakalondo. Nakalondo is the fetish which a medicine-man uses when he is asked to discover who the culprit is that has caused the death of any one. The medicine-man goes to the house in which the dead man lies, or, should it be after the funeral has taken place, he repairs to the house in which the man died; he calls the relatives of the deceased together and in the evening they cover the doorway with a bark-cloth, sit in the dark and sing songs which the medicine-man leads, clapping their hands as they sing to the time of the songs. After some time the medicine-man calls for silence, and all sit listening. They may be kept waiting some time or they may receive the answer after a few moments of waiting; the answer comes in distinct words, spoken at the door, telling the name of the person who made the magic and caused the death. A reason frequently pleaded by a person who is thus accused of causing the death of a man is that the deceased contemplated murdering him and that in self-defence he was forced to work magic. He had been warned of the contemplated murder and acted first, thus causing the man's death.

The fetish Nambaga. Nambaga is the fetish that brings wealth to a man. The owner sits outside his house in the

Plate XX

(1) Fetish drum
(*Basoga Tribe*)

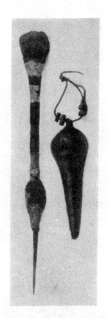

(2) Basoga fetishes

evening, smokes his pipe and holds his fetish in both hands, waving it to and fro as he puffs smoke on it. After a time the spirit of the fetish comes upon the man and instructs him how to act that he may become wealthy.

Gomba, the fetish of women. Gomba is a fetish which is able to assist women to become mothers. Women, especially young and newly-married women, seek the aid of this fetish. They tie a string of cowry-shells round it and make their requests to it for a child. Should the prayer be answered the woman after her purification shaves her head, pares the nails of both hands and feet, takes the hair and parings, ties them up into a ball with a strip of bark-cloth covering, and fastens them to the fetish. The woman's husband, or the owner of the fetish, now carries the ball and throws it away upon waste land, because it contains the evil that was upon the woman and which may work harm to other people if left about.

Fetishes of the Central District. In the Central District Gomba is a fetish said to protect the family. It is a long wand decorated with ivory discs, which are glued to the fetish with blood of goats and fowls which have been offered to it. The discs themselves are money offerings, being a kind of early currency. One end of the fetish has an iron prod, which can be stuck into the ground; and thus the fetish is made to stand upright, a position necessary for daily use. The fetish is used each morning to cleanse the family and remove any magical spell which may have been worked upon them during the night. Each morning the owner carries the fetish and places it by the door outside the house; and, as each member of the family passes it, he or she is cleansed, should there be any spell resting upon them which would have caused sickness and possibly death.

There are two fetishes of great renown, Nambaga and Namusisi, which are used in warfare. These fetishes are always made of sheep's horns. Warriors carry them about with them to make them brave and also to give them strength of arm and a sure aim when they direct their blow at a man. When a man carries either of these, the foe is also rendered incapable of injuring the wearer of the fetish.

Kazimba Kuigira is the fetish which protects the army against surprise and assures victory.

Kalera Baba is a fetish to guard children against illness in general, against evil-disposed persons and against ghosts. The child wears the fetish and is thus placed under the protection of the god.

Rain-making.

Rain-making. In the Central District there are very special ceremonies for rain-making. The chief of the district is responsible for the weather. He is believed to have power to send either rain or sunshine at will; he can give or withhold as he pleases. Hence, when there is a prolonged drought and the crops are suffering, the people go in a body and beg rain from him, asking him to use his influence to make the rain fall. Should it come in a few days, they are happy; but, should it still delay, they re-assemble and abuse the chief roundly for his callous behaviour and demand that he shall exert himself and cease to be so idle. This generally has the effect of rousing the chief, who makes an effort to obtain the needed rain. He calls together the leading medicine-men of the district and commands them to bring the herbs needed for the great ceremony of rain-making. Three black animals are brought, a black cow, goat, and fowl; these are killed and their blood is caught in vessels. Fires are lighted in an open space near the chief's house and large pots are set on them containing the blood of the animals, mixed with water and herbs, which is boiled until only a thick substance remains. As the steam rises, prayers are offered to the god of rain. The meat of these animals is eaten by the chief and the medicine-men. The medicine-men mix the blood and the herbs from the pots into two balls, one for the house of the chief and the other for the house of the principal medicine-man. Each ball has a stick in it, and a medicine-man carries them and puts one on each house. Each day these balls are smeared with some of the fat taken from the animals sacrificed, until the rain comes. When rain comes and food is obtained, the people take pots of beer to the chief as a thank offering, and a black ox to the medicine-man, in order that he may have fat for his fetishes.

Human sacrifice for rain-making. Another way of obtaining rain is by offering a human sacrifice to the god Kahango. This god is said to live in a deep hole in a part of the country known as *The Pit of Kahango*, where a priest dwells. A man is chosen by divination and is carried to the place of sacrifice. The victim is usually a cripple. He is laid near the edge of the pit on a bed of wild gourd creepers. The bearers are from a special clan who have this duty to perform. They also take with them an offering of a goat for a sacrifice and to supply the sacred meal with meat. As the victim is laid by the pit, the people say: "You, Kahango, if it is you who are keeping off the rain, accept this offering and let the rain come. If it is not you, then give this man strength to get up and walk back to us." The people retire some distance away, and after a reasonable time has been given and the man has not come, they look to see whether he has been drawn into the pit or not. Should he be missing, they kill the ox and eat a meal near the pit. The people say that it is seldom a man returns: he usually falls into the pit. The rain, they assert, invariably comes after such an offering. When the first-fruits are ready, some are taken to the god and presented to the priest, and afterwards the food may be consumed by all the clans concerned.

STATISTICS FROM THE NORTH-WESTERN DISTRICT

Women Questioned. No.	Children Born	Boys	Girls	Died in Infancy	Died Young	Grew to Maturity
1	3	2	1	1	1	1
2	7	2	5	5	—	2
3	7	4	3	4	1	2
4	6	3	3	—	4	2
5	8	5	3	2	—	6
6	10	5	5	4	—	6
7	2	1	1	2	—	—
8	8	5	3	2	—	6
9	6	4	2	1	—	5
10	2	1	1	1	—	1
11	5	3	2	3	—	2
12	6	2	4	2	—	4
13	4	2	2	1	—	3
14	6	4	2	2	3	1
15	10	4	6	3	4	3
16	5	2	3	2	2	1
17	7	4	3	2	2	3
18	8	3	5	4	3	1
19	4	2	2	—	1	3
20	8	5	3	3	2	3
21	7	3	4	4	3	—
22	10	4	6	3	4	3
23	9	5	4	2	3	4
24	6	2	4	3	1	2
25	15	6	9	8	2	5
26	8	4	4	3	3	2
27	10	4	6	5	2	3
28	4	3	1	2	2	—
29	6	2	4	1	3	2
30	6	4	2	4	1	1
31	8	3	5	3	2	3
32	5	3	2	4	1	—
33	10	5	5	2	4	4
34	11	5	6	4	5	2
35	7	4	3	2	3	2
36	9	6	3	4	2	3
	253	126	127	98	64	91

PART VI

THE NILOTIC TRIBES

THE BATESO

AND

THE KAVIRONDO

Plate XXI

(1) Nilotic Bateso

(2) Basoga band

CHAPTER XXIV

THE BATESO AND THEIR COUNTRY, GOVERNMENT, SOCIAL CUSTOMS AND RELIGION

The Bateso and their country. The Bateso are a tribe belonging to the Nilotic group, living in the Central Province of the Uganda Protectorate, and are supposed to number about a million people. Their country borders on Lake Kyoga and extends some miles to the north of it. The country is almost level, but has a few rocky hills with megaliths supported upon each other and looking as though a slight breeze would dislodge them and hurl them into the fields below. Many of the rocks have sacred associations connected with them, though there is no definite belief that they are tenanted by spirits. There is little wood in the country for household use and cooking, and timber for building purposes has to be carried long distances. The seasons are clearly defined: rain seldom falls during the dry season, but a strong dry wind blows daily. The people are commonly known as Bakedi, that is, 'naked people,' by their Bantu neighbours, because they wear no clothing. Both men and women are well built, their height being from five feet six inches to six feet; their features approach more nearly the Hamitic type than do those of the Bantu tribes; their lips are not so prominent nor are their noses so broad, and there appears to be a nearer approach to a nasal bridge. In other respects they resemble Bantu peoples, having dark skin and short woolly hair. They are neither cleanly in person nor sanitary in their habits, and they suffer considerably from syphilis, which, they say, was introduced into their country from Egypt. They are a quiet, inoffensive people who dislike war and have never intermarried with Bantu tribes.

Form of government. There are six principal chiefs who claim to be the owners of the land, and each of whom has a large tract of country which he governs through sub-chiefs. The people of a sub-district appeal to the principal chief for justice when they are dissatisfied with the ruling of a sub-chief, or when they desire to have a case tried and the person accused belongs to another sub-chief over whom their own sub-chief exercises no control. The principal chief levies no taxes, but his subjects make him presents of cattle, and also of grain after each harvest. The Bateso live in communities having numbers of families within a growing stockade. The stockade has a gate which can be closed by night or when there is danger. It is the duty of the chief of the community to try all cases within his village, to punish wrongdoing, to see that peace is kept, and to put down theft. The method of punishment is invariably by fine; there are no places of detention, and people are seldom executed for crime. The chief tries all cases of dispute about land, and he is the guardian of the rights of his village. The fields are often at a distance from the village; and, as people from different villages have fields in the same locality which often border on those of their neighbours from other parts, it thus frequently happens that one family tries to encroach upon the rights of another, making the intervention of a chief, and at times arbitration, necessary, in order to settle some boundary dispute.

Murder. Murder is punished by death, unless the relations of the murderer are able to appease the members of the murdered man's clan by sending offerings. These include a marriageable girl for the bereaved father, and also cattle for the other clan-members.

Adultery. Adultery is punished by fine; but there is little morality among young unmarried women, who are allowed to follow their own inclinations until claimed in marriage, after which they become wonderfully moral.

Inheritance. The eldest son inherits his father's property. If a man is childless, he sometimes adopts a slave to be his son and makes him heir to his property. It sometimes happens that a girl is adopted and is recognised as a man's daughter so that when she marries her adoptive father demands the full wedding-fee for her. Women seldom inherit property, though they are not prohibited by law from doing so. In a few isolated cases men have been known to give their property to their daughters; such property is managed by their husbands.

Clans.

Totemism. The Bateso are divided into a number of totemic clans, the general clan-names of which are well known, and in fact it is by the clan-name that a family is ordinarily distinguished; but, as several clans bear the same name yet have different totems, it is at times necessary to mention the totem for the sake of more exact distinction. Few people know the totems of other clans and, owing to the difficulty of understanding the language and the limited time available for seeking information, it was out of question to pursue the subject very far, and therefore only the names of a few clans with their totems, about which opinion was unanimous, are here given. It is impossible, with this limited knowledge, to say whether the groups which bear the same name are one clan with sub-divisions or whether they are distinct clans. On the other hand, certain groups have the same totems, but bear different clan-names. As in Busoga the children take the totems of their father. Descent in the clans is in the paternal line; that is, the children belong to the clan of their father, not of their mother. The names of the clans, with their totems, are:

1. The *Katikoko*, who take the Sheep and the Edoro tree for their totems.

2. The *Parama*, who take the Tamarind tree for their totem.

3.   The *Maditoko*, who take the Bones of animals for their totem; they avoid contact with the bones of animals.

4.   The *Eraraka*, who take for their totem the Gazelle, which they may not look at nor touch.

5.   The *Koroko*, who take for their totem the Gazelle, of which they may not eat the flesh.

6.   The *Kiribwoko*, who take the Mushroom for their totem; they abstain from eating mushrooms.

7.   The *Bararaka*, who take Broken Bones of animals for their totem; they avoid all contact with the bones of animals.

8.   The *Igorya*, who take Antelopes for their totem; they may not eat the flesh of Antelopes.

9.   The *Pokoro*, who may not shave the heads of their babies.

10.   The *Madokya*, who take Antelopes for their totem and may not eat the flesh.

11.   The *Katikoko*, who take the Edoro tree for their totem; they will not use the timber for any purpose.

Marriage.

Marriage customs.   The totemic clans of the Bateso are exogamous, that is, no man may marry a woman of his own clan. There are, however, no restrictions as to the number of women a man may marry; but he is forbidden to marry more than one daughter of the same man.   Each wife likes to have her own house, but she will live in the same enclosure with her husband's other wives.   It is the regular custom for a wife to leave her own home and clan at marriage and join that of her husband.   As soon as a man marries a woman, he is forbidden to speak to his mother-in-law or to pass her on the same path; he must turn out of the path, should he chance to find her coming in his direction.   Parents betroth their children in infancy, who frequently grow up together, if they belong to the same district, and play together while they are small.   The boy's father, usually, bespeaks another man's daughter, and, if the man and his wife consent to the arrangement, the boy's father gives them a cow which is the token of the formal betrothal of the children. In some instances a grown man becomes engaged to an infant, making his arrangements with the child's parents and waiting until she grows up, when he marries her. Children thus engaged in infancy are made acquainted with the fact when they are old enough to understand it; and, when they come to years of puberty, they marry. Widows belong to the heir, and should the clan select as heir a brother of the deceased, he marries the childless widows as a matter of course.

With regard to cousin marriages the rule of the Bateso seems to agree with that of the Basoga; that is, first cousins, the children of a brother and a sister respectively, are forbidden to marry each other; but second cousins are allowed to marry each other, provided that they are the grandchildren of a brother and a sister respectively, and that the father of the one was the son of that brother, and that the mother of the other was a daughter of that sister. In other words, a man's children may not marry his sister's children, but a man's son's children may marry his sister's daughter's children.

Before marriage the boy takes the marriage-fee which is ten cows, fifty goats, two pots of beer and a quantity of grain to the bride's parents. The month previous to the marriage the bride spends in seclusion, during which time she is daily washed and oiled from head to foot. On the day of her marriage a bride is conducted to her new home by many friends and relations who remain with her two days; she is not veiled when going to her husband, for, according to the custom of her tribe, she wears no clothing, only an abundance of ornaments, numbers of them being lent by friends. A party of girls accompanies the bride and remains with her a few days, and a house is placed at their disposal. Early each morning they go out to dig a plot of ground which is to be the bride's field; after their morning's work they return to the bridegroom's village where the bridegroom's mother entertains them. After a meal they spend the day and most of the night dancing and singing. For two days the bride's party work hard in the field, and each afternoon and evening feast and dance; on the third day the bridegroom presents four of the bride's

sisters with a goat each, which they kill and cook for a final
wedding feast. Some of the meat is reserved and carried
to the bride's parents. When the bride first enters her
husband's house, he presents her with a goat which she keeps
alive for breeding. During the first month the bride is treated
as a child at meals; her mother-in-law sits beside her and
feeds her, nor is she allowed to touch any food with her hands.
At the end of the month she enters upon her ordinary life.

Birth.

Birth customs. Should a woman show no signs of pregnancy
when she has been married some six months, her husband
consults a medicine-man who supplies him with medicine for
his wife to produce the desired effect. The medicine-man is
rewarded at the time with a meal only; but, when a child is
born, he is paid three goats. When a woman becomes aware
that she is with child, she leaves her husband and lives in a
separate house near, and has no further sexual relations with
him until she has weaned her child. Some two or three weeks
before the birth of her child a trustworthy woman, who is
herself a mother and has had experience as a midwife, is called
in and remains in the house with the expectant mother to
attend to her and direct her how to act. At the time of birth
a second woman is called in to assist. The expectant mother
sits on the floor with her back resting against the assistant
who kneels to support her; the midwife stands in front and
delivers the mother. The umbilical cord is cut with a blade
of coarse grass and the afterbirth is buried near the door
outside the house, on the left side as the house is entered.
When the stump of umbilical cord falls from the child, it is
placed upon the spot where the afterbirth is buried. For
three days the mother and child remain secluded with the
midwife, who attends upon the mother and does the cooking.
On the fourth day the husband's mother comes and washes her
daughter-in-law outside the house with warm water. During
the time she is thus engaged other women sweep the house

out and throw the sweepings into the cow-kraal. Should the woman who has become a mother be a second wife, the husband's first wife comes and washes her in the place of her mother-in-law. It is the duty of the husband's mother to name the child soon after its birth.

It is considered unlucky for a child to be born feet first; parents like such a child to die in infancy. A mother does no cooking for her husband for a period of two months after the birth of a child.

Birth of twins. The birth of twins is a welcome event. The midwife announces the fact to the father, who immediately orders the special drum-rhythm to be beaten to make the fact known, and women soon gather at the house uttering a peculiar shrill cry of pleasure. The mother remains secluded for three months, and during this time the father pays visits to members of his own and of his wife's clans, from whom he receives presents of food and animals for a special feast to be held when the period of seclusion is ended and the twins are presented to the members of the clans. Should no hospitality be offered to the father and no present be given at a place when he is making his round of visits, he refuses to enter the house and passes on elsewhere. This is regarded by its occupants as a loss, because the blessing of increase which rests upon the father of twins is not communicated to the inhospitable family. The day before the period of seclusion ends the husband's sister's son closes the door of the house in which the mother and twins are living, and on the following morning he opens it for them to be brought out and presented to the members of the clan. The mother now brings out her children for inspection, and members of both the husband's and the wife's clans meet for the purpose; and a sham-fight takes place which is rather rough play, and often during the fight some of the people are wounded by stones or by the spears which are at times used. One twin is claimed by the members of each clan, though it is not taken away from its parents, and each clan provides a nurse to take care of their particular child. The husband's mother names the twins before the sham-fight takes place, and after the fight there is a dance.

At this dance there is the great feast and the clans bring two fine sheep, one from each clan; these are killed and their meat is added to the meat which the father of the twins provides. The skins from these two sheep are presented to the nurses of the children to make the slings in which to carry the children on their backs. The husband's sister's son is given a goat for closing and opening the door. These ceremonies appear to be imitations borrowed from the Basoga, though it is possible that they are purely Nilotic.

Sickness and Death.

Treatment of sickness. There are no particular ceremonies connected with sickness. The medicine-man is called in and tries by various tests to discover whether the cause is magic, and also to find the nature of the illness. Members of the sick man's clan assemble to assist in carrying out the treatment prescribed by the medicine-man and also to sympathise with the patient.

Death customs. When death takes place, wailing commences at once and some of the widows wash the body, straighten the limbs and bend the left arm, if it be a man, or the right arm, if it is a woman, so as to put it under the head. An ox and a sheep are killed, the skin of the sheep is wrapped round the dead man's head and that of the ox is wrapped round the body. The grave is dug in the house in which the man lived and died, and the widows continue to live in it during the time of mourning. It is necessary to guard widows when the funeral takes place to prevent them from committing suicide. The mourning for a rich man may last twelve months, and seldom less than six months even for a poor man. The heir occupies a house near that which contains the grave and he conducts the mourning ceremonies. After the body is committed to the grave the mourners shave their heads; but, from that time until the mourning ends, they neither shave any part of their body nor do they pare their nails. Each morning at daybreak a drum sounds, and the mourners assemble at the grave and wail for fully an hour. During the rest of the day the women go to cultivate their fields and the men pursue their ordinary occupations. Strict rules of chastity are observed during the season of mourning. Should the deceased man have been a chief, his relations and friends send an ox daily for the mourners' food; other kinds of food and beer are freely supplied as offerings to the dead, and some portion is left by the grave for the ghost. The heir gives notice when the mourning is to end. For three days after the notice is given the mourners remain wailing at the grave a much longer time each day; on the fourth day they shave their heads and bodies, cut their nails and wash, and are then free to return to their homes.

Disposal of widows. The widows take up their abode with the heir as his wives, unless they wish to return to their relatives, in which case the original sum paid for them at their marriage has to be refunded. The children and property pass to the heir. As soon as the mourning ends the house in which the grave lies is deserted and falls into decay, no one attempting to keep it in repair.

Building.

Methods of building. Bateso houses are round huts with conical roofs. They are built by planting a circle of stakes four feet long and two inches thick some two or three inches deep in the ground. These form the outer wall. The roof may be compared to a huge umbrella, the central pole being the stick, the stout rafters radiating from it to the wall being the ribs and the grass thatch the cloth covering of the umbrella. The size of a house is determined by the builder, who is either the man who intends to live in it or some one who is providing it for one of his wives. He marks out a circle on the ground and digs holes a few inches deep for the stakes which he plants side by side, leaving a space for the doorway. The stakes are bound together at the top and bottom by a cord-like creeper. A long stout pole is erected in the centre of the house which has to support the roof, and to this pole strong saplings are tied at the height which will give the desired pitch to the roof and radiating to different points of the wall. Between the saplings either reeds or sticks fill in the interstices to carry the thatch, while the ends of the saplings, which serve as roof timbers, are left long enough to project twelve inches over the wall so as to protect the sides of the house from rain. The thatch is laid on with the stem-ends of the grass downwards, and the ends are evenly cut. Each succeeding layer of thatch is laid with the ends ten inches higher than the last layer so that when the thatching is done, it presents a series of ridges like the rows of slates on a roof. When the top is reached at the central pole, the thatch is tied neatly round it and the summit of the pole is often rudely carved, or it may have the horns of some animal put on it or be ornamented with large snail-shells. The walls are plastered with mud which is thrown with force against the stakes from within the house. This mud fills all the crevices and is smoothed with the hand on the inside but left rough on the outside of the house. The floor is dug up, levelled and beaten hard, and is finally smeared with a mixture of cow-dung and clay. A rough door is made of basket-work which is secured in the doorway by night and also during the day when the family is absent. A man is welcome to build his house in any village, but the newcomer must recognise the headman as chief of the community. When a man marries another wife he builds a house for her near his first wife's house. Sometimes a person prefers to begin house-keeping away from other people and builds his house upon a site which he selects at a distance from any village. As he adds houses for his wives, or as other people join him, he plants a growing fence of euphorbia round the houses which becomes a living stockade, and inside it he makes a kraal for his cattle.

Agriculture.

Agricultural pursuits. The Bateso are mainly an agricultural people. Both men and women spend most of their time in the fields while the crops are growing, and their chief food is porridge made from flour of millet. Each year when the rains are expected, the men and the women work together in the fields and roughly hoe up the ground. The seed is sown as soon as the rains begin, small holes being made in the ground with a hoe and two or three grains of seed dropped into each hole and covered with the foot. The crops are weeded once or twice until the corn is strong enough to suffer no harm from further growths, when it is left to fight its own battle. The people erect temporary huts in the fields and live in them for a time when the crops spring up and begin to put forth the ears, in order to protect them against wild animals by night and to frighten off the birds by day, pigeons being especially guarded against as great robbers. Millet is reaped by both men and women, who cut off the heads of grain and carry them to the threshing-floors, which are usually level places in the field beaten hard and in some cases smeared over with cow-dung to get a smooth surface. The grain is beaten out of the husk with a stick, each head of corn being held and beaten, and is winnowed by pouring it from a basket held up into a basket set on the ground, and the wind carries off the chaff. The granaries are large wicker-baskets six feet deep by four feet wide, smeared inside with clay and cow-dung and having conical thatched lids which project and carry off rain from the sides of the baskets. The granaries are placed near the owner's house in the compound, and are raised one or two feet from the ground to keep them dry. Each wife has her own granary and corn-supply. Other grains grown are maize and sesame, though these cereals are not regarded as staple food. Sweet potatoes are freely grown and two or three kinds of beans and marrows, which add to the variety of their vegetable diet. The sower, when sowing the crops, wears a gourd vine round his or her waist and arms, and mixes powdered herbs with the seed to fructify it. At harvest the people kill a goat, make some of the grain into porridge and eat the meal in the field, throwing a little of the grain into the road leading to the field and along the border of the field. Potatoes and other vegetables are welcomed as a change of diet, for there are several months when they live almost entirely upon porridge made from millet-flour. Women grind the flour daily between two stones. A large smooth stone is sought for the under stone, and is slightly raised at one end where the woman kneels as she grinds with a smaller hard stone. She pours the grain on the large stone from a basket at her side, grinds it into flour and sweeps it down into a small basket set at the lower end of the stone to catch it. As the flour accumulates, it is shaken in the basket and the coarser meal and husks are re-ground, but women do not trouble to grind the flour very fine except for their husbands or masters. The porridge made from millet is red, coarse and gritty, and only people accustomed to it can digest it.

Brewing and beer-drinking. After a good harvest a quantity of beer is brewed and villagers enjoy themselves for a time, as no work can be done in the fields from harvest until sowing-time comes round again, a period of six months. During the dry season men spend most of their days in going from village to village drinking beer: a large pot is placed in some open space either in the village or near the gate, and the men sit round and put the ends of their long beer-tubes into the pot and suck the beer through them, while they discuss public affairs. Sometimes these tubes are six feet long; they are neatly made from a stick from which the pith is extracted, and are encased with plaited palm fronds to strengthen and decorate them. The end put into the pot has a finely worked cane sieve which prevents the thick fluid from entering the tube, whose orifice is the eighth of an inch in diameter, being the thickness of the pith which has been pushed out of the thin cane-like stick. When not in use, the tube is inserted into a bamboo-rod which is the usual staff carried when men go to a beer-drinking feast. Women do not attend the public drinking, as they have their own beer-pots in some house where they drink as freely as the men. There is not so much drunkenness as might be expected when these feasts are going forward, nor do men often quarrel over their drink, though they may be going about from place to place for several weeks. Weapons are not taken to a drinking-party, it being a recognised rule that they shall be left behind lest a man should use them when under the influence of drink.

Cows and Domestic Animals.

Cow-keeping. The Bateso keep cows in almost every village in addition to large flocks of goats and sheep. Boys herd the animals. There is no attempt to keep the herds and flocks separate, so that cows, goats and sheep are to be found together in one pasture. The boys may often be seen riding on the backs of the cows as they wander grazing quite regardless of their burdens Women are not allowed to herd cattle nor to go among them. After a cow has calved, the calf is given all the milk for three days; on the fourth day the animal is milked, the milk is boiled and both husband and wife partake of it; after this ceremony the milk may be drunk by any of the family. Both goat and sheep mutton is eaten in common by men and women alike without any restrictions.

Hunting.

Huntsmen and methods of hunting. There is no distinct class of huntsmen among the tribe, but small game is hunted for the sake of meat by any man who wants it. Men armed with clubs and spears surround a space in which some small animal is thought to be lurking, the grass is beaten down as they advance, and, should an animal be found, it is clubbed or speared. The men are swift of foot and sure of aim so that an animal has little chance of escape. A few men hunt elephants from time to time when a herd passes through the country. The men go where there are trees, climb up into them, wait for the animals to pass beneath, and spear them from their point of vantage. Wounded animals are followed for several days until they sicken and can be surrounded and speared to death. The man who first spears an animal claims one tusk; the second tusk and the flesh belong to the party.

Warfare.

Methods of fighting. The Bateso are a pacific tribe, who rarely make war upon other tribes and prefer to live at peace with all men. From time to time, however, tribal quarrels arise owing to some conjugal dispute or to men quarrelling under the influence of drink. Begun in words between individuals, their clans take up the dispute and eventually resort to arms. The weapons carried by each warrior are a large leather shield five feet long and eighteen inches wide, two spears and a club, and often a warrior is further armed with a sling for hurling stones. In their fights one or two men are often badly bruised by the stones from the slings, it is seldom a man is killed. As a rule the fight ends on the same day; after the fight a conference is held where the parties meet, share a sacred meal, settle their differences, and take leave of each other amicably.

Ornaments.

Love of ornaments. Though neithér of the sexes wear any clothing, they are particularly fond of ornaments. Both men and women wear their hair long and twist string into it to increase its length, and on the string they thread cowry-shells. The edges of the ears are perforated with a number of small holes through which they run iron rings with beads on them or insert pieces of grass, when they are unable to obtain wire and beads. The lobes of the ears are often greatly enlarged by having these weighty rings of beads hung upon them. The neck-ornaments vary greatly: some people wear large coils of wire made into collars, while others have only strings of beads or cowry-shells round their necks. Many women wear small brass rings through the tips of their tongues; they also have the lower lip pierced for a stone, and almost all women have the cartilage of the nose pierced for a ring. Some women pinch up the flesh on the chest, pierce it and put a ring through the hole. Strings of beads are worn round the waist, and often a small bead or string apron four inches wide and two inches deep is also worn. On the wrists and ankles they wear brass and iron rings. Ornaments are often bartered, when the wearer is in need.

Religion.

Undeveloped religious ideas. The religious ideas of the Bateso are less developed than those of their Bantu neighbours; they have no temples nor shrines nor indeed any sacred cere-monies apart from mourning and rain-making. Rain-making is the chief ceremony observed.   The medicine-man calls the people together to some rock, the chief of the district supplies an animal, usually an ox, for a sacred meal to be eaten by the people, the medicine-man sprinkles water on all sides, and the people dance and sing during the rest of the day.   It was impossible to find the name of any supreme being whom they recognise.   There seems to be no idea of a deity apart from ghosts, and the rain-making ceremony has more the nature of public magic than of worship.   A Muganda teacher who had lived some years among these people said he had been unable to find any word for god.   We may with some degree of certainty say that there is no active belief in any higher powers, and worship is almost entirely restricted to ghosts and the dead.

Terms of Relationship.

The following table of relationships was made by the Rev. L. Kitching on a form supplied by Dr Rivers, Fellow of St John's College, Cambridge:

(m.s. = man speaks; w.s. = woman speaks).

Father, Paka, Okoka.
Mother, Totoka, Okoka.
Elder brother (m.s.), Onacika,. Onacika.
Elder sister (w.s.), Kinacika, Konacika.
Sister (m.s.), Kinacika, Onacika.
Father's brother, Onaci kapaka, Okoka or amororuka.
Father's sister, Ejaka, Ojojayitika.
Father's sister's child, Onacika (fem. Kivacika).
Mother's brother, Mamayika, Ocenika.
Mother's brother's wife, Amororuka.
Mother's sister, Totoka.
Mother's sister's husband, Paka, Okoka.
Mother's sister's child, Onacika (fem. Kivacika).
Sister's son's wife (m.s.), Amororuka.
Sister's son's child, Etatayitika, Pataka.
Sister's daughter's child, Epapayutika, Epapataka.
Father's father, Papaka, Okokokoka.
Father's mother, Tataka, Otatayitika.

Mother's father, Papaka.
Mother's mother, Tataka.
Husband, Okilinika, Aberoka.
Wife's father, Akamuranika.
Wife's mother, Akamuranika.
Husband's father, Papaka.
Husband's mother, Tataka.
Wife's brother, Ekamuran.
Wife's sister, Akamuran.
Husband's brother, Ekamuran.
Husband's sister, Akamuran

CHAPTER XXV

THE NILOTIC KAVIRONDO AND THEIR COUNTRY, GOVERNMENT, MARRIAGE, BIRTH AND PUBERTY

The tribe and their district—origin of the tribe—chiefs as rulers—land tenure—the local chief as the magistrate of his village—courts and court fees—making peace between two sections of the tribe—theft—adultery—murder—inheritance—marriage customs—distinctive dress of married women—birth customs—birth of twins—initiation at puberty.

The tribe and their district. The Nilotic Kavirondo are so named to distinguish them from the Bantu tribes of Kavirondo. They are a branch of the great family known as Nilotic tribes or tribes of the Nile Valley, and are quite distinct in language and custom from Bantu tribes. This particular branch may be found extending southwards from Mount Elgon along the coast of Lake Victoria Nyanza into German territory. They are settled in groups of villages among the Bantu and yet are quite distinct from them and do not intermarry with them. The clans met with live chiefly in the hills bordering on Lake Victoria. The mornings and evenings are comparatively cold in these hills, yet the people are absolutely destitute of clothing; indeed they consider clothing as indecent, and members who have been abroad and have adopted clothing are requested to put it away during their residence in their old homes. The features of the people are more closely allied to those of the pastoral tribes than to the Bantu. In stature the men are not, however, quite so tall as the Bahima, few of them reach six feet, five feet six to five feet eight being more usual. Their frame is slim like that of the Bahima, and the nose inclined to have a bridge. Again their love for cows is stronger than that of the Bantu. The women are shorter than the men, they are slim and athletic, a stout woman being seldom found; this may be accounted for by the amount of exercise they take and their constant activity in the field and home. The freedom with which the young women mingle with the men is striking, they may be seen among them, leaning on their shoulders when standing, as unrestrainedly as the men with men. The absence of clothing in no wise embarrasses them nor does it cause either sex a moment's thought; they are accustomed to this state of nature from childhood and feel no constraint in mingling freely together. They are extremely fond of ornaments and of painting themselves with different coloured clays, and often make patterns upon their bodies which they retain until the clay wears off. Their hair is often allowed to grow long, and youths frequently increase the length of it by twisting cords into it, greasing the whole with castor or other vegetable oil and rubbing red clay into it. Men and women mix freely together and often work in parties on the same field, singing songs as they work and keeping time with their hoes as they dig. Their homes in the hills are exposed and cold. Still, they do not appear to feel the cold winds and move about and work as freely as well-clothed tribes. As a tribe they combine agriculture with pastoral pursuits and their diet consists of milk and vegetables.

Origin of the tribe. According to their traditions they come from the north-west. Their ancestor Ramogi, they say, had seven sons named Kwenda, Nyakal, Owede, Nyadwat, Sakwa, Alego and Langho; and he adopted another son, Ugenya. Langho, they say, is the father of the Masai and Setik tribes. They trace their own descent from Owede who had two sons, Omwa and Sagam. We thus have two groups forming the tribe, as follows: Omwa, whose descendants formed eight clans; Sagam, whose descendants form seven.

The descendants of Omwa:

1. Dongo	2. Nyuto	3. Orando
4. Kwamudi	5. Nyamwegi	6. Ndalo
7. Ogonyo	8. Nyakwal	

The descendants of Sagam:

1. Pwonja	2. Hadedi	3. Waranja
4. Rateng	5. Wango	6. Menya
7. Nyameda		

Plate XXII

(1) Nilotic Kavirondo girls

(2) Young women ready for initiation ceremony
(Bagesu Tribe)

Government.

Chiefs as rulers. There is no king of the country, nor is there any single paramount chief; the Bantu chiefs claim equal, if not superior, rights to the land. Certain chiefs rule over extensive districts inhabited by the Nilotics, and their rights as leaders are considered to be hereditary; they are also looked to in cases requiring settlement or legislation.

Land tenure. Land which has not been cultivated in the past may be tilled by any family; but, when once it has been tilled, the community regard it as the property of the family whose ancestor first cultivated it. Should it be left fallow for a number of years, no other family may appropriate and till it without first obtaining the original owner's permission. Few people seek such permission, preferring to dig virgin-land which will afterwards belong to their children.

Local chiefs as the magistrates. The people live in communities. They build their houses in close proximity and in most cases surround them with a growing fence, leaving a gateway which can be closed during the night or in times of danger. Such a village group is ruled by a sub-chief who is under the authority of the district-chief. The chief of a village is magistrate and controls the general affairs of his people. This chief levies no taxes, but his people make him presents of goats and sheep, and of grain also at harvest time.

Courts and court fees. Any person wishing to bring a charge against another for any offence, real or imaginary, pays a small fee to the chief of the village before whom he lays his complaint or accusation. The chief or elder then summons the accused person and appoints a time when the case shall be heard. The chief sits with one or two village elders and gives his judgment. A person may appeal from a village chief to the principal chief in the district, and the elder who first tried the case will then go to the superior chief to be present when the case is reheard. The parties appealing have to pay fresh court-fees before the case is retried. The punishment in almost every case is a fine and the amount is determined by the gravity of the case. The losing party has to pay the fine, and from the amount the judge takes a portion for himself and passes the remainder to the successful litigant.

Making peace between sections of the tribe. Should there be a quarrel between two sections of the tribe and a desire be felt to end the strife, the chief of one section goes to the chief of the other with a few of his principal men, and they spend the afternoon and night together discussing the difficulty and finally coming to terms. The following day a goat is killed, some of the contents of the stomach are smeared over the chests of those present, and a little of the meat is pounded in a mortar and eaten as a sacred meal to ratify the terms of peace. As they eat the meal, they promise to live at peace, the form of oath taken being "By the dead dog."

Theft. Cattle lifting is the most common form of serious theft. Men seek to steal cattle from members of the same tribe living at a distance from their own district, because the animals stolen can thus be more easily secreted. A man who intends to rob a kraal first visits the place with his son in order to work magic and to make his preparations. He takes with him a number of sticks pointed and prepared for the magic, and indicates certain spots to his son, who drives a stick into the ground at each place. These are magical sticks which cast a spell upon owners of cattle. The magic is followed up at night by the man's going to the kraal, opening the gate and driving away the cattle while the people are sleeping. Should the animals make any noise or prove stubborn and refuse to leave the kraal, it is a sign that the owners have received some intimation of the intended theft and have taken precautions to make more potent magic to frustrate the robbery. Under such circumstances the cattle-lifter beats a hasty retreat before he is discovered and captured, as he knows that he will receive no quarter, but will certainly be put to death.

Chiefs possessing large herds of cattle take the precaution to keep a supply of powerful medicine over the gateway leading into the kraal, and also place it in various parts of the kraal so that, when a thief enters the kraal, he loses his strength, is unable to walk and so is captured and put to death. A successful cattle-lifter soon becomes a noted man and secures a large following, and thus becomes a powerful chief.

Petty thefts from houses are dealt with by a medicine-man who discovers the culprit. He goes to the village in which the suspected person lives, takes an ordinary stool, sets it in an open space in the village, fills the hollow of the seat with water and covers it with an inverted cooking-pot. Having done this he goes through a formula mentioning the names of the families of the village, and at length mentions the names of the suspected family individually, until at last he names the person accused. When the name of the guilty person is mentioned, the water on the stool is said to flow from under the pot. The person thus convicted is fined and, in addition to his fine, he is compelled to restore the full amount of property he has stolen.

Adultery. When a man is accused of adultery, he is tried and, if found guilty, is fined an ox which is given to the injured man. An unfaithful wife, who leaves her husband, may be restored to him and he will not think the worse of her. Should she refuse to return to her husband, her father must either supply the husband with another wife, a sister of his former wife, or restore the marriage-fee. Unmarried women are given great license and are not considered guilty of an immoral action when they have sexual relations before marriage.

Murder. A murderer is discovered by means of the oracle. A medicine-man is asked to discover the murderer and, when he names the person, the relatives of the murdered man accuse the murderer. The accused is ordered to bring his son, and the medicine-man, after making incantations over a pot of drugs, gives the boy a cup of it to drink. If the father is guilty, the son will die at once; whereas, if he is innocent, the boy will suffer no harm. When a man is proved to be guilty or acknowledges his guilt, he is fined a number of cows and has to give his daughter or sister to the father of the murdered man. A murderer seldom seeks safety by flight when he has committed his deed, and often confesses his guilt without any trial, avowing the motives of his act. There is a special ceremony to purify a murderer. He is first separated from the members

of his village and lives in a hut with an old woman who attends
to his wants, cooks for him and also feeds him, because he may
not touch food with his hands.   Separation lasts for three days,
and on the fourth day a man who is himself a murderer, or
who has at some time killed a man in battle, takes the murderer
to a stream where he washes him all over.   He then kills a
goat and cooks the meat, takes four sticks and places a piece
of meat on each stick and gives the man the meat to eat from
each in turn.   When the meat has been eaten, he gives him four
pieces of porridge made into balls and put on the sticks.
After this meal the goat-skin is cut into strips, one strip
being put on the neck and one strip round each wrist of the
murderer.   This ceremony is performed by the two men who
are alone at the river, and after it the murderer is free to
return home.   It is said that, until this ceremony is performed,
the ghost cannot take its departure for the place of the dead,
but hovers about the murderer.

Inheritance.   It is usual for a son to inherit property.
While a man is still in health, he makes known his wishes as
to whom he desires to inherit his property, and his wishes will
be observed.   Should a son be too young to succeed to his
father's estate at the time of death, the deceased man's brother
manages the property until the son is old enough to take
control.   Should a man with property die intestate, the members of his clan elect one of his sons to be heir.   There is no
fixed law as to which son shall inherit.   It is not a question
of age nor may the son of a particular wife claim precedence
over the sons of other wives, but the clan-members are at
liberty to choose the man they consider the most suited for
the office.   Women never inherit or hold property.   The
father's stool and bracelet are given to the heir and are the
insignia of lawful succession.

Marriage, Birth and Puberty.

Marriage customs.   It was impossible to discover the
ritual of marriage or the groups into which a man might or
might not marry, all that could with certainty be learned
being that there are exogamous divisions within the tribe.

There are no restrictions as to the number of women a man may marry nor as to the number of his wife's sisters whom he may take to wife.   Previous to her marriage a young woman may have as many lovers as she wishes, she is only careful to avoid incestuous connections.   The unmarried women have their own quarters in a village and the young men theirs, and they seldom have any further intercourse than that of brothers and sisters; the young men, however, from another village pay visits to the young women during the day and make love to them, and in the evening the women return the men's visit and have sexual relations with them, while other young people sing songs of an obscene character and dance outside the house.   Such intercourse is not stopped nor discountenanced by the elder people, as it is a recognised custom.   Should any children be born from such relations, no punishment ensues nor are the couple blamed. When a father considers his son old enough to marry, he chooses a woman to be his wife.   He then takes a cow and a goat to the parents of the young woman and arranges with them the amount to be paid for the marriage-fee.   If the parents consent to the match, when an instalment of the fee has been paid, the bride is conducted by her friends to the home of the young man and lives with him as his wife for ten days : during this time there is daily singing and dancing outside the house where the bride and bridegroom reside, and they take part in the dances.   At the end of ten days the bridegroom's parents give a feast to all those who have gathered, and after the feast the friends of the bride escort her back to her parents, who in turn give a feast to the people that accompany their daughter. The bride remains with her parents until her husband is able to obtain and pay the full sum asked for as the marriage-fee. During this time, while the bride is waiting for her husband to bring the marriage-fee, there is no obligation upon her to live a chaste life, and she is free to have as many lovers as before.   When, however, the fee has been paid and the bride claimed, she ceases to live a loose life and becomes most chaste. The husband builds his house, either in or near his father's village, and his wife is brought thither.   When a man marries a second or third wife, he may select another place for his new wife, either in the village near his former wife, or he may elect to take her to some other village. A man who has wives dwelling in different places lives with them in turn. Married women are careful in regard to their relations with men. Should a woman be lax in her behaviour or encourage men to visit her, her husband will send her back to her parents and divorce her.

A wife who is proved to be sterile is not divorced, but her parents send her sister to become the man's wife, and he is expected to pay another sum as a marriage-fee for her; but there is no stated time when the sum shall be paid after the woman goes to live with him. The former wife continues to live with him as his wife.

Distinctive dress of married women. Each woman after marriage makes a girdle with a long fringe at the back and ties the ends together, which gives it the appearance of a tail. The girdle is worn constantly during the husband's life-time, but, should he die, she takes it off and puts it on the house-roof over the door during the season of mourning to show that she is a widow and is mourning. After marriage a wife scarifies her sides and back in addition to the scarifications she made at puberty. When a woman has a son born, she makes a clay-mound in the middle of the floor in her house for the food pot to rest on when the family are at meals.

Birth customs. A wife who expects her confinement calls in an elderly woman to act as midwife. This woman is a person who has had experience in such matters and is herself a mother. When the child is born, the midwife cuts the umbilical cord on an axe handle if the child is a boy, and on a hoe handle if it is a girl. The placenta of a boy is buried outside on the right side of the doorway and that of a girl on the left side. During the first three days the father remains near the house in which his wife and child lie, but the midwife alone enters and attends to the wants of the mother and child. On the third day the father takes a fowl and rubs it on the child's chest and turns it loose, when it becomes the property of the child. When the new moon appears, the parents bathe, and

shave their heads, taking care to keep separate the hair which
is cut off.   This hair is hidden away in some place near,
by preference in a rat-hole or in some hole where it is not
likely to be found again.

Birth of twins. At the birth of twins the parents remain
together in one house for ten days, and the midwife waits on
them. When this time of seclusion ends, a small pot of blood is
drawn from the neck of an ox, cooked and given to the parents
to eat. After the meal they are escorted to the river, washed,
and their heads shaved. Their house is then swept and the
floor smeared with cow-dung, and friends come and dance in
the village and drink beer. The mother takes the twins a
round of visits which lasts several days, but she returns home
each night to sleep. At each house she visits the people give
her presents of grain. When the visits have been made the
mother brews beer with the grain she has received in presents,
and her friends again gather to dance and to drink the beer.

Initiation ceremonies. Children live in the same village
with their parents and under their control. Until marriage
they lead a free and happy life, with few wants and cares.
The boys assist in herding cattle, and the girls help their mothers
in their fields and also carry wood and water and assist in
cooking. Their duties are light and there is no force beyond
argument used to make them work. Children imitate their
elders in seeking ornaments to wear and in smearing their
bodies with oil and red or white paint. When they come
to the age of puberty, their four front teeth in the lower
jaw are extracted and they are initiated in the customs of the
clan. For four days they remain in the house, after which
they go about visiting their friends and receive presents of
fowls. Girls go through the same ceremony as boys in having
their teeth extracted, but, in addition, their bodies are scarified
on the sides and back. Should there be excessive haemorrhage
when teeth are extracted, the parents send to the man who
has the bracelets of the deceased person after whom the boy
is named and borrow them, and the youth wears them until
the bleeding ceases. When the ceremony of extracting the
teeth is over, the boys are sent to live in the boys' quarters

with the youths of the village, and girls go to the young women's quarters, and both cease to live in the house of their parents. From this time until marriage these young people live in their communities and have much freedom, their morals not being considered, but each following the leading of natural impulse.

CHAPTER XXVI

SICKNESS, DEATH, BURIAL, WARFARE, INDUSTRIES, RELIGION AND RELATIONSHIPS

Treatment of the sick—ghostly possession—death and mourning—
death of a wife—manner of conducting warfare—treatment of a
warrior who has slain one of the enemy—agricultural pursuits—
cow-keeping—oxen used as riding animals—mode of building—
religious beliefs—terms of relationships.

Treatment of the sick. Sickness is thought to be due to
one of two causes: it may be, and the people think most
frequently is, the result of magic which has been worked by
some person who wishes to give pain or even to cause death
because of a grievance, real or imaginary; or it may be due to
some ghost. Under either circumstance, when a serious case
of sickness occurs, the family seek the aid of a medicine-man
who by his various tests and incantations discovers the cause;
and, in a case where magic has been worked, he not only
discovers the cause but also discloses the name of the culprit,
who is thereupon sought and asked to give his motive for
afflicting the sick person, and is paid to release him from the
spell. Should the man have intended to kill the other because
he has suffered some discourtesy or received some offence at
his hands, he would probably have speared his shadow, so that
the sick person will die unless the spell or magic is removed.
Again, it may be that some magic has been worked and
certain objects have been hidden near the house which are
causing the sickness; these have to be removed and the spell
broken before any drugs or treatment will avail the sick man.
The perpetrator will only remove these when his grievance
has been settled and he has received the needful compensation.
In the case of a ghost, the medicine-man will tell which ghost
is working the trouble and why it is thus causing sickness.

The ghosts are usually those of grandparents who afflict grandchildren because their father has failed to fulfil the duties of a son to his father in his old age, either by direct unkindness or by neglect. The medicine-man will now order a shrine to be built by the grave of the grandparent concerned, and the sick person's father offers a goat or a sheep at the grave, pouring out the blood as an offering upon the ground, and then eating the meat on the spot with a few relatives. The medicine-man is afterwards able to treat the sick man with reasonable hope of restoring him to health, because the offended ghost has now been pacified and will allow the sick man to benefit by the treatment. Sometimes sickness is transferred to another person by rubbing herbs over the sick man and burying them in the road for some other person to walk over and thus contract the disease.

Ghostly possession. Fits are supposed to be the manifestation of ghostly possession. They can often be overcome by giving the person warm blood to drink drawn from the veins of an ox and by feeding the patient with a generous diet. During the time a fit lasts the man is held down, if he is violent, until the attack is over. Should a man fall into the fire during a fit, no help is rendered and he is allowed to burn to death, because it is said that the ghost has claimed him and would resent any interference and would affect the person who attempted to rescue the stricken man with a similar malady. A drum beaten near a person subject to fits is said to bring on an attack of the malady.

Death and mourning. When a person dies, his legs are bent up into a squatting posture, the right arm is raised under the head and the death-wail commences. The dead are not washed but merely have their ornaments stripped off; an ox or a cow is then killed and the body is wrapped in the skin and is stitched up tightly in it. The grave is dug in the house. When the body is laid in it, all the relatives stand round with their backs towards it and, at a given signal, they stoop down and with their hands scrape the earth into the grave without looking where it falls. After they have scraped in earth for some moments they walk out of the house, and the brother of the deceased enters with a son of the dead man and together they fill in the grave and beat the floor hard. Some of the blood of the animal that was killed is poured into the grave as it is being filled with earth; and, after the grave is filled up, four pieces of meat are taken and one piece is placed at each corner of it. A pot of newly brewed beer is placed on the grave and left to ferment until it runs over the sides when the relatives drink it. When the duty of filling in the grave is completed, all the mourners wash, shave their heads and have a meal of the meat of the animal that was killed. The widows remove their girdles and place them on the roof of the house containing the grave. A goat is killed, and an elderly woman related to the deceased man ties a portion of the entrails of the goat round the waist and neck of each widow, and also winds a portion round her own neck; and this is worn by each widow during the period of mourning. On the following morning a grandson climbs the house and breaks the end off the central pole which stands out above the thatch; he also breaks the cooking-pot in which the deceased man's food was cooked. On the second day after the funeral a goat is brought into the house and each of the mourners strikes it with his fist and kicks it; it is then taken and killed, and its flesh is cooked in part of the broken cooking-pot and eaten by the mourners. After this meal the male relatives go to war against some group of their tribe who are said to have been the cause of the man's death. After mourning four days the party shave their heads and continue to the end of the mourning period without further shaving their heads or paring their nails. The widows continue to live in the house which contains the grave. When the ox or cow for the funeral ceremonies is killed, if the deceased is a man, it is speared to the heart; but, when the deceased is a woman, it is speared in the head between the horns. When the mourning ceremonies are ended, each widow makes a girdle, with the fringe at the back, which she wears for a year while she continues to live in the house containing the grave. At the end of the year she burns the girdle, goes to the river and washes, takes her old girdle from the house-roof with her and leaves it in the river-bed. After washing she makes a new girdle from papyrus while still at the river, and wears it as she returns to her village. She is then free to remarry.

Dead people are sometimes said to come to life again. This is reported to take place within a short time after death. It is said that the spirit had gone on a journey and had returned after the man was thought to be dead, but in time to stop the funeral. The supposed dead person sneezes and revives, the sneezing being thought to be the signal that the spirit has returned from his journey.

Death of a wife. Should a wife die before her husband, her body is buried in the house, and, when the husband dies, he is buried in the goat-house near. He may not be buried in the same house with his wife. The animal offered at a man's funeral is always an ox, while it is an old cow that is offered at a woman's funeral. The skin from the animal is used to wrap the body as a shroud. The meat from the animal is divided in the following manner: a shoulder is retained for the dead and is eaten by the mourners at the grave, the second shoulder is for the relatives in the village, and the remainder, with the exception of the neck, is for the guests who live at a distance: the neck is given to the medicine-man.

A suicide is buried in the open, never in a house. Should the death have taken place in a house, it is burned down, for no one will live in it.

Warfare.

Mode of conducting wars. The people are not fond of war and fortunately their wars are never very serious matters. Cattle-lifting and women-stealing are the chief causes of fighting. The battles take place after short notice, when it is found that cattle have been robbed or when the alarm is given that a woman has been captured by some other clan. When a fight is impending, the attacking party drive a few cows to some spot where the other party may see them and challenge the others to come and take them. The party challenged must either attempt to carry off the cows while the others protect them, or they must pay a fine imposed by the attacking army.

The warriors are armed with long-bladed spears and use large shields three feet high and of a **V** shape, behind which the bearer crouches and is completely hidden. The shields are made of cow-hide and are so dried that they are hard enough to resist a spear-thrust. Each warrior is painted with red and white clay in fantastic designs and wears a head-dress. Some of the head-dresses are like helmets adorned with ostrich feathers, while others are small straw hats such as a child's doll might wear.

The battle is decided when the cattle are carried off by the one party or when the other party prove themselves strong enough to retain them. The victors dictate terms of peace and the vanquished pay a fine in cattle and women.

Treatment of a warrior who has slain one of the enemy. When a warrior kills another in battle, he is isolated from his village, lives in a separate hut some four days, and an old woman cooks his food and feeds him like a child because he is forbidden to touch any food. On the fifth day he is escorted to the river by another man who washes him, a white goat is killed and cooked by the attendant, who feeds the man with the meat, the goat-skin is cut into strips and put upon the man's wrists and round his head, and he returns to his temporary home for the night. The next day he is again taken to the river and washed, and a white fowl is presented him. He kills it and it is cooked for him, and he is again fed with the meat. He is then pronounced to be clean and may return to his home. It sometimes happens that a warrior spears another man in battle and the latter dies from the wound some time after. When death takes place, the relatives go to the warrior and tell him of the death, and he is separated at once from the community until the ceremonies above described have been performed. The people say that the ceremonies are necessary in order to release the ghost of the dead man, which is bound to the warrior who slew him and is only released on the fulfilment of the ceremonies. Should a warrior refuse to fulfil the ceremonies, the ghost will ask, "Why don't you fulfil the ceremonies and let me go?" Should the man still refuse to comply, the ghost will take him by the throat and strangle him.

Industries.

Agricultural pursuits. Agriculture is the principal pursuit of the people and they have now become dependant upon their crops for the grain which forms their chief food. Millet and maize are grown freely and are ground into flour for making porridge. Men and women work together in the fields and dig them for the seed. They use the common hoe with a long handle when digging, and roughly hoe the ground, when rains are expected. Sweet potatoes, beans and sesame are grown more for change of diet and as additions, such as we should call savouries, to the porridge than as necessaries of life. When the crops are a few inches high, the chief and all his people shave their heads, and from that time till harvest no one is allowed to shave again. After harvest the headman shaves and all the people follow his example. Should any one neglect this custom and shave before the time, it is said to be injurious to the crops and to prevent the grain from ripening. The culprit is therefore fined for his heedless conduct. When the corn is in the ear, a goat is killed and the contents of the stomach are scattered about the field to prevent blight and to preserve the crops from being injured by hail-storms.

Cow-keeping. Cows form the principal wealth of the people. The numbers vary in a village according to the prosperity and success of the community. Milk is used as an article of food, especially when sour and clotted, but it is more of a luxury, in the present progressive stage of the tribe, than a necessity; and the meat of the animals is almost entirely reserved for ceremonial use. Cattle are herded by boys and young men, who mix their herds and flocks of goats and sheep. Women and girls are strictly forbidden to herd or to milk cows; they may churn and wash the milk-vessels, but there their duties in connection with cows end. Each village has its cattle, and the young men and boys of the place are responsible for their safety during the day, while they graze on the hill-side. When a cow calves, the calf is left with the dam during the first ten days and the cow is not milked. On the morning of the eleventh day the cow is milked and the milk is churned, the

butter being used for cooking a special meal which is eaten
by the owner of the cow and his wife; a little of the butter
is set aside and they smear it on their lips, but none of it may
be smeared on their bodies. After the meal has been eaten,
the cow is milked regularly and the milk may now be drunk
by all the family.

Oxen used for riding.   Oxen are frequently used for riding.
The young men train the animals to this and ride them constantly. They turn them as they wish by prodding the side
of the animal's cheek with a stick from which it turns away.
The animals are trained, however, to obey the voice rather
than wait for the stick. They trot along at a fast rate and
cover the ground quicker than a man can walk.

Sheep and goats.   Sheep and goats are kept by all villagers.
Goats especially are eaten by men and women without any
restrictions. Fowls are also kept, though, as is usual among
most African tribes, fowls have to find their own food, and
their chickens are constantly preyed upon by hawks and kites,
and those that grow up are of a poor and miserable kind.

Building.

Architecture and mode of building.   The houses are round
huts with conical thatched roofs They have an outer wall
of stakes three and sometimes four feet high with mud smeared
over them on the inside and a central pole passing through
the roof, to which the rafters are attached. The roof is thatched
with grass and the end of the central pole, which passes through
the roof, is rudely carved. The houses are grouped together,
leaving room enough to pass between them, and a growing fence
surrounds them. Many villages have no outer fence, but are
built high up the hill-sides for protection from hostile clans.

Religion.

Religious beliefs.   Apart from worship of the dead and a
belief in ghosts, the people have little religion. They call the
supreme being Nyasi, who, they say, is to be found in large
trees. In times of trouble or sickness they make offerings to
him of an animal which is killed under a large tree, and the

flesh is cooked and eaten near by, though sometimes the meat
is taken a little distance away and is not eaten under the
shadow of the tree.

Rain-making. Rain-making is an important ceremony,
but it is performed by a Musoga priest who lives among the
people for the purpose of assisting them in discharging those
religious obligations which they consider necessary yet do not
themselves understand how to perform. The man is treated
with great respect and has a comfortable existence among them.

Relationships.

Terms of relationship. The following terms of relationship
were supplied by the Rev. J. J. Willis, now Bishop of Uganda,
formerly a C.M.S. Missionary at Maseno, Kavirondo, who says
that the pronominal forms for Father and Mother are used,
that is, each person says "My father" or "My mother" (m.s.
= man speaks, w.s. = woman speaks).

Father, won, wora
Mother, min, mama
Eldest brother (m.s.), kayo, ng'amodwong'ena
Eldest sister (w.s.), nyamin madwong', nyamera madwong'
Sister (m.s.), Nyamin, Nyamera.
Father's brother, omin won, omin worwa
Father's brother's wife, min, minwa mama
Father's brother's child, owat, owadwa
Father's sister, wa, waya
Father's sister's husband, chwor wa, chwor waya
Father's sister's child (boy), wod wa, wod waya
Father's sister's child (girl), nyar wa, nyar waya
Mother's brother, ner, nera
Mother's brother's wife, chi ner, chi nera
Mother's brother's child (boy), woda ner, woda nera
Mother's brother's child (girl), min, mama
Mother's sister, min, mama
Mother's sister's husband, won, wonwa
Mother's sister's child (boy), owat mar nyina hao, owadwa
    mar nyina hao

Mother's sister's child (girl), nyamin mar nyina hao, ny-
    amera mar nyina hao
Sister's son's wife (m.s.), chi nyakweo, chi nyakwewa
Sister's son's child (m.s.), nyakwar, nyakwara
Sister's daughter's husband (m.s.), chwor nyakewo,
    chwor nyakewa
Sister's daughter's child (m.s.), nyakwar, nyakwara
Father's father, Kwar, kwara
Father's mother, da, dana
Mother's father, Kwar, kwara
Mother's mother, da, dana
Husband, chwor, chwora
Wife's father, or, ora
Wife's mother, mar, mara
Husband's mother, mar, mara
Husband's father, or kwar, ora kwara
Wife's brother, or, ora
Wife's sister, yu or, yu ora
Husband's brother, yu or, yu ora
Husband's sister, yu or, yu ora
Wife's sister's husband, omin, omera
Husband's brother's wife, nyek, nyeka
Son's wife's parents, nyawana, nyawanana

INDEX

Boy attached to the special herdsman
11; substitute for the father of
twins 46
Brewing beer 72, 270
Bride accepted as a daughter by her
mother-in-law 40; in agricultural
clan 41; and her companions 39;
carried off to her husband 120;
entering upon normal duties 41;
fed like a child 210; home of 40;
in tears 39; secluded 150, 263;
taken to her husband 149; treated
as a child 120; bridal party
263
Bridegroom of the pastoral clan 39,
119; of the agricultural clans 41;
of the Bakene 150; of the Bagesu
172; of the Basoga 209; of the
Kavirondo 281
Brother the person to sanction his
sister's marriage 150
Building 191, 240, 267; canoes 79;
a kraal 63; houses 73; huts 63;
mode of 291
Bunyoro, Bacwezi, the priestly clan
of 6; boundaries 5; burial-place
of kings 5; class distinctions 27;
extent of 3; four dynasties of
kings given of 5; its geographical
position 3; name of a dead
king never mentioned 5; origin
of the royal house 5; physical
features 5; rocky hills venerated
in 5; royal house 5; story of the
first two kings of 6; terms of
relationship 32
Burial 129, 224; customs 58; customs among agricultural people
61; customs in Central Busoga
227; customs of women and
unmarried men 228; of a chief of
Busoga 201; a fallen warrior 83;
of dead 286; of a king 52, 60,
128; of a suicide 288; of twins
48; of women 61; place of placenta 45
Burning iron used in sickness 54
Butter making 108; smeared on the
body 104
Busoga 197; architecture 240; chief,
mourning for a 201; chiefs of the
Central District 204; districts
197; fetishes 251; owner of land
230; physical features of 199;
rain makers 254; rock spirits
250; statistics 256

Calves fed by cow 106; treatment
of 107
Cannibalism of the Bagesu 161

Canoes 79; and rafts of the Bakene
157; building 79; travelling 147
Capital punishment of chiefs 111;
for theft 25
Capturing a ghost 56, 136, 180
Cases of appeals brought to the king
113; tried in court 22
Cattle belonging to a ghost 132;
divided into herds of one hundred
138; given to a bride 120; given
to chiefs in lieu of land 110;
lifting 22; lifting a cause of war
288; long-horned 118; observance of colour of 38; offered to
the dead king 53; owned by the
king 111; rearing 63, 168; sickness 136; rules for breeding 38;
totems 118
Causes for divorce 114, 151, 174, 213,
232
Causes of war 81, 190, 242, 271, 288
Caves on Mount Elgon 162
Central District of Busoga 198;
burial customs 227
Ceremonies at birth 43, 123, 174,
213, 264, 282; before childbirth 174
Ceremony at the birth of twins 126,
152, 175, 217; at the birth of a
calf 133, 236; at burial of the dead
224, 287; at new moon 97; for
cleansing men 138; for ending
marriage seclusion 211; of Bagesu
marriage 173; of making blood-
brothers 138; of eating the dead
178; of first fruits 235; of
initiation 184, 283; of marriage
149; of naming children born
during twin birth ceremonies 221;
of naming twins 153, 217; of
purification after childbirth 124;
of purification after initiation
187; of smearing butter on the
body when sowing beans 236;
of adopting children 114; performed over newly cultivated
land 166; to announce the new
moon 139; to avert famine 95; to
bring rain 183, 292; to celebrate
a child's first tooth 125; to
cleanse a warrior who has killed
a man 190; to discover cause of
sickness 222; to end mourning
226; to ensure a chief's health
203; to heal sick cattle 136;
to keep birds from crops 235; to
make peace 170; to make known
the death of the king 14; to
obtain good crops 234; to prevent
war 96; to prove a man guilty of
adultery 216; to purify a man guilty

of manslaughter 171; to purify a murderer 280; to purify mourners 60; to purify the parents of twins 175; to release a ghost 225, 280, 287; to secure freehold land 231; to stave off evil during feasts 95; to stay sickness 94; when a child is named 214
Charcoal making 74
Chief of Busoga, death of a 201
Chiefs appointed to rule over cattle 110; giving the body of the dead king to the victorious prince 51; guarding the king's body 51; huts surrounding the royal enclosure 73; in Busoga 200, 230; killed at the king's grave 52; not allowed to take part in the civil wars 15; of the Central District of Busoga 204; of the Kavirondo 276; the guardian of the body of the dead king 15
Childbirth customs 215
Childless wife discarded 151
Children betrothed 118; forced to drink large quantities of milk 71, 125; given a portion of their father's property 232; living at home until marriage 214; playing in canoes 147
Choosing a wife 149, 172, 208, 211
Churning 41, 66
Churns 108
Circumcision 184
Civil wars 81; to secure the throne 14
Claims on the children of a woman by the clan 217
Clan family names 29; gods 133; in Bunyoro 27; obligations in a case of murder 115
Clans and totems 28, 116; of the Bagesu 164; of the Bakene 148; of Busoga 204
Clothing of Bakene women 158; of the Kavirondo 276; of men 158; of the Bagesu 164
Companion to the king's ghost 52
Compensation for manslaughter 116
Conception 42, 123, 174, 213, 264, 282
Confirming the betrothal promise made in infancy 119
Consent of a woman sought in marriage 212
Consummation of marriage 40
Contest for the vacant throne 51
Cooking never done by women in pastoral clans 41
Corn stored 69; threshing 69
Counting 138

Country of the Bateso 259
Court fees 22, 277; held in the open 112; houses 21; house for state secrets 22
Courts of appeal 22; of the Bagesu 169
Cousin marriage 38, 209, 262
Cowardice in war punished 84
Cow-dung as fuel 64
Cow-keeping 62, 271, 290; in Central Busoga 236; by peasants 67
Cow kraal 105
Cows, amount of milk from 106; for milk in the capital 74; given salt 77, 105; love for a fire 64; love for smoke 105; made to low on the day of a death 59; never fed in a kraal 66; not milked on the day of a death 58; offered to dead king 128; rarely killed 68; treatment of sick 68
Cow-skins, garments made of 77; placed in the grave 58; robes of pastoral women 5
Creator without a temple 131
Creditors claim upon an estate 60
Crowning the new king 15
Cultivation of millet 70; of sweet potatoes 70
Custom of awe and reverence when the king took a meal of milk 12; of bleeding bulls 168; of choosing a wife 208; of extracting lower teeth 157, 187; of making peace 278; of marriage 39, 119, 148, 210, 281; of marriage in Bagesu 172; of marriage in the Central District 211; of placing a child to sit alone 44; of placing a pot of milk at a kraal fire for warriors to drink 132
Customs adopted during period of menstruation 42; adopted to obtain children 42; followed at childbirth 123, 213, 215, 264, 282; followed by pregnant women 44; at death 266; at harvest 269; of building in Central Busoga 241; of burial of women and unmarried men 228; of hospitality 122; of hunting 193, 238; of sowing and of harvest 235
Cutting the teeth 217

Dances 189; drums used in 88; in connection with twins 47; to end initiation ceremony 187
Daughter-in-law received by her husband's parents 120
Dead buried in the dung-hill 58;